State Capacity, Economic Control, and Authoritarian Elections

Although the phenomenon of authoritarian elections has been a focal point for the literature on authoritarian institutions for more than a decade, our understanding of the effect of authoritarian elections is still limited.

Combining evidence from cross-national studies with studies on selected cases relying on recent field work, this book suggests a solution to the "paradox of authoritarian elections." Rather than focusing on authoritarian elections as a uniform phenomenon, it focuses on the differing conditions under which authoritarian elections occur. It demonstrates that the capacities available to authoritarian rulers shape the effect of elections and high levels of state capacity and control over the economy increase the probability that authoritarian multi-party elections will stabilize the regime. Where these capacities are limited, the regime is more likely to succumb in the face of elections. The findings imply that although multi-party competition and state strength may be important prerequisites for democracy, they can under some circumstances obstruct democratization by preventing the demise of dictatorships.

This text will be of key interest to scholars, students, and practitioners of democratization, and to those who study autocracy and electoral authoritarianism, as well as comparative politics more broadly.

Merete Bech Seeberg is Assistant Professor at Aarhus University, Denmark.

Routledge Studies in Elections, Democracy and Autocracy
Series Editors:
Pippa Norris, *Harvard University, USA, and the University of Sydney, Australia*
Carolien van Ham, *the University of New South Wales, Australia.*

This series addresses the quality of elections, how and why electoral contests fall short of international standards, and the implications of flawed elections for democracy and autocracy. The series is published in association with the Electoral Integrity Project.

1 **Election Administration and the Politics of Voter Access**
   Kevin Pallister

2 **Electoral Rights in Europe**
   Advances and Challenges
   Edited by Helen Hardman and Brice Dickson

3 **Electoral Integrity and Political Regimes**
   Actors, Strategies and Consequences
   Edited by Holly Ann Garnett and Margarita Zavadskaya

4 **State Capacity, Economic Control, and Authoritarian Elections**
   Merete Bech Seeberg

For more information on this series please visit: www.routledge.com/Routledge-Studies-in-Elections-Democracy-and-Autocracy/book-series/REDA

State Capacity, Economic Control, and Authoritarian Elections

Merete Bech Seeberg

LONDON AND NEW YORK

First published 2018
by Routledge
2 Park Square, Milton Park, Abingdon, Oxon OX14 4RN

and by Routledge
711 Third Avenue, New York, NY 10017

Routledge is an imprint of the Taylor & Francis Group, an informa business

© 2018 Merete Bech Seeberg

The right of Merete Bech Seeberg to be identified as author of this work has been asserted by her in accordance with sections 77 and 78 of the Copyright, Designs and Patents Act 1988.

All rights reserved. No part of this book may be reprinted or reproduced or utilised in any form or by any electronic, mechanical, or other means, now known or hereafter invented, including photocopying and recording, or in any information storage or retrieval system, without permission in writing from the publishers.

Trademark notice: Product or corporate names may be trademarks or registered trademarks, and are used only for identification and explanation without intent to infringe.

British Library Cataloguing-in-Publication Data
A catalogue record for this book is available from the British Library

Library of Congress Cataloging-in-Publication Data
Names: Seeberg, Merete Bech, author.
Title: State capacity, economic control, and authoritarian elections / Merete Bech Seeberg.
Description: Abingdon, Oxon ; New York, NY : Routledge, 2018. | Series: Routledge studies in elections, democracy and autocracy ; 4 | Includes bibliographical references and index.
Identifiers: LCCN 2017051285 | ISBN 9781138202696 (hardback) | ISBN 9781315473413 (ebook)
Subjects: LCSH: Authoritarianism—Economic aspects. | Elections—Economic aspects. | Voting—Economic aspects. | Democratization—Economic aspects. | Economic development—Political aspects.
Classification: LCC JC480 .S4 2018 | DDC 324.9—dc23
LC record available at https://lccn.loc.gov/2017051285

ISBN: 978-1-138-20269-6 (hbk)
ISBN: 978-1-315-47341-3 (ebk)

Typeset in Times New Roman
by Apex CoVantage, LLC

Contents

List of figures ix
List of tables xi
Acknowledgements xiii

1 The puzzle of authoritarian elections 1

The puzzle 1
The argument 2
Time period and cases 6
The concepts: authoritarianism, elections, and regime breakdown 8
  Authoritarian regimes 8
  The dependent variable: regime stability and breakdown 12
  The independent variable: authoritarian multi-party elections 13
    Measuring multi-party elections 15
  One- and no-party elections and non-electoral regimes 16
The spread of authoritarian elections 17
  Elections over time 18
  Elections across regions 21
  Elections across authoritarian regime types 23
The plan of the book 27
Notes 29
References 30

2 Authoritarian capacities and regime stabilization through elections 35

Threats to power and survival strategies in authoritarian regimes 36
The existing literature on authoritarian elections 37
  Regime-sustaining elections 37
  Regime-subverting elections 39

vi *Contents*

  Empirical evidence 40
  A conditional effect 42
 The argument: authoritarian capacities and the conditional effect of elections 44
 Voting choices, elite defections, opposition mobilization, and voter protests 45
  (1) Voter choice 46
  (2) Candidate choice 47
  (3) Protester choice 48
 Authoritarian capacities and electoral strategies 49
  State capacity 50
  Economic control 51
  Authoritarian capacities, vote choice, supermajority victories, and the effect on candidate choice 53
  Authoritarian capacities and increased costs of being in opposition and protesting 58
  Hypotheses 59
  The costs of violence and fraud 60
 Typical cases and observable implications 63
  Three scenarios of authoritarian capacities 63
  Stabilization by election: high administrative capacity and/or economic control 64
  Breakdown by election: limited capacities 64
  Electoral survival: high coercive capacity but limited administrative capacity and economic control 65
 Notes 66
 References 67

3 State capacity and the effect of elections in authoritarian regimes   73

 Method and data 73
 Administrative capacity, elections, and regime breakdown 80
 Coercive capacity, elections, and regime breakdown 89
 Conclusion 94
 Notes 95
 References 96

4 Economic control and the effect of elections in authoritarian regimes   99

 Method and data 100
 Economic control, elections, and regime breakdown 102
  The subcomponents of economic control 108

Testing the effect of elections where all capacities are low 110
Conclusion 112
Notes 113
References 113

5 State capacity, economic control, and two divergent elections in Malaysia and the Philippines — 115

Method and case selection: Malaysia and the Philippines in the late 1980s 116
   State capacity and economic control in Malaysia and the Philippines 117
Theoretical expectations 120
Electoral dynamics 121
   Managed elections and authoritarian stability in Malaysia 121
   Post-electoral collapse in the Philippines 125
Conclusion 129
References 130

6 Electoral ups and downs, state capacity, and economic control in Zimbabwe — 133

Method and case selection: Zimbabwe in the 2000s 134
The 2008 elections in Zimbabwe: winning office, losing legitimacy 135
   Authoritarian capacities in Zimbabwe prior to the 2008 elections 135
      Administrative capacity 135
      Coercive capacity 137
      Economic control 138
      Theoretical expectations for the 2008 elections 141
   Electoral dynamics in 2008 142
      Government strategies and resources in the second round of the 2008 elections 142
      The effect of the 2008 electoral turmoil 147
The 2013 elections in Zimbabwe: reinstating power through a supermajority victory 148
   The GPA and the Inclusive Government 148
   A changed environment? ZANU(PF)'s coercive and administrative capacity and economic control during the IG 149
   Theoretical expectations to the 2013 elections 151
   Electoral dynamics in 2013 152
      Systemic manipulation 153

Manipulation of voters' preference formation 154
Manipulation of voters' preference expression 155
Restricting access to the vote 156
Manipulation of tabulating and counting 157
Economic and legal harassment of the opposition 157
Physical harassment of the opposition 158
The effect of the 2013 electoral dominance 159
Conclusion 160
Note 162
References 162

7 **Conclusion: authoritarian elections, capacities, and regime stability**   167

The findings and the need for further research 168
Implications for the literature on authoritarian elections 172
Authoritarian elections, violence, and standards of living 175
What are the implications for the study and promotion of democracy? 176
References 178

Appendix   182
Index   187

Figures

1.1a	Authoritarianism, elections, and regime breakdown by country, 1946–2008	9
1.1b	Authoritarianism, elections, and regime breakdown by country, 1946–2008 (continued)	10
1.1c	Authoritarianism, elections, and regime breakdown by country, 1946–2008 (continued)	10
1.1d	Authoritarianism, elections, and regime breakdown by country, 1946–2008 (continued)	11
1.1e	Authoritarianism, elections, and regime breakdown by country, 1946–2008 (continued)	11
1.1f	Authoritarianism, elections, and regime breakdown by country, 1946–2008 (continued)	12
1.2	Development in authoritarian elections, 1947–2008, count	18
1.3	Development in authoritarian elections, 1947–2008, percent	19
1.4	Development in authoritarian elections across regions, 1947–2008, percent	21
1.5	Development in authoritarian elections across regime types, 1947–2008, count	25
2.1	Actors' choices and regime stability	46
2.2	The conditioning effect of state capacity and incumbent economic control	50
3.1	The spread of elections across levels of capacities	79
3.2	Marginal effect of elections for increasing levels of administrative capacity	86
3.3	Predicted probability of breakdown for low and high administrative capacity	87
3.4	Marginal effect of elections (held within the past year) for increasing levels of coercive capacity	93
4.1	Marginal effect of elections for increasing levels of economic control – varying time horizons	106
4.2	Predicted probability of breakdown for regime with high and low levels of economic control	107

4.3 Marginal effect of elections for increasing levels of government spending 110
4.4 Predicted probability of regime breakdown where authoritarian capacities are low 111

Tables

1.1	Classification of autocracies, electoral dimension	17
1.2	Elections across authoritarian regime 1946–2008, illustrative examples	24
1.3	Elections across authoritarian regime types	26
2.1	Mechanisms linking elections to authoritarian regime stability	38
2.2	Strategies of electoral control and their effects	53
2.3	Hypotheses	62
2.4	Observable implications of the theory for each combination of capacities	66
3.1	Operationalizations	77
3.2	Multi-party elections, administrative capacity, and regime breakdown	81
3.3	Multi-party elections, administrative capacity, and regime breakdown – alternative controls	83
3.4	Multi-party elections, administrative capacity, and regime breakdown – varying time horizons	84
3.5	Multi-party elections, administrative capacity, and regime breakdown – robustness checks	88
3.6	Multi-party elections, coercive capacity, and regime breakdown	90
3.7	Multi-party elections, coercive capacity, and regime breakdown – varying time horizons	92
4.1	Multi-party elections, economic control, and regime breakdown	103
4.2	Multi-party elections, economic control, and regime breakdown – varying time horizons	104
4.3	Multi-party elections, subcomponents of economic control, and regime breakdown	109
5.1	Capacities, election strategies, and effects – Malaysia and the Philippines	128
6.1	Capacities, election strategies, and effects – Zimbabwe	146

Appendix

A	Multi-party elections, coercive capacity, and regime breakdown – alternative controls	182
B	Multi-party elections, military personnel, and regime breakdown	183
C	Multi-party elections (3 years), economic control, and regime breakdown – alternative controls	184
D	Multi-party elections (5 years), economic control, and regime breakdown – alternative controls	185
E	Multi-party elections (1 year), government spending, and regime breakdown – alternative controls	186

Acknowledgements

Elections. They are the cornerstone of any democracy; yet the existence of elections by no means guarantees citizens an actual, democratic choice. In too many places on our globe, elections have been bent so thoroughly out of shape that the reminiscence of a democratic competition is fleeting. At the age of 18 years and three days, I voted for the first time in local and parliamentary elections in Denmark – my proud father brought along his camera and I still have the picture of me leaving the voting booth with a big smile on my face. I have later observed elections in Denmark and around the world, but at 18, I was unaware of the concept of *electoral authoritarianism*. Authoritarian elections first came to my attention a few years later when I was a student at the London School of Economics (LSE). I crisscrossed the LSE library reading everything I could find on the topic and was intrigued by Beatriz Magaloni and Kenneth Greene's books on Mexico in the twentieth century describing voting experiences very different from what I had grown up with. How could some leaders thoroughly control electoral processes and outcomes? The question became the focal point of my PhD studies and eventually of this book.

I am very grateful to the many people who have helped me along the way. At the Department of Political Science, Aarhus University, I have found what I suspect is one of the best research and work environments that the world of academia has to offer. I wish to thank the department for financial support for my endeavors ranging from stat courses to field work. My dissertation advisors, Jørgen Elklit and Svend-Erik Skaaning, have been encouraging, supportive and constructive in their criticism throughout the process. The members of my committee, Jørgen Møller, Gerry Munck, and Carl Henrik Knutsen have expertly and generously advised me on how to turn a thesis into a book. A range of colleagues in Aarhus have commented on parts of the manuscript along the way, and I am thankful to David Andersen, Mette Kjær, Lasse Rørbæk, Jakob Tolstrup, the entire comparative politics section, and the excellent PhD group. I am also indebted to Annette Andersen for her excellent and speedy editing work.

Along the way, I have benefited from visiting fellowships in rewarding research environments. Larry Diamond kindly hosted me at the Center for Democracy, Development, and the Rule of Law at Stanford University. Pippa Norris, who – along with Carolien van Ham – has also supported me as editor on the Routledge series *Elections, Democracy, and Autocracy*, hosted me at the Electoral Integrity Project at University of Sydney. During these stays abroad and at international conferences and workshops, the manuscript has benefited from conversations with or comments from Rasmus Fonnesbæk Andersen, Jason Brownlee, Aurel Croissant, Daniella Donno, Francis Fukuyama, Barbara Geddes, Kenneth Greene, Judith Kelley, Staffan Lindberg, Beatriz Magaloni, Michael Miller, Lise Rakner, Lars Svåsand, Michael Wahman, Joseph Wright, and a number of other brilliant junior and senior scholars in the field. Finally, a very special thank you goes to the many Zimbabweans who openly and patiently shared their wisdom and stories with me.

Furthermore, parts of this book draw on research that has been published and I am indebted to the anonymous reviewers who helped improve the argument. Chapter 5 has been published in a different version as Seeberg, Merete Bech. 2014. "State capacity and the paradox of authoritarian elections." *Democratization* 21(7): 1265–1285. Parts of Chapter 2 and 4 have been published as Seeberg, Merete Bech. 2018. "Electoral Authoritarianism and Economic Control." *International Political Science Review* 39(1) 33–48: 1265–1285.

After many years of reading the acknowledgements of various publications in comparative politics because I was too tired to dive straight into the extensive formal models that typically extend from page 17 onwards, I have noted that academics, at least in the social sciences, often thank their children. My children have in no way contributed to my academic work nor have they been the least bit overbearing with me throughout the process. In fact, I think I would have gotten a lot more work done had it not been for colicky infants, long nights pacing the floors with a child suffering from the zillionth inner ear infection of the season, and hours spent building Lego rather than writing. But of course, I am eternally grateful to Harald and Bjørk for making all aspects of my life apart from academia so much more joyful. And finally: Henrik, *tusind tak*.

1 The puzzle of authoritarian elections

The puzzle

Dictators hold elections. They have done so since the late 19th century, and in many instances they have allowed the opposition to participate. Today, multi-party elections are the rule rather than the exception in authoritarian regimes. While non-electoral authoritarian regimes still exist, the majority of autocracies today have recently held a national-level election in which parties from outside the ruling front fielded candidates and were allowed to run. While dictators also win these elections thanks to various means of repression and manipulation – they are dictators, after all – the effects of elections on authoritarian regime stability are disputed.

In the aftermath of the Serbian parliamentary and presidential elections of September 2000, hundreds of thousands of protesters stormed the federal Parliament building in Belgrade. While the electoral commission abandoned the tallying of votes as they realized that the results were not in favor of incumbent President Slobodan Milosevic and a second round was hastily prepared, the people took to the streets to protest electoral manipulation (Birch 2002, 505). Coal miners went on strike, thus threatening the continued running of major power plants, and key elites of the authoritarian regime defected (Kuntz and Thompson 2009, 167–8; Bunce and Wolchik 2011, 110–11). Within weeks of the elections, Milosevic had given up power in what became known as the "Bulldozer Revolution." The dramatic events allowed observers to link the holding of non-democratic elections with the breakdown of the authoritarian regime.

Although perhaps less dramatic, the Senegalese President and dictator Abdou Diouf also gave up power in the context of elections in the very same year. In Senegal, the process was slower as "the gradual creation of democratic institutions precede[d] and contribute[d] to political culture change" (Vengroff and Magala 2001, 129). After a string of authoritarian elections, manipulated and won by the rulers, and a gradual process of reform, the opposition won the second round of the democratic elections in 2000, and Diouf graciously handed over power to opposition leader Abdoulaye Wade. The authoritarian regime had broken down and a process of democratization had started, exemplified by the competitive elections in 2000.

These and numerous other cases, including the "Rose Revolution" in Georgia, the "People Power Revolution" in the Philippines, and the gradual liberalizations in sub-Saharan Africa, have spurred a belief in elections as a force for transforming dictatorships. In this research tradition, elections are theorized to destabilize and sometimes even democratize authoritarian regimes (e.g., Lindberg 2006, 2009; Howard and Roessler 2006; Bunce and Wolchik 2011; Levitsky and Way 2010; Schedler 2006; Kuntz and Thompson 2009).

While some autocrats have given up power following a manipulated election or have gradually liberalized elections to the degree that they have become democratic, other rulers show no signs of conceding power in spite of multi-party elections; quite the contrary. From Asia to the Middle East, Africa, and Latin America, multi-party elections have been used to sustain authoritarian rule. In Zimbabwe, President Robert Mugabe, to the surprise of many observers, cemented his rule by winning the heavily manipulated yet relatively peaceful 2013 elections. The ruling Zimbabwe African National Union-Patriotic Front's (ZANU[PF]) 62% majority robbed the largest opposition party, the Movement for Democratic Change-Tsvangirai (MDC-T), of 30 parliamentary seats and sent the opposition into a tumultuous period of internal squabbles. Disagreeing over electoral tactics and blaming the electoral loss on opposition leader Morgan Tsvangirai, the opposition split in April 2014, leaving ZANU(PF) as Zimbabwe's strongest party in spite of a looming succession crisis.[1] Similar dynamics have been witnessed in cases as different as the party regimes of Malaysia and Singapore, Egypt under Hosni Mubarak, and Mexico in the 20th century. Although some of these regimes eventually collapsed, the rulers used regular multi-party elections to their advantage, sabotaging the opposition, creating legitimacy, and demonstrating superiority. Such cases have led many scholars to conclude that authoritarian elections are just another tool adopted and adapted to sustain authoritarian rule (e.g., Magaloni 2006; Gandhi and Lust-Okar 2009; Blaydes 2011).

The two claims are paradoxical: authoritarian elections both stabilize and undermine authoritarian rule. The paradox of authoritarian elections is the topic of this book. But rather than arguing that the effect of authoritarian elections on regime stability always works in a particular direction, the book asks: Why do multi-party elections sometimes stabilize authoritarian regimes and at other times lead to their demise?

The argument

I argue that the effect of authoritarian elections on regime stability depends on the central capacities that the rulers have at their disposal. Such capacities enable autocrats to carry out strategies of electoral manipulation that shape the choices of key actors, thus impacting the long-term effects of elections. Specifically, I argue that higher levels of administrative and coercive capacity, jointly referred to as state capacity, and control over the economy increase the probability that authoritarian multi-party elections will stabilize the regime. Where these capacities are lacking, the regime is more likely to succumb in the face of elections.

In the parliamentary elections in Malaysia in March 2004, the party regime drew on both its strong administrative and coercive force and control over the economy to dominate the election and control its long-term effects. Its strategies were targeted at voters, opposition, and internal elites. Leading opposition figure Anwar Ibrahim was in prison, convicted of sodomy. His opposition *Reformasi* movement that had challenged the ruling United Malays National Organization (UMNO) in the late 1990s had partly been co-opted into the regime, and the remaining opposition was split (Welsh 2005, 154–5). The media was biased (Case 2005), and opposition campaigning was obstructed by police and special branch personnel (Lee 2007). The ruling group's control over resources was abused to persuade voters to support the party, and in case this was not enough to secure a supermajority victory, the electoral commission was dominated by UMNO loyalists, and constituency boundaries were drawn to the advantage of the ruling coalition (Wong 2005, 317). In the end, the Barisan Nasional (BN), the coalition dominated by UMNO, secured 63.9% of votes, its largest majority in 25 years, and no major post-electoral protests occurred.

Only two years later in Singapore, a similar scenario played out. The ruling People's Action Party (PAP) relied on its state capacity and economic monopoly to limit opposition activity and lure voters into supporting the ruling party. Although the coercive apparatus was less visible, one of the major opposition parties was sued for defamation, leading to a rupture of its campaign and deterring others from representing the opposition (Chin 2007, 704–5). Gerrymandering of districts and ethnic quotas have traditionally been used to restrict the opposition, and the ruling party's control over resources was used to secure votes, as housing upgrades were reserved for districts that supported PAP (Ong and Tim 2014; Chin 2007; Tan 2013). As a result, the ruling party won over 66.6% of votes and 82 out of 84 seats.

These dynamics stand in contrast to the elections that toppled dictators in the post-communist world in the 2000s. In Georgia, incumbent President Eduard Shevardnadze was unable to curb elite defections, and former Minister of Justice Mikheil Saakashvili headed the opposition in the 2003 parliamentary elections. The ruling elites' attempts to take over the media and to inhibit opposition parties' ability to gain parliamentary seats through changes to the constitution failed (Bunce and Wolchik 2011, 156–7). Instead, the rulers relied more heavily on visible and blatant electoral fraud (OSCE/ODIHR 2004), thus spurring the post-electoral protests that became known as the "Rose Revolution." Facing angry citizens and with pro-opposition media broadcasting the "revolution" 24 hours a day, the poorly paid security forces proved disloyal and defected (Mitchell 2004; Bunce and Wolchik 2011, 165). Within weeks of the election, President Shevardnadze had resigned, and the opposition took over power.

These contrasting cases illustrate the argument that the capacities available to ruling elites, namely levels of state capacity and control over the economy, condition the effect of authoritarian elections. Such capacities enable and constrain electoral strategies aimed at affecting choices made by internal regime elites, opposition candidates, and ordinary citizens, and in turn affect the likelihood that the regime stabilizes through elections.

The literature on electoral authoritarianism has increasingly recognized the paradox of authoritarian elections. Schedler argues that elections are arenas of struggle between regime and opposition actors. Where the regime wins, elections may serve to stabilize its rule. But if the opposition comes out victorious, elections cause change (Schedler 2013). I agree with Schedler's notion that elections are a double-edged sword, holding the potential to both sustain and subvert authoritarian regimes. However, I disagree with Schedler's main claim that the result of this struggle between opposition and regime, playing out in the context of authoritarian uncertainty, is determined primarily by actors' choices (Schedler 2013, 141). I argue that deeper-running factors affect the probability that elections support authoritarian regimes because they affect the choices made by central actors. Just as Svolik argues that the occurrence of personalist rule is not only a function of the individual leader's ambitions and personal abilities to concentrate power or the elites' attempts to reign him in, but depends on the conditions of authoritarian rule (Svolik 2012, 55), this book presents the claim that the effect of authoritarian elections is shaped by the circumstances under which the elections play out. This approach turns the "paradox" of authoritarian elections into a theory of a conditional effect of authoritarian elections.

Why focus on authoritarian capacities? A number of factors may likely affect electoral dynamics. The international environment, the strength of the ruling party, the existence of an opposition coalition, and the levels of legitimacy that the incumbent enjoys have previously been proposed as factors affecting whether electoral authoritarian regimes democratize (Howard and Roessler 2006; Levitsky and Way 2010; Donno 2013; Flores and Nooruddin 2016). I argue that in investigating the effects of authoritarian elections on the likelihood of regime breakdown, we have failed to take into account the capacities available to the ruling group – in particular the strength of the state apparatus and the rulers' degree of control over the economy. These factors matter because they affect the electoral strategies available to rulers when they are challenged by the opposition in what Schedler terms a two-level game of authoritarian elections (Schedler 2013, 115–17). By presiding over a strong state apparatus, both its administrative and its coercive arm, and by dominating the economy, autocrats may affect the electoral game (the fight over votes) and the institutional game (the fight over rules).

The electoral strategies employed to do so are targeted at the three main actor groups of the authoritarian regime: the internal elites, the opposition, and the voters. Relying on state capacity and control over the economy to conduct electoral strategies of voter manipulation and opposition repression, autocrats affect the individual-level choices made by regime elites, opposition actors, and citizens. Thus, the UMNO leadership in Malaysia was dependent on its strong coercive force, both the police corps and the special branch, to subtly and effectively disrupt the opposition's political campaign, thus attempting to affect voters' preference formation, intimidate potential opposition activists, and prevent regime elites from defecting (Lee 2007). And in both Malaysia and Singapore, a loyal civil service and resources stemming from the ruling party's control over the economy were crucial in diverting economic benefits to supporters of the incumbents, thus subtly manipulating voters' preference formation (Ong and Tim 2014; Chin 2007).

In Georgia, unlike in Malaysia and Singapore, the opposition was not effectively harassed by the courts, and the collapsing state apparatus did not allow for subtle manipulation of voters' preference formation or discreet rewriting of electoral laws to the ruling party's advantage. Instead, the state apparatus was employed to steal votes on election day (OSCE/ODIHR 2004). While this maneuver ensured electoral victory, the failing coercive apparatus could not prevent citizens from taking to the streets, and when protests escalated, the underpaid military was not willing to put them down. The autocrat did not have the capacities to manage elections.

Thus, Schedler may be right when he states that actors' choices determine the effect of authoritarian elections. However, I attempt to identify the structures that shape these choices. The theoretical argument is not at odds with Howard and Roessler's (2006) and Donno's (2013) findings that opposition coalitions are crucial in bringing down electoral authoritarian regimes. The theory highlights that high levels of state capacity and control over the economy enable repressive and manipulative strategies that affect the likelihood that such a coalition occurs in the first place.

By assessing the effect of authoritarian capacities on electoral dynamics, the theory does not rule out actor-centered explanations. These explanations are taken into account as the capacities available to autocrats are theorized to impact the effect of elections exactly because they affect choices on the micro level. Furthermore, the book does not claim that authoritarian capacities are the sole factors conditioning the effect of authoritarian elections. The strength of the party and the involvement of the international community may also affect the two-level game of elections. These explanatory factors are not universal, however. The organization and strength of the ruling party may indeed be relevant in party regimes, but as shall be demonstrated later, numerous authoritarian regimes without a dominant ruling party, including personalist and military regimes, hold elections. Furthermore, elections have undergirded authoritarian stability in electoral autocracies both with and without the involvement of the international community. Thus, whereas additional factors affecting the role of elections undoubtedly exist, the claim of this book is that by not analyzing the conditioning effect of authoritarian capacities, namely the capacity of the state and the control over the economy, we have overlooked important factors that can help explain the apparent paradox of authoritarian elections.

The effect of authoritarian elections on regime stability presents a puzzle that this book seeks to resolve. But why does the puzzle need a solution? In an interview in 2007, Adam Przeworskii deemed dictatorships the most "understudied area in comparative politics" (Munck and Snyder 2007, 473). In particular, he referred to the prevailing notion in 20th century comparative politics that institutions in authoritarian regimes are *pro forma* and have no actual effects on regime dynamics. However, since the publication of a seminal article by Geddes (1999), research on authoritarian institutions has increased dramatically. This development is dubbed "the institutional turn" of a subfield now known as "comparative authoritarianism" (Pepinsky 2014; see also Gandhi and Lust-Okar 2009; Brancati 2014). As researchers have acknowledged that "the end of history" (Fukuyama 1992) did not put an end to authoritarianism, and that this regime form is prevalent across the globe, focus has turned to the inner workings of authoritarian regimes (Geddes 1999; Svolik 2012, 27–8; Gandhi 2008, 18–21; Ulfelder 2005; Weeks 2012; Wright 2009; Escribà-Folch and Wright 2010; Gandhi and Przeworski 2007). Geddes has pointed out how "different kinds of authoritarianism differ from each other as much as they differ from democracy" (Geddes 1999, 121). The fact that more than a third of the world's population lives under some form of authoritarian rule in itself justifies an increased focus on the dynamics of authoritarianism.

This book contributes to the research agenda on institutions in authoritarian regimes. It focuses not only on the workings of authoritarian systems and the effect of institutions, but more specifically on the effect of authoritarian institutions on the prospects for change. Just as there is a need to know how one of the world's most prevalent political systems works, we must also know more about how and why it sometimes ends.

The aim of this book is to disentangle the conditional effect of authoritarian elections on regime stability. But the outcomes of authoritarian regime breakdowns vary. Whereas some electoral authoritarian regimes, such as Mexico in the 20th century, collapse and emerge as democracies, many others, such as Egypt following the Arab Spring, make room for a new form of authoritarian rule. The end result of an authoritarian regime breakdown greatly affects the lives of many people. Why authoritarian regimes break down, and what takes their place once they have succumbed, however, are two different research questions. I cannot fully account for both within the scope of this book. By focusing on the determinants of authoritarian stability through elections, and thus also the conditions under which electoral authoritarian regimes collapse, I leave aside the equally interesting and perhaps even more important question of the circumstances under which authoritarian elections may promote democratization. The analyses restrict the focus to the circumstances under which autocracies break down regardless of what comes in their place, be it democracy, a new authoritarian system, or collapse into civil war. After all, the end of an authoritarian regime is a necessary precondition for the emergence of a new democracy. In the conclusion, I reflect upon the prospects for democratization by elections and avenues for further research.

Time period and cases

To scrutinize the theoretical claims, the book engages in cross-national studies of all authoritarian regimes from 1946–2008 and in-depth studies of four cases of authoritarian elections. This combination of cases and cross-national studies is an improvement over many studies of electoral autocracies. Theoretically and empirically rigorous studies of authoritarian elections have taken us far (i.e., Lindberg 2006; Magaloni 2006; Greene 2007; Blaydes 2011), but have focused on certain countries or regions. Thus, we are left wondering whether the diverging effects of authoritarian elections that they unravel may be a function of the cases they study. I owe great debts to these works as my theoretical apparatus builds on their findings, but I add to them by theorizing the conditions, namely the varying degrees of authoritarian capacities, under which elections have such diverging effects and by testing the theory across the entire population of autocracies. Unlike existing cross-national studies (i.e., Brownlee 2009b; Hadenius and Teorell 2009; Knutsen, Nygård, and Wig 2017), however, the case analyses allow me to test the proposed theoretical mechanisms through which authoritarian capacities condition the effect of elections. Whereas the statistical studies deal with the overall relationship between elections, capacities, and stability, the case studies tune in on the effect of capacities on the ruler's electoral strategies and its effects on voters, political candidates, and potential protesters.

The chosen time period is largely an effect of data availability. However, it is an improvement over many studies of electoral autocracies that are limited to the post-Cold War era, in which a unique liberal hegemony has undoubtedly shaped regime developments, and in particular the spread of democratic institutions across the globe (Schedler 2013, 57). Thus, in some respects, these analyses meet the call for studies of authoritarian elections that go further back in time (Møller 2014).

On the other hand, the Cold War period may very well be as unique a period as – if not, historically speaking, even more unique than – the last decade of the 20th century. Authoritarian politics across the globe, including their institutional characteristics, capacities, and longevity, were profoundly shaped by the two superpowers of the East and the West, both of which supported, inspired, and in other ways affected their share of authoritarian regimes. Thus, the time period under study will likely affect both descriptive and causal inferences (Boix 2011). In the cross-national analyses in Chapters 3–4, a control for the Cold War era is introduced to account for the changing world order. But as data on elections, capacities, and regime stability before 1946 are not yet available, the scope condition for this book is the post-World War II era, spanning both a bipolar world order and a period of liberal hegemony.

Within this period, I also choose four cases of authoritarian elections in which to test the plausibility of the proposed theoretical mechanisms. The authoritarian multi-party elections in the Philippines in 1986, Malaysia in 1990, and Zimbabwe in 2008 and 2013 all represent typical cases of the argument. In the Philippines, President Marcos prevailed over a weakened bureaucracy and a failing army and did not have the means to control the economy. Shortly after holding multi-party elections, he was forced to flee, and his regime collapsed. If the collapse was indeed partly attributable to the combination of limited capacities and multi-party elections, a number of observable implications follow from the theoretical apparatus. If we track events in the Philippines in the months and weeks surrounding the 1986 elections, these implications should be detectable. This is the topic of the first part of Chapter 5.

Malaysia under the rule of UMNO and Prime Minister Muhammad Mahatir in 1990 and the two most recent elections in Zimbabwe under President Robert Mugabe's reign, on the other hand, represent typical cases of regime stabilization through elections. In Malaysia, the administrative and coercive force at the disposal of the rulers was impressive and the regime displayed extensive control over the economy through government interventions and the introduction of state-owned enterprises. In Zimbabwe, Mugabe displayed heavy control over the administrative apparatus and particularly the strong coercive force comprising the military, the police force, war veterans, and various youth militias, which were commonly employed to intervene in politics. Although the economy was in shambles, Mugabe and his allies successfully controlled a significant part of the economic activity left on the territory through measures such as land redistribution, price regulations, and control over licenses. But rulers may use different capacities, and use them in different ways, in order to abuse elections to stabilize the regime. The latter three cases provide an opportunity to test the various theoretical mechanisms related to stabilization by elections. Such analyses are carried out in the latter part of Chapter 5 and in Chapter 6.

The concepts: authoritarianism, elections, and regime breakdown

Before presenting and testing the argument, I unfold the central concepts and turn to an analysis of the spread of authoritarian elections across regions and over time so as to demonstrate that the phenomenon of authoritarian elections, and thus its effects, is too widespread to be ignored.

Authoritarian regimes

A *regime* is defined as the set of formal and informal rules that structure the access to political power (Mazzuca 2010, 342; Geddes, Wright, and Frantz 2014a, 314–15). To define an authoritarian regime,[2] I rely on the Schumpeterian understanding of democracy as an "institutional arrangement for arriving at political decisions in which individuals acquire the power to decide by means of a competitive struggle for the people's vote" (Schumpeter 1974 [1942], 269). Following the conventions in the literature, I define *authoritarianism* as a residual category (e.g., Svolik 2012, 20; Gandhi 2008, 7–8).[3] Thus, autocracies are regimes in which leaders are not chosen through elections with uncertainty over outcome.

The minimalist definition of democracy is chosen to enable a focus on truly *authoritarian* elections. Much work on authoritarian elections and their effects on democratization rests on a Dahlian definition of democracy (e.g., Brownlee 2009b; Hadenius and Teorell 2007; Donno 2013; Levitsky and Way 2010), which demands that democratic regimes not only feature competition but also protect certain political rights, namely freedom of expression, association, and the right to seek alternative information (Dahl 1989, 220–2). Thus, the term *competitive authoritarianism* emerges, covering regimes that are authoritarian yet hold competitive elections (Levitsky and Way 2010; Diamond 2002). This definition is in sync with a Dahlian understanding of democracy but leaves studies of the effects of authoritarian elections on regime breakdown and democratization vulnerable to endogeneity claims. Did competitive elections lead to democracy? Or was democracy already present – partly in the form of competitive elections – and spurred by a completely different process? A minimalist definition of democracy ensures that authoritarian elections are uncompetitive, and the concept thus does not overlap with aspects of a democratization process.

The puzzle of authoritarian elections 9

To identify authoritarian regimes, I rely on the Autocratic Regimes Dataset (GWF). Geddes and collaborators code a country-year as authoritarian if the leader did not acquire power through a reasonably competitive election in which at least 10% of the population had the right to vote or succeeded a democratically elected leader following constitutional rules; if a democratically elected government circumvents electoral competition (for instance, by banning opposition parties or annulling results); or if the military wields substantial power, for instance, by banning parties from participating in elections or dictating economic policies (Geddes, Wright, and Frantz 2014b, 6–7). With the requirement of at least 10% suffrage, the measure departs slightly from the strictly Schumpeterian definition of democracy. However, few electoral regimes fall short of this requirement in the covered period (after World War II). Further, the measure excludes from the category of authoritarian regimes country-years in which no government controlled the majority of the territory, the regime was foreign-occupied, or a provisional government was in place to oversee a transition to democracy. In this and the following chapters, I include in the analyses all country-years classified as authoritarian based on GWF data.

The GWF data count 4,587 authoritarian country-years from 1946–2010. Authoritarian spells – that is, periods of authoritarian rule – occurred in 118 different countries. Figures 1.1a–1.1f illustrate authoritarian regime spells across

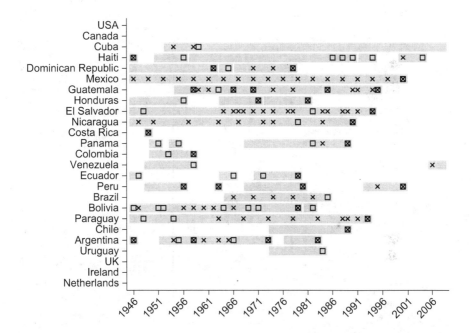

Figure 1.1a Authoritarianism, elections, and regime breakdown by country, 1946–2008

Note: grey = authoritarian. ▫ = breakdown (only for autocracies). **x** = multi-party election (only for autocracies). Data on elections from NELDA (Hyde and Marinov 2012), number of parties from CGV (Cheibub, Gandhi, and Vreeland 2010), and authoritarianism and breakdown from GWF (Geddes, Wright, and Frantz 2014a).

Figure 1.1b Authoritarianism, elections, and regime breakdown by country, 1946–2008 (continued)

Note: grey = authoritarian. □ = breakdown (only for autocracies). **x** = multi-party election (only for autocracies). Data on elections from NELDA, number of parties from CGV, and authoritarianism and breakdown from GWF.

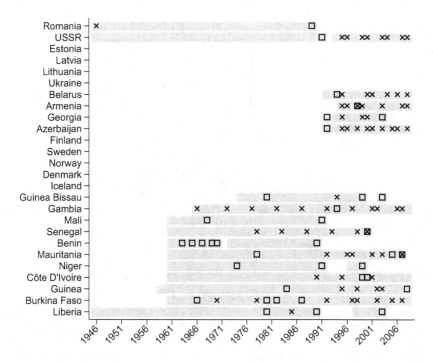

Figure 1.1c Authoritarianism, elections, and regime breakdown by country, 1946–2008 (continued)

Note: grey = authoritarian. □ = breakdown (only for autocracies). **x** = multi-party election (only for autocracies). Data on elections from NELDA, number of parties from CGV, and authoritarianism and breakdown from GWF.

Figure 1.1d Authoritarianism, elections, and regime breakdown by country, 1946–2008 (continued)

Note: grey = authoritarian. □ = breakdown (only for autocracies). **x** = multi-party election (only for autocracies). Data on elections from NELDA, number of parties from CGV, and authoritarianism and breakdown from GWF.

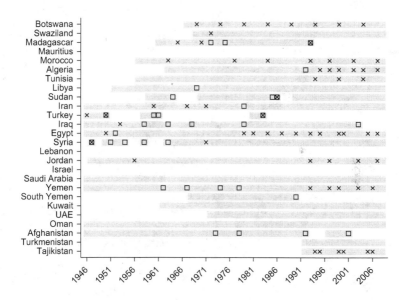

Figure 1.1e Authoritarianism, elections, and regime breakdown by country, 1946–2008 (continued)

Note: grey = authoritarian. □ = breakdown (only for autocracies). **x** = multi-party election (only for autocracies). Data on elections from NELDA, number of parties from CGV, and authoritarianism and breakdown from GWF.

12 *The puzzle of authoritarian elections*

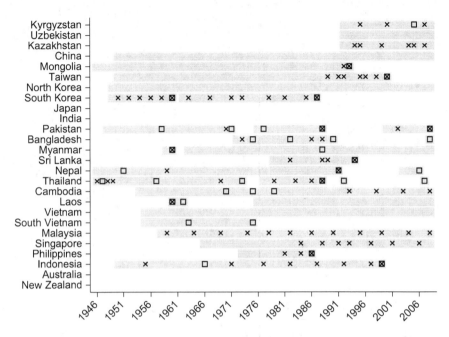

Figure 1.1f Authoritarianism, elections, and regime breakdown by country, 1946–2008 (continued)

Note: grey = authoritarian. □ = breakdown (only for autocracies). **x** = multi-party election (only for autocracies). Data on elections from NELDA, number of parties from CGV, and authoritarianism and breakdown from GWF.

countries. Grey areas indicate authoritarian rule. These countries include classic cases of authoritarian rule, such as Cuba and North Korea; well-known examples of electoral autocracies such as Mexico until 2000, Russia since 1994, and Zimbabwe since 1980; and also cases that some datasets would count as democratic, perhaps the most prominent example being Venezuela since 2006.

The dependent variable: regime stability and breakdown

When are authoritarian regimes stable? Regime *stability*, like consolidation, is difficult to gauge. The clearest evidence of instability is the collapse of the regime. Vice versa, if the regime does not break down, it is likely stable. To simplify matters, regime stability is here defined as continuity. Stability is the absence of breakdown. Thus, when I analyze the effect of multi-party elections on regime stability, I investigate how the holding of elections affects the likelihood that the regime breaks down.

A regime *breakdown* is any transition from one regime to another; that is, a change to the rules guiding the access to power (Mazzuca 2010, 336). The most well-researched transitions in authoritarian regimes are democratizations, but the most common forms are the transitions from one authoritarian regime to the next (Geddes, Wright, and Frantz 2014a). Such transitions between autocratic regimes may occur as a government elected in uncompetitive elections is ousted, exemplifying a change to the formal rules of access to power. But transitions from one authoritarian regime to the next also occur when a coup changes the informal rules of power so that rulers following the coup are selected from a new group of people (Geddes, Wright, and Frantz 2014a, 315). This book analyzes the effect of authoritarian multi-party elections on the likelihood of any of these types of transitions, as they all exemplify the breakdown of the existing regime.

The authoritarian breakdowns were spread across 93 different countries and are marked by a square in Figures 1.1a–1.1f. It is clear that far from all breakdowns led to democratization – a great number of the breakdowns occurred during a prolonged period of autocracy, marked by the grey color in Figure 1.1. For instance, Mobutu's autocracy in the DRC collapsed in 1997 following the civil war of the 1990s but was replaced by another dictatorship led by Kabila. The transition from Mobutu to Kabila in the DRC is marked in Figure 1.1d by a square in 1997 punctuating the grey area of authoritarian rule in the DRC. In other cases, authoritarian breakdowns were followed by democratic rule. The transition from the authoritarian regime under PRI to democracy in Mexico in 2000 is marked by a square in Figure 1.1a, and the following years of democratic rule are white rather than grey. The prospects for democratization following breakdown by elections are discussed in the conclusion. Here, I turn to the spread of multi-party elections across authoritarian regimes.

The independent variable: authoritarian multi-party elections

The main explanatory variable investigated in this book is the holding of *multi-party elections* in authoritarian regimes. The role played by one- and no-party elections has been the topic of an older literature on authoritarian elections (see Hermet, Rouquie, and Rose 1978), and a few prominent pieces have also brought the role of one-party elections into the recent literature on authoritarian institutions (see Malesky and Schuler 2010, 2011). However, most of the recent literature on authoritarian elections or "electoral authoritarianism" centers on some form of multi-party elections (e.g., Schedler 2006, 2013; Brownlee 2009a; Lindberg 2009, 2006; Howard and Roessler 2006; Levitsky and Way 2010; Donno 2013; Magaloni 2006; Greene 2007; Blaydes 2011). Whereas some of the effects of elections may be identical independent of the number of parties participating, others will be unique to multi-party elections. This book focuses on the effect of elections in which opposition parties are allowed to participate. As shown later, such regimes are the most common form of authoritarianism today, and they are also the form most closely resembling democracy.

Multi-party elections are defined as elections in which competitors from outside the ruling front participate. They are distinct from one-party elections or no-party elections, where all registered competitors support the ruling front. Multi-party elections occurring under authoritarian rule as defined previously are per definition authoritarian elections. They may break with only a few of the characteristics of "free and fair" elections (Elklit and Svensson 1997) or with most of them. Most importantly, given the definition of authoritarianism, multi-party elections in authoritarian regimes are in essence uncompetitive. If the opposition were to win and take over power, the regime would have been classified as a minimalist democracy rather than an autocracy.

How does the concept of multi-party elections relate to previous work on elections in authoritarian regimes – what has been dubbed "electoral authoritarianism"? Schedler introduces the term "electoral authoritarianism" to cover regimes that hold multi-party elections yet "violate the liberal-democratic principles of freedom and fairness so profoundly and systematically as to render elections instruments of authoritarian rule rather than 'instruments of democracy'" (2006, 3). But the notion of electoral authoritarianism covers great variation in especially the competitiveness of elections. Diamond divides electoral authoritarianism into two subgroups (2002, 5). The non-competitive group, *hegemonic* authoritarianism, Sartori originally described as "A two-level system in which one party tolerates and discretionally allocates a fraction of its power to subordinate political groups . . . The hegemonic party formula may afford the appearance but surely does not afford the substance of competitive politics" (Sartori 2005, 205). Thus, hegemonic regimes are non-democratic according to a Schumpeterian definition of democracy: there is no uncertainty over who will hold power after the election.

The conceptualization of the competitive subgroup, *competitive* electoral authoritarianism, is developed by Levitsky and Way. These regimes are characterized by the lack of free and fair elections, but "arenas of contestation exist through which opposition forces may periodically challenge, weaken, and occasionally even defeat autocratic incumbents" (Levitsky and Way 2002, 54). In contrast to their hegemonic counterparts, their level of competition qualifies at least some competitive autocracies as democratic when a Schumpeterian notion of democracy is applied.

My definition of multi-party authoritarian elections largely corresponds to that of hegemonic autocracies. However, I do not distinguish hegemonic autocracies from competitive autocracies based on the incumbents' margins of victory, as is common in the literature on electoral authoritarianism (e.g., Diamond 2002; Roessler and Howard 2009; Brownlee 2009a). Instead, both hegemonic regimes and those competitive regimes that do not have uncertainty over electoral outcome qualify as multi-party electoral authoritarian according to the definition presented here. Those of Levitsky and Way's competitive regimes in which elections have uncertainty over outcomes are considered democratic following the Schumpeterian understanding and are thus excluded from the analysis. This restriction of the category of authoritarian multi-party elections allows me to explore the effect of multi-party elections in authoritarian regimes regardless of the incumbent's margin of victory in such elections. Instead, both margins of victory and the effect of elections on regime stability may be explained by other factors. The theoretical argument of Chapter 2 takes advantage of this approach and theorizes how the

The puzzle of authoritarian elections 15

capacities available to the autocrat condition the effect of multi-party elections, among other things because they enable supermajority victories.

Measuring multi-party elections

How do we know a multi-party election when we see it? I define it as an election in which competitors from outside the ruling front participate. There are thus two questions to be answered: What counts as an election, and how does one know that a real competitor is represented?

To answer the first question, I rely on the NELDA dataset, which identifies all direct, national elections in countries with more than 500,000 inhabitants between 1945 and 2010 (Hyde and Marinov 2012). Thus, it includes both executive and legislative elections, as well as constituent assemblies as long as these were directly elected by the people (regardless of franchise requirement) as opposed to election by members of a council or the like (Hyde and Marinov 2012, 1). Referenda are only included when they are votes on the continued rule of the incumbent.[4]

How many elections does it take for a regime to be "electoral"? Hadenius and Teorell have rightly pointed to confusion over the explanatory variable in studies of authoritarian elections: Is it the holding of a single election or the cumulative number of elections that affects authoritarian regime outcomes (Hadenius and Teorell 2009)? It is primarily theories of elections as levers of democratization that are concerned with the cumulative number of elections held in a country (e.g., Lindberg 2006). For studies of elections as causes of stability or breakdown of autocracies, the dependent variable is often the regime's status as "electoral" (e.g., Brownlee 2009b; Magaloni 2008). The exception is studies that focus on electoral outcomes, in which case the unit of analysis is the election, and the independent variables take on other forms, such as actors' strategies or international interventions (e.g., Donno 2013; Howard and Roessler 2006).

Rather than scoring a regime as electoral if it has held an election at any point during its rule, I code regimes as electoral if they have held more recent elections. The threshold for what counts as a recent election will inevitably be somewhat arbitrary. In the descriptive analyses, I code regimes as electoral if they have held at least one executive or legislative election within the past seven years. Seven years is a rather large interval. However, it ensures that autocracies holding regular elections with intervals longer than what is the most common in democracies are still classified as having elections (e.g., Mexico held presidential elections every six years during the 20th century – see Figure 1.1a).[5] Furthermore, only elections held under the current authoritarian regime count. That is, elections held within the past seven years but during a democratic phase or held under a previous authoritarian regime do not qualify a regime as electoral authoritarian.[6][7]

Elections taking place in regimes recorded as authoritarian by the GWF measure are counted as authoritarian elections. But are they multi-party elections? To answer the second question and capture whether an election featured competitors from outside the ruling front, I rely on two variables from the data collected by Cheibub, Gandhi, and Vreeland (CGV). "Defacto2" registers whether parties outside the ruling front exist and "lparty" records whether non-ruling front parties are represented in the legislature (Cheibub, Gandhi, and Vreeland 2010). Multi-party electoral regimes score 2 on both variables, indicating that even though the winner of the elections is known *a priori*, opposition candidates run and win votes. An example would be Singapore since 1984 or Egypt from 1981 until the ousting of Mubarak in 2011, where the opposition ran and won votes, yet the regime remained authoritarian as there was no real uncertainty over electoral outcomes.

To sum up, a multi-party election is one in which non-ruling front parties are elected into the legislature. Multi-party elections occurring in authoritarian regimes are marked by a black X in Figures 1.1a–1.1f. If there was more than one election in a single year, this is only marked by one cross. It is evident that breakdowns – as well as long spells of stability – occurred in both electoral and non-electoral regimes. For example, the communist party dictatorship of China has ruled in the entire period under investigation without holding national, multi-party elections and without breaking down. The party dictatorship of Malaysia displays the same level of stability (understood as the absence of breakdown) but has seen regular multi-party elections (see Figure 1.1f). During the uninterrupted period of authoritarian rule in Bolivia lasting until 1979 (marked by the grey shaded area), both elections and breakdowns occurred, and in Uruguay in 1984, the military regime broke down without ever having held an election (see Figure 1.1a). Thus, there is great variation in terms of both elections and breakdown.

In the following descriptive analyses, a regime is counted as having multi-party elections if such an election has been held under the regime within the past seven years (in the causal analyses of Chapters 3–4, I estimate the effect of elections across various time horizons). Based on these measures, all authoritarian regimes from 1946–2008[8] can be classified as either having or not having multi-party elections.

One- and no-party elections and non-electoral regimes

Multi-party elections are the independent variable of the analyses of the following chapters. But the group of regimes without multi-party elections also covers variation. Previously, multi-party elections were distinguished not only from non-electoral regimes but also from those in which elections are held but no parties from outside the ruling front are allowed to participate. For the purpose of the causal analyses in the following chapters, no distinction will be made between *non-electoral* and *one- and no-party electoral* regimes. To assess the spread of authoritarian multi-party elections to other categories of authoritarian regimes, the concepts of non-electoral autocracies and one- and no-party electoral autocracies are briefly operationalized here.

The regimes in which no national elections were recorded in the past seven years according to the NELDA data are counted as non-electoral. An example is Saudi Arabia, a monarchy that holds local but not national elections. Along with the multi-party regimes that have been operationalized previously, this leaves a

Table 1.1 Classification of autocracies, electoral dimension

	Non-electoral autocracy	One- and no-party electoral autocracy	Multi-party electoral autocracy
Elections	-	+	+
Multi-party elections	-	-	+
Uncertainty in elections	-	-	-

residual group that holds elections yet does not feature parties from outside the ruling front in the legislature. In their typology of authoritarian regimes, Hadenius and Teorell include a category for one-party regimes in which "all parties but *one* are forbidden (whether formally or de facto) from taking part in elections." They also have a category for no-party regimes defined as electoral regimes in which "*all* political parties (or at least candidates representing a party) are prohibited" (Hadenius and Teorell 2007, 147). Interesting nuances indeed exist between one-party regimes on the one hand and partyless regimes on the other. Nonetheless, I collapse them into one subgroup, as I am primarily interested in comparing the development in authoritarian elections to that of non-electoral and non-multi-party electoral autocracies. This residual group can be termed one- and no-party electoral regimes. It comprises both Hadenius and Teorell's one-party electoral regimes and no-party electoral regimes.[9] This category includes cases such as Syria (before the ongoing civil war), which held regular legislative and executive elections yet tolerated no opposition to the incumbent president, and Uzbekistan, formally a four-party system but with all parties belonging to the ruling front. The distinction between non-electoral, one- and no-party electoral, and multi-party electoral autocracies is summarized in Table 1.1.

In Figures 1.1a–1.1f, non-electoral and one- and no-party electoral regimes are indistinguishable, as none of them have held multi-party elections. The development of all three subgroups of autocracy is explored in the following analysis. However, the chapters that follow focus on the effect of the third class of elections. That is, the independent variable is the holding of multi-party elections (those indicated in Figures 1.1a–1.1f), and regimes in which no such elections are held are collapsed into one group whether they hold one-party elections or no elections at all.

The spread of authoritarian elections

This book examines the effect of authoritarian multi-party elections on regime stability. But how common are such elections? Are authoritarian elections a new phenomenon? Are some authoritarian regime types or some regions more prone to holding elections? And do autocrats perhaps prefer one-party elections over more risky multi-party competitions, such as those investigated in the following chapters?

18 *The puzzle of authoritarian elections*

Elections over time

How have authoritarian elections developed over the course of the past half century? Figure 1.2 presents developments in authoritarian elections from 1947–2008 in frequencies and Figure 1.3 shows the same development in percentages. As revealed by Figure 1.2, the absolute number of authoritarian regimes peaked in the late 1970s, when 99 of the world's regimes did not have leaders selected through competitive elections. In earlier periods, autocracies likely comprised a greater percentage of the world's regimes, but decolonization from the early 1960s onward produced an increase both in the overall number of independent regimes and in autocracies. However, as found by previous studies mapping the development of democracy in the late 20th century (see Møller and Skaaning 2013; Hadenius and Teorell 2007), the effects of the third wave of democratization are undeniable: since the late 1970s, authoritarianism has been on the decline, as exemplified by the collapse of the Latin American military dictatorships, the democratization of a great number of the post-communist regimes, and the spread of somewhat free and fair multi-party elections across sub-Saharan Africa and Asia. In 2008, there were 59 autocracies worldwide.

Thus, the trend of authoritarian decline did not kick in following the end of the Cold War, but started even earlier. Yet if we turn instead to the distribution of elections across authoritarian regimes, the breakdown of the Soviet empire and the beginning of liberal hegemony have clearer effects.

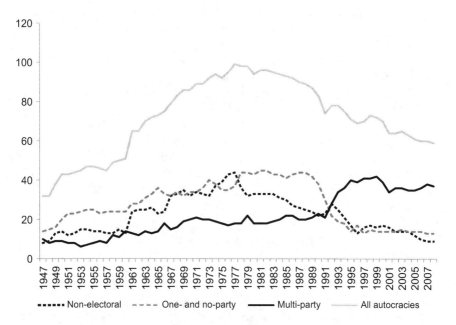

Figure 1.2 Development in authoritarian elections, 1947–2008, count

Note: Number of regimes with different types of elections over time. Data on regimes from GWF, data on elections from NELDA, and data on number of parties from CGV.

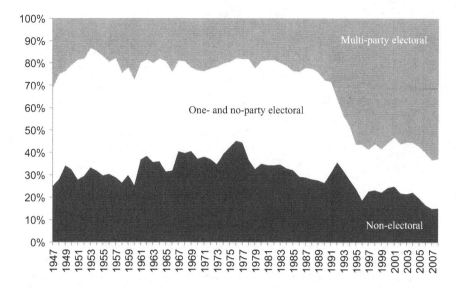

Figure 1.3 Development in authoritarian elections, 1947–2008, percent

Note: Percent of regimes with different types of elections over time. Data on regimes from GWF, data on elections from NELDA, and data on number of parties from CGV.

Figure 1.3 shows that just as the number of autocracies peaked in the late 1970s, this was also the period in which the majority of these regimes did not feature elections (apart from the few years immediately following World War II). In 1976, 45% of authoritarian regimes were non-electoral. The non-electoral regimes of the 1970s include China, Cuba under Fidel Castro, and the military regimes of Guatemala, Peru, Chile, and a number of other Latin American countries. A few of the communist party regimes of Eastern Europe, such as Yugoslavia, and a range of personalist regimes in Africa, including Libya and Uganda, as well as the Middle Eastern monarchies were also non-electoral.

Previous studies, dating back to 1972 at the earliest (the year the first Freedom House rating was released), have shown a marked decrease in the number of what is often termed "closed authoritarianism," comprising non-electoral, no-party electoral, and one-party electoral autocracies (e.g., Roessler and Howard 2009). My data confirm the trend and date the beginning of the decline of non-electoral authoritarianism to the mid-1970s – but the drop in non-electoral regimes is accompanied by the general decline of authoritarianism worldwide. Thus, although non-electoral autocracies disappear, the number of electoral authoritarian regimes does not increase until 1991. Throughout the 1990s, however, electoral autocracies as a share of authoritarian regimes increased dramatically: 36% of autocracies had not held an election within the past seven years in 1992 compared to 15% in 2008.

The most noticeable development, however, is not the decline of non-electoral regimes but the rise of multi-party autocracies. Regimes in which authoritarian rule was mixed with multi-party elections comprised 28% of autocracies in 1991. In the following two decades, when the liberal world order became dominant, international institutions started to attach conditions of at least formal democratic-institutional progress to aid and loans. As there was no longer a rival superpower to which distressed dictatorships could turn for support (Joseph 1997; Levitsky and Way 2010; Carothers 2002), multi-party elections in authoritarian regimes expanded by no less than 35 percentage points. Authoritarian regimes from Singapore to Senegal introduced multi-party elections during this period (indicated by the Xs in Figures 1.1a–1.1f), and in 2008, 63% of autocracies had held a multi-party election within the past seven years.

This trend largely corresponds to the findings of Roessler and Howard, who present a marked increase in the two groups they term hegemonic and competitive authoritarian regimes (Roessler and Howard 2009). My data confirm that although the number of minimalist democracies did grow rapidly in the very same period (Møller and Skaaning 2013; Seeberg 2013), the increase found by Roessler and Howard in electoral authoritarian regimes cannot be accounted for by the minimalist democracies that they include in this subgroup under the label of competitive authoritarianism. Instead, it is indeed an increase in authoritarian elections. Furthermore, by distinguishing between non-electoral and one- and no-party electoral regimes, my analysis reveals that in opposition to the decline of non-electoral regimes, one- and no-party regimes flourished until the end of the Cold War. Following 1990, however, the group of one- and no-party electoral regimes rapidly declined to the same level as the non-electoral subgroup. This corresponds to the trend unveiled by Hadenius and Teorell, although it is slightly conflated in their analysis due to their partly overlapping groups of military and monarchic regimes that may also hold one- or no-party elections (Hadenius and Teorell 2007). Thus, the rise of electoral authoritarianism does not represent an increase in autocratic elections as such. Rather, it is an increase in restricted multi-party competition under authoritarianism.

Two important points should be made. In spite of the renewed focus on electoral authoritarianism, non-democratic elections are not a new phenomenon. In the aftermath of World War II, elections were held in almost half of all authoritarian regimes. The more striking development, and perhaps the empirical catalyst of the renewed research on the effect of non-democratic elections, is the recent rise in multi-party elections in authoritarian regimes. While non-electoral and one- and no-party electoral regimes have steadily declined since the 1970s, multi-party elections have been on the rise. This finding may also be an artefact of the period under investigation – multi-party elections in authoritarian regimes were also known before World War II. Regardless of whether the new increase in authoritarian multi-party elections simply represents a return to the pre-Cold War norm, the fact that multi-party elections are now held in more than 60% of the world's autocracies merits a study of their effect.

Elections across regions

Is the tendency to hold authoritarian elections confined to certain regions? Can the increase in multi-party authoritarianism be attributed to stalled democratization processes in Africa and the post-communist world after 1990? Figure 1.4 shows the development in authoritarian elections over time across six politico-geographic

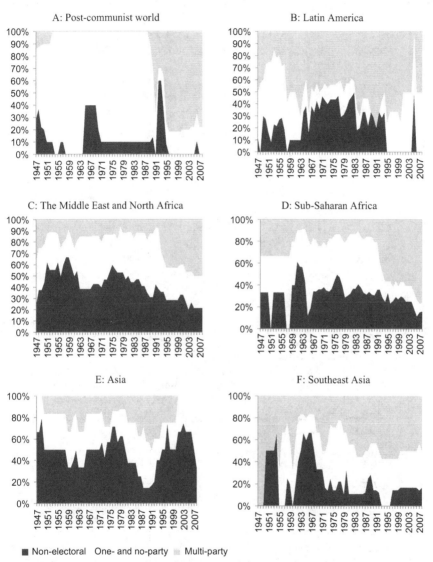

Figure 1.4 Development in authoritarian elections across regions, 1947–2008, percent

Note: Percent of regimes with different types of elections over time and across regions. Data on regimes from GWF, data on elections from NELDA, and data on number of parties from CGV.

regions.[10] Western Europe is not represented in the figure as there were only three Western European dictatorships after World War II (Greece, Portugal, and Spain) and the region did not host any autocracies after Franco's death in 1975. None of the Southern European dictatorships ever held multi-party elections. This region aside, the figure clearly illustrates that authoritarian multi-party elections are not confined to certain regions. In the dictatorships of the post-communist world, there were no multi-party elections held during the Cold War, as most of the communist regimes instead held elections with only one party represented. All regions (except the West) experienced all types of authoritarian regimes at some point after World War II.

The figure also reveals that the increase in multi-party electoral authoritarianism is driven by its expansion as a share of autocracies in the post-communist world, the Middle East and North Africa (MENA), and sub-Saharan Africa. The post-communist world in particular experienced a great increase in multi-party elections and a decline in one-party elections following the dissolution of the USSR. Whereas many Eastern European regimes democratized after the fall of the Berlin Wall, other post-communist regimes, such as Belarus, Armenia, and Georgia, opened up elections for opposition candidates but did not allow the real competition that would qualify them as minimalist democracies. Similarly, in the 1990s, elections were opened up for multiple parties across the African continent from Kenya and Tanzania to Senegal. The tendency also spread to the monarchies of the Middle East, some of which eventually allowed multiple parties to compete in parliamentary elections. In 2008, 78% of autocracies in the post-communist world had held multi-party elections within the past seven years (the only exceptions were Turkmenistan and Uzbekistan) and in sub-Saharan Africa, 77% had held a recent multi-party election (exceptions being Côte d'Ivoire, Ethiopia, Eritrea, Somalia, Sudan, and Swaziland). In the MENA region, 50% of autocracies were multi-party electoral in 2008.

The other regions did not see a similar increase in multi-party authoritarianism in the 1990s. In Asia, few autocracies hold multi-party elections (examples include Taiwan in the 1990s and South Korea until 1987). In Latin America and Southeast Asia, multi-party elections have been relatively common since the end of World War II, and there was thus no significant increase after the Cold War. In Southeast Asia, regimes such as Malaysia, Singapore, and Indonesia have held authoritarian multi-party elections for decades.

In Latin America, there were only two autocracies left in 2008, multi-party electoral Venezuela and one-party electoral Cuba, and the shares would change dramatically if one of these regimes were to democratize or abandon elections. Thus, the disappearance of multi-party electoral autocracies from Latin America in 2005 stems from the fact that Haiti, the only multi-party electoral regime in the region in the early 2000s, experienced a coup in 2004 and was ruled by a provisional government in the following years. The share of multi-party electoral regimes then increased to 50% again in 2006, when Venezuela was coded as authoritarian because of increasing repression and electoral manipulation. Importantly, though, although not all regions experience an increase in the share of multi-party regimes, such elections have taken place in authoritarian contexts across all regions.

In spite of the global spread of multi-party elections, non-electoral regimes are still in existence. Whereas there were no non-electoral regimes left in Latin America in 2008, the greatest share was found in Asia (33%) and MENA (21%). In Asia, these are accounted for by regimes such as China, but also the Nepalese monarchy of the early 2000s. In the MENA region, more recent non-electoral regimes are the Gulf monarchies of Saudi Arabia, the United Arab Emirates, and Oman until 2002, as well as Libya. However, the share of non-electoral regimes declined in all regions.

Similarly, one- and no-party electoral regimes as a share of all authoritarian regimes have also diminished in all regions, although they are still relatively common in MENA, Asia, and Southeast Asia.[11] They include one-party elections such as those that took place under Saddam Hussein's Baath party in Iraq and the communist parties of Laos and Vietnam, and parliamentary elections in Kuwait where political parties are illegal and candidates run as individuals, perhaps with an attachment to a looser alliance (Koch 2001, 162). In spite of different tendencies across regions, authoritarian multi-party elections are thus not confined to certain regional settings. This finding underscores the importance of a global inquiry into the effect of multi-party authoritarian elections. Before engaging in such analyses, however, I explore whether multi-party elections – although they have spread across all regions of the globe – remain confined to certain authoritarian regime types.

Elections across authoritarian regime types

In the new literature on authoritarian institutions, authoritarian regime type is commonly presented as the cause of phenomena as different as regime stability (Geddes 2003; Magaloni 2008), civil war (Fjelde 2010), investment and growth (Wright 2008), property rights (Knutsen and Fjelde 2013), and the propensity to go to war (Weeks 2012). But are some authoritarian regime types more likely to host elections than others? As different types of authoritarian regimes are argued to have different propensities to break down, authoritarian regime types could confound the relationship between elections and regime stability if some types of autocracies are more likely to hold elections than others.

Authoritarian regime type is most commonly used to refer to the organizational roots or origins of the people in control of policies and political appointments (Geddes, Wright, and Frantz 2014a, 5). I explore whether elections map differently across the four different types of authoritarian regimes identified by Geddes and collaborators. Where a royal family controls policy and leadership selection, the regime is a monarchy. If control instead resides with the military (or a group thereof), a ruling party, or a narrow circle of the dictator's supporters, the regime is classified as military, party, or personalist, respectively (Geddes, Wright, and Frantz 2014a, 15). Combining this regime classification with the categorization of elections results in the simple typology illustrated in Table 1.2.

24 *The puzzle of authoritarian elections*

Table 1.2 Elections across authoritarian regime 1946–2008, illustrative examples

	Party	Military	Monarchy	Personalist
Non-electoral	China, 1950– Cuba, 1960–1992 Eritrea, 1994–	Chile, 1974–1987 Nigeria, 1984–1991 Pakistan, 1978–1984	Nepal, 2003–2006 Saudi Arabia, 1946– Swaziland, 1979–1992	Spain, 1952–1976 Uganda, 1967–1993 Libya, 1970–
One- and no-party electoral	Poland, 1947–1988 Tanzania, 1965–1994 Turkmenistan, 1992–2008	Myanmar, 1974–1988 Panama, 1972–1982 Rwanda, 1978–1994	Afghanistan, 1947–1973 Ethiopia, 1957–1974 Kuwait, 1963–	DRC, 1965–1993 Iraq, 1980–2003 Philippines, 1973–1980
Multi-party electoral	Egypt, 1979– Mexico, 1946–2000 Zimbabwe, 1981–	Algeria, 1995– Brazil, 1966–1985 South Korea, 1963–1987	Iran, 1960–1977 Jordan, 1993– Morocco, 1993–	Cameroon, 1992– Haiti, 2000–2004 Russia, 1995–

Note: Data on regimes from GWF, data on elections from NELDA, and data on number of parties from CGV.

The table illustrates that the authoritarian regimes marked in grey in Figures 1.1a–1.1f may not only be split into various types of elections but also demarcated based on the ruling group. Some authoritarian multi-party elections, such as those in Algeria after 1995 and in Brazil prior to 1985, took place under military rule, while others have been held under a party regime, a personalist ruler, or even a monarch, as is the case in Jordan and Morocco. Importantly, all three types of elections have occurred under all four types of authoritarian rule. Figure 1.5 thus examines the development in authoritarian elections over time in each of the four authoritarian subtypes.

In each subtype, the distribution of elections largely follows the trends described previously: non-electoral regimes declined and the tendency to hold multi-party elections increased after 1990 (although for monarchic and military regimes there are very few regimes in each group after 1990). This development is particularly striking for personalist regimes. There were no multi-party personalist regimes in 1991; in 2008, there were 19. In the same period, the number of non-electoral personalist regimes dropped from eight to three.

Although the different types of elections follow largely the same trend over time in the various subtypes, Figure 1.5 also reveals that party, military, personalist, and monarchic autocracies have different propensities to hold elections. Monarchic regimes form a curious subgroup, in which one- and no-party elections are still the most common, and the proportion of non-electoral regimes equals that of multi-party electoral. The relationship between regime type and election type is explored further in Table 1.3.

The puzzle of authoritarian elections 25

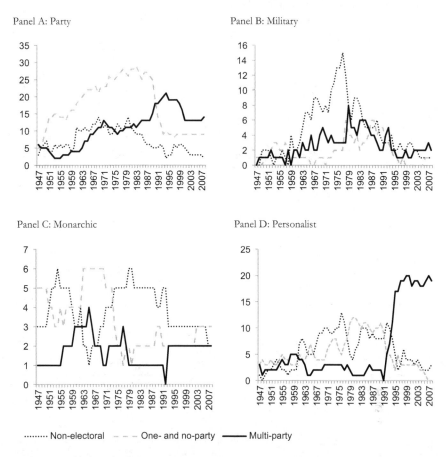

Figure 1.5 Development in authoritarian elections across regime types, 1947–2008, count
Note: Number of regimes with different types of elections over time and across regime types. Data on regime types from GWF, data on elections from NELDA, and data on number of parties from CGV.

During the Cold War, military regimes had the greatest share of non-electoral country-years (53% in all). After 1989, monarchies were more likely to be non-electoral than military regimes: 43% of all country-years were non-electoral in the world's monarchies compared to 41% of military country-years and only 13% of country-years in which a party-led regime ruled (Table 1.3, Panel B). This is not surprising since legitimacy in monarchies is derived not from popular elections but mainly from the historic roots of the dynasty, and succession issues are largely resolved within the royal family (Gandhi 2008, 23–5), rendering elections as a means for solving elite crises obsolete. Thus, in spite of its regular parliamentary elections, the Moroccan monarchy emphasizes its genealogical descent from the Prophet Muhammad and "an unbroken dynastic history stretching back to the seventeenth century" (Joffe 1988, 201). In Saudi Arabia, where no national elections

Table 1.3 Elections across authoritarian regime types

Panel A: Cold War era, 1947–1989

	Party	Military	Monarchy	Personalist
Non-electoral	23%	53%	43%	41%
	(366)	(242)	(176)	(264)
One- and no-party electoral	55%	20%	39%	42%
	(884)	(90)	(160)	(267)
Multi-party electoral	22%	27%	18%	17%
	(349)	(123)	(73)	(107)
Total	100%	100%	100%	100%
	(1,599)	(455)	(409)	(638)

Panel B: Post-Cold War era, 1990–2008

	Party	Military	Monarchy	Personalist
Non-electoral	13%	41%	43%	21%
	(78)	(43)	(60)	(92)
One- and no-party electoral	33%	23%	32%	15%
	(189)	(24)	(45)	(67)
Multi-party electoral	54%	37%	24%	64%
	(311)	(39)	(34)	(287)
Total	100%	100%	100%	100%
	(578)	(106)	(139)	(446)

Note: Observations are country-years. Data on regime types from GWF, data on elections from NELDA, and data on number of parties from CGV.

are held, in 2006 King Abdullah instated the Allegiance Council, consisting of princes of the Al Saud to advise the king on succession and lead the process if the king dies (Henderson 2009, 13–15).

In contrast, in party regimes, here included in the group of civilian regimes, the right to rule is based on a claim of serving "on behalf of 'the people'" (Ulfelder 2005, 17), a claim that – unlike the historical source of legitimacy in monarchies – can be underpinned by constructing elections (or rather, election victories, as discussed in Chapters 3–4). Indeed, party regimes were the group most likely to have held some form of election within the past seven years (adding together the groups holding one- and no-party and multi-party elections), both during and after the Cold War (Table 1.3). A large number of the one- and no-party elections that occurred in these party regimes took place in communist systems across the regions, as discussed previously.

However, the limited expansion of elections within the group of monarchies is also striking. Whereas the other groups saw a marked decline in non-electoral regimes, during the Cold War 43% of monarchic country-years succeeded at least a seven-year period in which no elections had been held. The number was the same after the Cold War. The prevalence of non-electoralism could also be seen as a manifestation of the fact that most of the monarchies are oil-rich states in the Middle East that may be less susceptible to international pressure for democratization and thus less likely to implement elections.

In the post-Cold War period, personalist regimes were most likely to feature multi-party competition (64% of country-years did so), followed by party regimes (54%) (Table 1.3, Panel B). The increase in multi-party elections among party regimes includes both post-Soviet states discussed previously and African regimes in which elections were opened up for competitors, as happened in Kenya in 1992 and Tanzania in 1995. The increase in multi-party elections among personalist regimes in the post-Cold War era is accounted for primarily by the introduction of multi-party elections in Africa and Central Asia under personalist leaders such as Nazarbayev of Kazakhstan and Biya of Cameroon, but also the multi-party elections in Russia under Putin. The same trends are visible for military regimes: while the share of military country-years that were non-electoral has declined, 37% of all military country-years after the Cold War have followed a seven-year period in which no multi-party elections were held.

Thus, although each regime type largely follows the pattern of a decline in non-electoralism and an expansion of multi-party elections, they differ markedly in their propensity to hold multi-party elections, with personalist and party regimes being more likely to do so. This trend is taken into account in the causal analyses in Chapters 3–4, where I control for regime type when I analyze the effect of elections on regime breakdown.

The plan of the book

Authoritarian elections are common today, where they occur in 85% of all autocracies, but they are not a new phenomenon. At the end of World War II, almost half of all autocracies had held some form of election within the past seven years. What is new is the dramatic increase in multi-party authoritarian elections – what the literature terms hegemonic (and in some instances competitive) regimes. Since the end of the Cold War, multi-party competition has increased its share among autocracies by 35 percentage points, and in 2008, more than 60% of authoritarian regimes had held a multi-party election within the past seven years. Moreover, multi-party authoritarian elections are occurring in all regions in which authoritarian regimes exist and across all types of autocracy. They have been introduced in the personalist regimes of sub-Saharan Africa, in the monarchies of the MENA region, and in party regimes across the globe. Even among the handful of military dictatorships left by 2008, both Algeria and Pakistan held multi-party elections. But what happens when autocrats open up for multi-party competition in elections? Do they open a window of opportunity for the opposition to challenge the rulers? Is it the first step toward authoritarian collapse? Or is it just another tool employed by adaptive autocrats to tie in the elite, co-opt the opposition, and dress the whole thing in a veil of legitimacy? It is to the effect of these authoritarian multi-party elections that the book now turns.

Chapter 2 unfolds the theoretical argument. Zooming in on the three core actor groups of an authoritarian regime – the internal elites, the opposition, and citizens – the chapter shows that the existing literature on authoritarian elections has uncovered plausible, theoretical mechanisms that link elections to both regime survival and regime breakdown. Furthermore, the empirical record is ambiguous. There is no clear evidence of either a regime-sustaining or a regime-subverting effect of authoritarian elections.

Building on the theoretical insights of the existing literature, the chapter presents the theory of a conditional effect of authoritarian elections. The starting point is the choices made on the individual level by voters deciding whether to support the regime or the opposition, regime elites deciding whether to defect or stay loyal, opposition candidates pondering whether to mobilize for the opposition or be co-opted into the ruling group, and citizens deciding whether or not to engage in post-electoral protests. I argue that administrative capacity, coercive capacity, and control over the economy shape the strategies available to autocrats who wish to affect these individual-level choices, and thus the effects of authoritarian elections. The higher these capacities are, the more likely it is that rulers subtly and successfully manipulate elections, and the less likely it is that the regime will break down following an election. The chapter results in six hypotheses and a number of observable implications that guide the quantitative, cross-national analyses and the case studies.

The second part of the book exposes the theoretical argument to empirical tests on a cross-national basis. The conditional effect of state capacity, both administrative and coercive, is put to the test in Chapter 3. Based on quantitative data on all authoritarian regimes from 1960–2006, the chapter finds evidence of a negative, conditional effect of administrative capacity on the relationship between elections and regime breakdown. As administrative capacity increases, authoritarian regimes are less likely to break down following an authoritarian election. Where administrative capacity is high, elections are associated with regime stability. This corroborates theoretical expectations. But no such effects can be found for coercive capacity. Higher levels of coercive capacity, at least as proxied by measures of military capacity, do not reduce the risk of electoral breakdown. This non-finding is explored further in the case studies.

Chapter 4 subjects the hypotheses on economic control to the same type of tests. Relying on data for all authoritarian regimes from 1970–2006, the analyses support the theoretical framework and find that the higher the degree of economic control, the less likely it is that regime collapse will follow a multi-party election. Regimes with low and medium degrees of economic control are more likely to break down if they have recently held a multi-party election than if no elections have been held. These results hold with various measures of economic control. Furthermore, there is evidence that in regimes where both state capacity and control over the economy are limited, elections are more likely to be associated with regime breakdown.

The third part of the book relies on evidence from four cases of authoritarian elections. It assesses whether the relationship between elections, capacities, and regime stability unraveled in the previous chapters may indeed be attributed to the theoretical apparatus. It investigates whether four cases of authoritarian elections show signs of the micro-level mechanisms that link state capacity and economic control to elections and regime stability. Based on observable implications of the theoretical framework, Chapter 5 assesses the theory of a conditional effect of authoritarian elections against the cases of the Philippine election in 1986 and the Malaysian election in 1990. The Philippines was a case of breakdown by elections; Malaysia a case of stabilization by elections. The strategies employed by the ruling UMNO and the effects of the electoral victory of 1990 on Malaysian elites, opposition, and citizens correspond well with the theoretical framework. The party leadership relied primarily on its administrative capacity but also its control over the economy to subtly manipulate elections. In the Philippines, the dynamics were more nuanced. Despite low levels of capacities, President Marcos's ruling elite pulled off a number of manipulative strategies. But in correspondence with theoretical expectations, the strategies eventually failed and the regime did not have the coercive power to quell the anti-Marcos protests, resulting ultimately in post-electoral collapse.

Chapter 6 nuances these findings by tuning in on another high-capacity case. Comparing the elections in Zimbabwe in 2008 and 2013, the chapter shows that the possession of authoritarian capacities does not correlate perfectly with the use of these capacities. In spite of their high degrees of economic control and moderate levels of administrative capacity, Mugabe and his ruling group in the 2008 elections – contrary to expectations – relied primarily on overt repression strategies and a strong coercive force to win the elections. But in correspondence with expectations, these strategies backfired. The regime survived but did not experience the full range of stabilizing effects of an electoral supermajority victory. Thus, the case also demonstrates the potential importance of coercive capacity. Although no conditional effect of coercive capacity is unraveled in Chapter 3, it is worthwhile to test this relationship with new measures of coercive capacity that go beyond the military. In the 2013 elections, Mugabe and his partners seemed to have learned their lesson and relied more heavily on subtle manipulation tactics afforded by both the state apparatus and control over the economy. These strategies largely worked as expected, contributing to the post-electoral stability of the regime. The case studies do not test the overall correlations between elections, capacities, and stability, but they lend credence to the suggested theoretical mechanisms through which capacities are argued to affect electoral dynamics.

Finally, Chapter 7 concludes and reflects upon the findings. It looks into the question of whether democratization can be expected to follow an electoral authoritarian regime breakdown, discusses the implications of the findings for the promotion of democracy and elections, and suggests avenues for future research.

Notes

1 A succession struggle that – as this book went into press – resulted in the military removing Mugabe from power to install the former vice president, Emmerson Mnangagwa, in the presidency.
2 Throughout the book, the terms *authoritarian regime*, *autocracy*, and *dictatorship* are used interchangeably. This terminology parts ways with Linz's original distinction between authoritarian and totalitarian regimes (2000) but is in line with the use of the concepts in newer research.

3 Periods in which the central authority lacks control over the territory, such as foreign occupation, are defined as neither authoritarian nor democratic.
4 The NELDA data have been collapsed into country-year format, with each country-year scoring 1 if at least one executive or legislative election occurred in the country during that year.
5 For the causal analyses in the following chapters, I test for the effect of various time horizons.
6 For every year in which both a regime change and an election occurred, I have gathered information on the timing of the election and the date of regime change and ascribed the election to the regime in place when the election occurred. As the GWF data code the regime in place on January 1, some regimes will only be classified as electoral in the year following the election. For example, the Azerbaijani leader as of January 1, 1993, Elchibey, was ousted in August following a military coup in June. In October, Aliyev was elected President, and these presidential elections are thus coded under the new regime (in place on January 1, 1994) rather than that of 1993. These decisions do not affect results but simply reflect the choice of whether to code regimes as of January 1 or December 31. Choosing January 1 ensures that for the causal analyses, the independent variable, elections, actually records the electoral regime in place when the breakdown occurs and not the one that takes over following the breakdown. In Figures 1.1a–1.1f, however, elections are marked in the actual year in which they occur, and if a country-year saw both a regime breakdown and an election, it is not possible to read from the figure which came first.
7 Finally, I have checked the record of elections in all regimes that I code as non-electoral when the analyses begin in 1946 (additional information from Nohlen, Thibaut, and Krennerich 1999; Nohlen, Grotz, and Hartmann 2001a, 2001b; Nohlen 2005a, 2005b; Nohlen and Stöver 2010). If an election had in fact occurred under that regime in the prior seven years and no coups or the like interrupted the regime in the meantime (data on irregular leadership changes from Goemans, Gleditsch, and Chiozza 2009), I have recoded the regime as electoral.
8 The CGV data are coded from 1946–2008.
9 Although interesting nuances indeed exist between one-party regimes on the one hand and partyless regimes on the other, I collapse them into one subgroup here, as I am primarily interested in comparing the development in authoritarian elections to that of non-electoral and non-multi-party electoral autocracies.
10 Data on regions are from Hadenius and Teorell (2005). I have collapsed South Asia and East Asia into the category termed "Asia" but it remains separate from Southeast Asia (SEA).
11 That 50% of all autocracies in Latin America in 2008 were one- and no-party electoral covers the aforementioned fact that the region saw only two autocracies that year, one of them the Cuban one-party regime.

References

Birch, Sarah. 2002. "The 2000 Elections in Yugoslavia: The 'Bulldozer Revolution'." *Electoral Studies* 21 (3): 499–511.

Blaydes, Lisa. 2011. *Elections and Distributive Politics in Mubarak's Egypt*. New York: Cambridge University Press.

Boix, Carles. 2011. "Democracy, Development, and the International System." *American Political Science Review* 105 (4): 809–28.

Brancati, Dawn. 2014. "Democratic Authoritarianism: Origins and Effects." *Annual Review of Political Science* 17 (1): 313–26. doi:10.1146/annurev-polisci-052013-115248.

Brownlee, Jason. 2009a. "Harbinger of Democracy: Competitive Elections before the End of Authoritarianism." In *Democratization by Elections: A New Mode of Transition*, edited by Staffan Lindberg, 128–47. Baltimore: The Johns Hopkins University Press.
———. 2009b. "Portents of Pluralism: How Hybrid Regimes Affect Democratic Transitions." *American Journal of Political Science* 55 (3): 515–32.
Bunce, Valerie, and Sharon Wolchik. 2011. *Defeating Authoritarian Leaders in Postcommunist Countries*. New York: Cambridge University Press.
Carothers, Thomas. 2002. "The End of the Transition Paradigm." *Journal of Democracy* 13 (1): 5–21.
Case, William. 2005. "Southeast Asia's Hybrid Regimes: When Do Voters Change Them?" *Journal of East Asian Studies* 5 (2): 215–37.
Cheibub, Jose, Jennifer Gandhi, and James Vreeland. 2010. "Democracy and Dictatorship Revisited." *Public Choice* 143 (1): 67–101.
Chin, James. 2007. "The General Election in Singapore, May 2006." *Electoral Studies* 26 (3): 703–7.
Dahl, Robert A. 1989. *Democracy and Its Critics*. New Haven: Yale University Press.
Diamond, Larry. 2002. "Elections without Democracy: Thinking about Hybrid Regimes." *Journal of Democracy* 13 (2): 21–34.
Donno, Daniela. 2013. "Elections and Democratization in Authoritarian Regimes." *American Journal of Political Science* 57 (3): 703–16.
Elklit, Jørgen, and Palle Svensson. 1997. "What Makes Elections Free and Fair?" *Journal of Democracy* 8 (3): 32–46. doi:10.1353/jod.1997.0041.
Escribà-Folch, Abel, and Joseph Wright. 2010. "Dealing with Tyranny: International Sanctions and the Survival of Authoritarian Rulers." *International Studies Quarterly* 54 (2): 335–59.
Fjelde, Hanne. 2010. "Generals, Dictators, and Kings Authoritarian Regimes and Civil Conflict, 1973–2004." *Conflict Management and Peace Science* 27 (3): 195–218.
Flores, Thomas Edward, and Irfan Nooruddin. 2016. *Elections in Hard Times: Building Stronger Democracies in the 21st Century*. Cambridge, New York, NY and Washington, DC: Cambridge University Press.
Fukuyama, Francis. 1992. *The End of History and the Last Man*. New York: Free Press.
Gandhi, Jennifer. 2008. *Political Institutions under Dictatorship*. New York: Cambridge University Press.
Gandhi, Jennifer, and Ellen Lust-Okar. 2009. "Elections under Authoritarianism." *Annual Review of Political Science* 12: 403–22.
Gandhi, Jennifer, and Adam Przeworski. 2007. "Authoritarian Institutions and the Survival of Autocrats." *Comparative Political Studies* 40 (11): 1279–301.
Geddes, Barbara. 1999. "What Do We Know about Democratization after Twenty Years?" *Annual Review of Political Science* 2 (1): 115–44.
———. 2003. *Paradigms and Sand Castles: Theory Building and Research Design in Comparative Politics*. Ann Arbor: University of Michigan Press.
Geddes, Barbara, Joseph Wright, and Erica Frantz. 2014a. "Autocratic Breakdown and Regime Transitions: A New Data Set." *Perspectives on Politics* 12 (2): 313–31.
———. 2014b. "Autocratic Regimes Code Book: Version 1.2." http://sites.psu.edu/dictators/.
Goemans, Henk E., Kristian Skrede Gleditsch, and Giacomo Chiozza. 2009. "Introducing Archigos: A Dataset of Political Leaders." *Journal of Peace Research* 46 (2): 269–83.
Greene, Kenneth. 2007. *Why Dominant Parties Lose: Mexico's Democratization in Comparative Perspective*. Cambridge: Cambridge University Press.

Hadenius, Axel and Jan Teorell. "Assessing Alternative Indices of Democracy", Concepts & Methods Working Papers 6, IPSA, August 2005. http://www.concepts-methods.org/Files/WorkingPaper/PC%206%20Hadenius%20Teorell.pdf

———. 2007. "Pathways from Authoritarianism." *Journal of Democracy* 18 (1): 143–56.

———. 2009. "Elections as Levers of Democratization: A Global Inquiry." In *Democratization by Elections: A New Mode of Transition*, 77–100. Baltimore: The Johns Hopkins University Press.

Henderson, Simon. 2009. "After King Abdullah: Succession in Saudi Arabia." 96. Policy Focus. Washington, DC: The Washington Institute for Near East Policy.

Hermet, Guy, Alain Rouquie, and Richard Rose. 1978. *Elections without Choice*. New York: Wiley.

Howard, Marc, and Philip Roessler. 2006. "Liberalizing Electoral Outcomes in Competitive Authoritarian Regimes." *American Journal of Political Science* 50 (2): 365–81.

Hyde, Susan, and Nikolay Marinov. 2012. "Codebook for the National Elections across Democracy and Autocracy (NELDA) Dataset." http://hyde.research.yale.edu/nelda/#.

Joffe, George. 1988. "Morocco: Monarchy, Legitimacy and Succession." *Third World Quarterly* 10 (1): 201–28.

Joseph, Richard. 1997. "Democratization in Africa after 1989: Comparative and Theoretical Perspectives." *Comparative Politics* 29 (3): 363–82. doi:10.2307/422126.

Knutsen, Carl Henrik, and Hanne Fjelde. 2013. "Property Rights in Dictatorships: Kings Protect Property Better Than Generals or Party Bosses." *Contemporary Politics* 19 (1): 94–114.

Knutsen, Carl Henrik, Håvard Mokleiv Nygård, and Tore Wig. 2017. "Autocratic Elections: Stabilizing Tool or Force for Change?" *World Politics* 69 (1): 98–143.

Koch, Christian. 2001. "Kuwait." In *Elections in Asia and the Pacific: A Data Handbook, Volume I: Middle East, Central Asia, and South Asia*, edited by Dieter Nohlen, Florian Grotz, and Christof Hartmann, 155–68. Oxford: Oxford University Press.

Kuntz, Philipp, and Mark Thompson. 2009. "More Than Just the Final Straw: Stolen Elections as Revolutionary Triggers." *Comparative Politics* 41 (3): 253–72.

Lee, Julian C.H. 2007. "Barisan Nasional – Political Dominance and the General Elections of 2004 in Malaysia". In *Südostasien aktuell : Journal of Current Southeast Asian Affairs* 26 (2): 38–65. URN: http://nbn-resolving.de/urn:nbn:de:0168-ssoar-336605

Levitsky, Steven, and Lucan Way. 2002. "The Rise of Competitive Authoritarianism." *Journal of Democracy* 13 (2): 51–65.

———. 2010. *Competitive Authoritarianism: Hybrid Regimes after the Cold War*. Cambridge: Cambridge University Press.

Lindberg, Staffan. 2006. *Democracy and Elections in Africa*. Baltimore: The Johns Hopkins University Press.

———, ed. 2009. *Democratization by Elections: A New Mode of Transition*. Baltimore: The Johns Hopkins University Press.

Linz, Juan José. 2000. *Totalitarian and Authoritarian Regimes*. Lynne Rienner Publishers. Boulder, Colorado and London.

Magaloni, Beatriz. 2006. *Voting for Autocracy*. New York: Cambridge University Press.

———. 2008. "Credible Power-Sharing and the Longevity of Authoritarian Rule." *Comparative Political Studies* 41 (4/5): 715–41.

Malesky, Edmund, and Paul Schuler. 2010. "Nodding or Needling: Analyzing Delegate Responsiveness in an Authoritarian Parliament." *American Political Science Review* 104 (3): 482–502.

———. 2011. "The Single-Party Dictator's Dilemma: Information in Elections without Opposition." *Legislative Studies Quarterly* 46 (4): 491–530.
Mazzuca, Sebastián L. 2010. "Access to Power versus Exercise of Power Reconceptualizing the Quality of Democracy in Latin America." *Studies in Comparative International Development* 45 (3): 334–57.
Mitchell, Lincoln. 2004. "Georgia's Rose Revolution." *Current History* 103 (675): 342–8.
Møller, Jørgen. 2014. "Review of the Politics of Uncertainty: Sustaining and Subverting Electoral Authoritarianism. By Andreas Schedler. New York: Oxford University Press, 2013." *Perspectives on Politics* 12 (4): 45–7.
Møller, Jørgen, and Svend-Erik Skaaning. 2013. "The Third Wave: Inside the Numbers." *Journal of Democracy* 24 (4): 97–109.
Munck, Gerardo, and Richard Snyder. 2007. *Passion, Craft and Method in Comparative Politics*. Baltimore: The Johns Hopkins University Press.
Nohlen, Dieter, ed. 2005a. *Elections in the Americas: A Data Handbook, Volume I: North America, Central America, and the Caribbean*. Oxford: Oxford University Press.
———, ed. 2005b. *Elections in the Americas: A Data Handbook, Volume II: South America*. Oxford: Oxford University Press.
Nohlen, Dieter, Florian Grotz, and Christof Hartmann, eds. 2001a. *Elections in Asia and the Pacific, Volume I: The Middle East, Central Asia, and South Asia*. Oxford: Oxford University Press.
———, eds. 2001b. *Elections in Asia and the Pacific: A Data Handbook, Volume II: South East Asia, East Asia, and the South Pacific*. Oxford: Oxford University Press.
Nohlen, Dieter, and Philip Stöver, eds. 2010. *Elections in Europe: A Data Handbook*. Baden-Baden, Germany: Nomos Publishers.
Nohlen, Dieter, Bernard Thibaut, and Michael Krennerich, eds. 1999. *Elections in Africa: A Data Handbook*. Oxford: Oxford University Press. www.oxfordscholarship.com/view/10.1093/0198296452.001.0001/acprof-9780198296454.
Ong, Elvin, and Mou Hui Tim. 2014. "Singapore's 2011 General Elections and Beyond: Beating the PAP at Its Own Game." *Asian Survey* 54 (4): 749–72.
OSCE/ODIHR. 2004. "Parliamentary Elections, Georgia: Post-Election Interim Report: 3–25 November 2003." Tbilisi: OSCE/ODIHR Election Observation Mission Georgia, Parliamentary Elections 2003. www.osce.org/odihr/elections/georgia/17822?download=true.
Pepinsky, Thomas. 2014. "The Institutional Turn in Comparative Authoritarianism." *British Journal of Political Science* 44 (3): 631–53.
Roessler, Philip, and Marc Howard. 2009. "Post-Cold War Political Regimes: When Do Elections Matter?" In *Democratization by Elections: A New Mode of Transition*, edited by Staffan Lindberg, 101–27. Baltimore: The Johns Hopkins University Press.
Sartori, Giovanni. 2005. *Parties and Party Systems: A Framework for Analysis*. Colchester: ECPR.
Schedler, Andreas. 2006. "The Logic of Electoral Authoritarianism: The Dynamics of Unfree Competition." In *Electoral Authoritarianism*, edited by Andreas Schedler, 1–23. Boulder: Lynne Rienner Publishers.
———. 2013. *The Politics of Uncertainty: Sustaining and Subverting Electoral Authoritarianism*. Oxford: Oxford University Press.
Schumpeter, Joseph. 1974 [1942]. *Capitalism, Socialism and Democracy*. London: Unwin University Books.
Seeberg, Merete Bech. 2013. "Authoritarianism and Elections during the Third Wave." *Statsvetenskaplig Tidskrift* 114 (4): 313–44.

Svolik, Milan W. 2012. *The Politics of Authoritarian Rule*. New York: Cambridge University Press.

Tan, Netina. 2013. "Manipulating Electoral Laws in Singapore." *Electoral Studies*, Special Symposium: The New Research Agenda on Electoral Integrity 32 (4): 632–43.

Ulfelder, Jay. 2005. "Contentious Collective Action and the Breakdown of Authoritarian Regimes." *International Political Science Review* 26 (3): 311–34.

Vengroff, Richard, and Michael Magala. 2001. "Democratic Reform, Transition and Consolidation: Evidence from Senegal's 2000 Presidential Election." *The Journal of Modern African Studies* 39 (1): 129–62.

Weeks, Jessica L. 2012. "Strongmen and Straw Men: Authoritarian Regimes and the Initiation of International Conflict." *American Political Science Review* 106 (2): 326–47.

Welsh, Bridget. 2005. "Malaysia in 2004: Out of Mahathir's Shadow?" *Asian Survey* 45 (1): 153–60.

Wong, Chin-Huat. 2005. "The Federal and State Elections in Malaysia, March 2004." *Electoral Studies* 24 (2): 311–19.

Wright, Joseph. 2008. "Do Authoritarian Institutions Constrain? How Legislatures Affect Economic Growth and Investment." *American Journal of Political Science* 52 (2): 322–43.

———. 2009. "How Foreign Aid Can Foster Democratization in Authoritarian Regimes." *American Journal of Political Science* 53 (3): 552–71.

2 Authoritarian capacities and regime stabilization through elections

In the Georgian parliamentary elections in November 2003, incumbent President Shevardnadze's support parties secured a combined majority of votes. But they were only able to do so by relying heavily on blatant electoral fraud. The quality of the state apparatus was summed up by an old joke: "The government was bad, but at least there was not much of it" (Mitchell 2004, 348; see also Bunce and Wolchik 2011, 153–4). With Shevardnadze declaring his victory in spite of national and international allegations of voting irregularities, voters took to the streets to protest the stolen elections. Protesters never numbered the hundreds of thousands known from other electoral revolutions, but pro-opposition media broadcast the "revolution" to the population 24 hours a day, and Shevardnadze's underpaid security forces quickly defected (Mitchell 2004; Bunce and Wolchik 2011, 165). The former minister of justice, Saakashvili, who had defected to head the opposition, presented Shevardnadze with a letter of resignation, and within three weeks of the election, the president had abandoned his post. The authoritarian regime had succumbed to what was later termed the "Rose Revolution."

Four months later, the Malaysian ruling coalition, the Barisan Nasional (BN), won a landslide victory by taking 65% of the votes and 90% of the seats in parliamentary elections. The opposition leader was in prison, and the ruling coalition controlled the media, the electoral commission, and the police force. It enjoyed economic support from major businesses that were rewarded with contracts and licenses. Electoral districts were gerrymandered in favor of the incumbents, and state support was doled out in return for votes (Lee 2007). Hardly any protests erupted following the elections, which had largely been successful in terms of co-opting the opposition *Reformasi* movement into the regime (Welsh 2005, 154–5). The BN is still in power today and continues to win elections, as it has done since independence.

These tales of two very different electoral settings neatly illustrate the apparent paradox of authoritarian elections. But they also hint at a potential solution: elections with very different consequences often take place under autocrats endowed with different levels of capacities, thus allowing for different levels of electoral control. Perhaps the paradox of authoritarian elections is not so paradoxical after all?

This chapter develops a theoretical framework aimed at clarifying the conditions under which elections stabilize dictatorial rule. It sets out by clarifying the underlying assumption of actor behavior in dictatorships, sketching the groups that compose the main threat to dictatorial survival in office and the strategies available to power-hungry dictators. On this basis, I review the existing literature on authoritarian elections to understand the mechanisms through which elections may affect regime stability.

I then theorize how the capacities available to autocrats, namely state capacity (both administrative and coercive) and control over the economy, enable them to control elections by affecting individual citizens' and politicians' decisions about whether to support or oppose the ruling front. The main argument is that the greater the administrative capacity or economic control autocrats have at their disposal, the more likely elections are to be regime stabilizing. Where administrative capacity and economic control are limited, autocrats may rely on their coercive apparatus to ensure short-term survival. When incumbents control neither the administrative or coercive apparatus nor the economy, they are more likely to succumb in the face of multi-party elections. The theory results in six hypotheses and a number of observable implications that are put to the test in the following chapters.

Threats to power and survival strategies in authoritarian regimes

This book works from the assumption that rulers, whether democratic or authoritarian, are office seeking. For dictators in particular, holding office enables the ruler to accumulate rents whereas losing office has dire consequences, including the prospects of exile, imprisonment, or even death (Goemans 2008). From Syria's Bashar Assad, who is, at the time of writing, literally fighting for his grasp on power, to the leadership of Malaysia's ruling coalition, BN, which recently secured another term in office, authoritarian leaders want first and foremost to ensure regime survival and entrench their position in power. This assumption of office-seeking rulers underlies much classic work on both democracy and dictatorship (Bueno de Mesquita et al. 2003; Downs 1957).

In their quest for power and regime stability, authoritarian rulers face three domestic groups that might wish to overthrow them.[1] The first group, the internal elite, has been identified as the greatest threat to the regime: in the second half of the 20th century, more than two-thirds of dictators who lost power unconstitutionally[2] were overthrown by elites internal to the ruling coalition (Svolik 2012, 4–5; see also Tullock 1987). This regime elite – the ruling coalition (Svolik 2012, 63), launching organization (Haber 2006, 696), or winning coalition (Bueno de Mesquita et al. 2003) – is the group "whose support is essential if the incumbent is to remain in power" (Bueno de Mesquita et al. 2003, 38). The internal elite, often the very group that brought the dictator to power, is integrated into the state apparatus, the military, and the economy to a degree that makes it able (though not necessarily willing) to bring down the regime (Haber 2006, 696).[3]

Second, dictators also face a vertical threat, a pressure from the masses. Whereas Svolik establishes the greatest threat against dictators in general to be the elite, personalist dictators (or established autocrats in Svolik's terms), who have centralized power in their own person, should be more likely to be overthrown by popular rebellion (Svolik 2012, 63). Although popular uprisings have been established as neither necessary nor sufficient for a transition to take place (Ulfelder 2005, 313; Goldstone 2001, 168), pressure from below has been identified as an initiator of elite splits that in turn bring down the regime (Bratton and van de Walle 1997, chap. 3; O'Donnell, Schmitter, and Whitehead 1986; Przeworski 1991; Diamond 1994). The so-called Colored Revolutions of the post-communist world and the Arab Spring provide recent empirical examples of this phenomenon.

Although the most common distinction is between the regime elites and the populace (Svolik 2012, 3–6; Gandhi 2008, 164; Magaloni 2006, 44; Blaydes 2011, 9), a third actor group also exists in multi-party autocracies: the established opposition. The threat constituted by this group becomes particularly prominent in multi-party electoral regimes (Schedler 2013, 118–19). Defecting regime elites often become the most prominent opposition leaders, and the active opposition draws heavily on the populace. Thus, the borders between regime elites and opposition elites on the one hand and opposition elites and the populace on the other hand are blurred. But established opposition figures can threaten the rulers by running against them in elections, stirring public protests, provoking anti-regime sentiments at home or abroad, or simply presenting a possible future alternative to the current regime.

The existing literature on authoritarian elections

This is the environment in which authoritarian multi-party elections are entrenched. Whether these elections are adopted by a power-hungry dictator hoping to derive some benefit from the electoral institution, forced upon the regime by democracy-promoting foreign powers, inherited from a preceding democratic regime, or installed by colonial rulers, Chapter 1 showed that 62% of all dictators today fight to maintain power in a context that also involves multi-party elections. How do multi-party elections affect the game between regime leadership, elites, opposition, and population? The existing literature is reviewed below and the mechanisms are summarized in Table 2.1.

Regime-sustaining elections

The idea that authoritarian elections serve the interests of the ruler is not new. In *Elections Without Choice*, Linz stated that "if there are elections they must have some functions from the point of view of the leadership" (Linz 1978, 36). In recent years, the literature on authoritarian institutions has proliferated, and numerous scholars have come to see formally democratic institutions as tools available to the ruling elite in their quest to hold on to power and maintain regime stability (Brownlee 2009; Gandhi and Lust-Okar 2009; Magaloni 2006; Geddes 2005; Gandhi and Przeworski 2006; Blaydes 2011; Gandhi 2008). Elections are essential in securing the cooperation of the masses and in deterring the ruling elite from defecting to the opposition. A number of potential mechanisms through

Table 2.1 Mechanisms linking elections to authoritarian regime stability

Actor group	Actor's choices	Mechanisms of stability	Mechanisms of subversion
Elite	Loyalty or defection?	Signaling Credible commitment Monitoring and power distribution	Information on regime weakness
Opposition	Co-optation or mobilization?	Exclusion Co-optation and division	Focal point for mobilization Visibility
Populace	Voting for regime or opposition? Protesting or staying quiet?	Legitimacy Rent distribution	Post-electoral protests Spread of democratic norms and capabilities

which nominally democratic elections may help sustain the authoritarian regime have been proposed. They concern the three main actor groups of the authoritarian regime: the internal elites, the opposition, and the populace.

Since rebellion by the *internal elite* is recognized as the greatest threat to autocrats (Svolik 2012, 4–5), a main concern of any autocrat is controlling the elites and avoiding defections. One obvious way in which authoritarian elections serve this purpose is through signaling. When the leadership is successful in winning (or creating) large majorities, it signals that there is no political future outside of the ruling front, and would-be defectors are thus discouraged (Magaloni 2006, 4–10, 16–19; Geddes 2005, 11–12). In order for this strategy to work, supermajorities and high voter turnouts (to signal that there is no remaining pool of votes for the opposition to tap into) are necessary (Magaloni 2006; Geddes 2005, 12).

Second, elections also function as a form of credible commitment between ruler and elites. To decrease the risk of violent rebellion from their own elites, dictators must make an unbreakable contract that limits their personal rule. Multi-party elections offer elites a credible threat of challenging the leadership in elections and simultaneously commit rulers to distributing power positions to the lower-level elites (Magaloni 2008, 724, 728).

Third, elections allow the incumbent to monitor elites and distribute power: they offer the leadership information on candidates' popularity among voters (or their ability to manipulate or coerce voters into supporting the incumbent) (Malesky and Schuler 2011, 495–7), they help distribute spoils and jobs among the elite (Magaloni 2006, 16–19; Gandhi and Lust-Okar 2009, 405), they can solve the potentially damaging issue of succession, and they can function as a recruitment device for lower-level officials (Geddes 2005, 13). The main goal of all three tactics is to avoid elite defections. The argument is not only that the risk of elite defections is high during election time and must thus be diminished, but that elections, through signaling, credible commitment, monitoring, and power distribution, can actually lower the likelihood of elite defections.

Elections may also help the leadership in controlling the *opposition* through the mechanisms of exclusion and co-optation. If the opposition takes part in elections, they legitimize the system (Linz 1978, 60; Magaloni 2006, 9–10, 258); if they boycott elections, they automatically exclude themselves from potential influence and visibility. Elections also provide rulers with an effective divide and rule strategy through co-optation. Access to either limited policy influence or spoils, through, for instance, an authoritarian Parliament, may be offered to only parts of the opposition or to prominent opposition figures, who are thus contained and the rest of the opposition is left out (Malesky and Schuler 2010, 482; Linz 1978, 62; Gandhi and Lust-Okar 2009, 405; Schedler 2013, 91; Bunce and Wolchik 2011, 95).[4]

Elections also affect the rulers' relationship with the third group – the *populace* – who, in the context of elections, are typically seen either in the role of voters or as potential protesters. Regardless of their different roles, these are one and the same group – the citizens. The most common voter-oriented argument for why elections sustain the regime is legitimation – the mere fact that voters can, at least supposedly, express their political preferences at the ballot box may serve to legitimate the regime and prevent public uprisings (Schedler 2002a, 36; Hermet 1978, 16).

Perhaps more important today is the role of elections as a tool for rent distribution. Elections deliver information about supporters and opponents or about whole districts that are either opposition strongholds or ruling party bases. This information allows the ruling elite to distribute spoils and punishments among constituents accordingly, thus tying voters to the ruling front and making citizen protests – or even voter defections in elections – even more unlikely (Magaloni 2006, 4–10; Lust 2009a, 124–31; Blaydes 2011). This system of competitive clientelism also undermines public support for democratically oriented candidates: voters only vote for candidates who can deliver state spoils, and state resources are only available to the candidates of the incumbent party (Lust 2009a, 124–31).

Elections thus affect all important internal actor groups in an authoritarian regime, and there are numerous mechanisms through which elections can be tamed into relatively unharmful creatures or even play an active part in sustaining an authoritarian regime.

Regime-subverting elections

In spite of the numerous arguments for why non-competitive, multi-party elections sustain authoritarian regimes, several authors argue for a new path toward regime change and in some instances even democratization through elections (Hadenius and Teorell 2009; Howard and Roessler 2006; Schedler 2006; Lindberg 2006; Bunce and Wolchik 2011; Thompson and Kuntz 2004). This has been guided by the idea that uncertainty is introduced through elections, or that elections open a window of opportunity for change (Schedler 2002b, 109). Like the regime-sustaining electoral effects, the mechanisms connecting elections to regime subversion also work through the three main actor groups of an authoritarian regime.

First, *internal elites* may abuse the informational role played by elections in a traditionally information-scarce society. If elections signal leadership weakness, there is a risk that the elite will split and turn against the dictator (Magaloni 2006, 258; Schedler 2009, 305–6).

Second, *opposition* forces will respond to these same signals. If they perceive victory as being within reach, they are more likely to fight (Howard and Roessler 2006, 369). A weak opposition has been identified as the main obstacle to democratization in many semi-authoritarian regimes (Rakner and van de Walle 2009, 205). But elections can become focal points that enable the opposition to overcome coordination problems (Pop-Eleches and Robertson 2009, 13). Further, even though non-competitive elections are defined by the very fact that the opposition does not win them, opposition candidates may still take advantage of the election and the visibility they may gain from it and seek to become "opinion leaders" (Linz 1978, 54–5).

Third, elections also have the capacity to spark massive protests among *the populace* that can in turn trigger regime breakdown (Kuntz and Thompson 2009; Tucker 2007). A state of chaos is more likely in electoral autocracies, according to Schedler, because elections in non-democracies involve all the structural opportunities for collective action: grievances (over lack of democratic rights), repertoires of collective action (demonstrations, strikes, etc.), and political opportunities are all present at the same time (Schedler 2009, 306–7; see also Bunce and Wolchik 2011, 15–16). But even in the absence of large-scale protests, the mere holding of repetitive elections may instill democratic norms in voters and spur the development of civic associations that, in turn, bolster citizens' capabilities. As the individual citizen is exposed to the norms of equality through elections, these ideas will spread in society. Groups will form and campaign for rights outside of elections, and the media often becomes more outspoken during elections, which may promote further democratization (Lindberg 2006, 111–15).

The contrasting effects of elections are summarized in Table 2.1: through signaling, credible commitment, monitoring, and power distribution, elections may bind elites to the ruling front. But they may also reveal information that spurs elite defections. Elections can de-fang the opposition through exclusion, co-optation, and divisions. However, they may become focal points for opposition mobilization and provide opposition visibility. Further, elections may either tie in the populace through legitimation processes and rent distribution or they may push voters away from the regime by provoking protests and spreading democratic norms throughout society.

Empirical evidence

Scholars have developed theoretical arguments for both a regime-sustaining and a regime-subverting effect of authoritarian elections. Some have ventured so far as to argue that unfree elections may even spur democratic developments. What have we actually seen? This section reviews existing, cross-national, empirical investigations of the relationship between authoritarian elections and regime developments.

Existing studies differ on several levels (see also Schedler 2013, 149–72). Some studies test the effect of all types of authoritarian elections, some focus only on multi-party elections, and some restrict the focus to competitive multi-party elections. Some researchers explore the effect of cumulative numbers of elections whereas others look at the propensity for regime breakdown based on the holding of elections regardless of electoral history. As for the dependent variable, some have explored the effect of elections on breakdown propensities, survival rate, or average age of authoritarian regimes, or, in some instances, individual dictators' tenure rates. Others have supplemented this with studies of elections' effects on a regime's propensity to transition to democracy after a breakdown. Still others have traced the effect of elections on developments in political rights and civil liberties. Drawing together this body of knowledge, this section proceeds to ask what we know about the effect of authoritarian elections on regime breakdown.

In the literature on democratization, the most pressing question has been whether the holding of non-democratic elections affects the likelihood of democratization. This question falls outside of the scope of this book, but the findings nonetheless affect the expectations generated here. The debate was sparked with Lindberg's findings that the cumulative number of consecutive multi-party elections improved levels of civil liberties in Africa between independence and 2003, regardless of the democratic qualities (or lack thereof) of these electoral contests (Lindberg 2006). Along the same lines, Hadenius and Teorell, in their study of transitions from different regime types, find that democratization is most common in authoritarian multi-party regimes without a dominant party (i.e., competitive regimes) (Hadenius and Teorell 2007, 152–3).

The finding has been contested by McCoy and Hartlyn's study of elections in Latin America, where they find that "there is no relationship between the number of elections a country has held and its democratic experience" (2009, 49). Similarly, Kaya and Bernhard (2013) have found that the repeated holding of authoritarian elections has not affected levels of civil liberties across the post-communist world. Finally, Bogaards has evaluated the claim based on Lindberg's original sample. He finds that of the 48 African cases, only two – Senegal and Ghana – have transitioned to democracy following repetitive multi-party elections (Bogaards 2013, 155).

However, Lindberg's original claim still finds support in global studies. Hadenius and Teorell find that the cumulative number of elections have a significant – although small – effect on civil liberties ratings (Hadenius and Teorell 2009, 95–8). Brownlee (2009) shows that competitive regimes may be more likely to democratize following an authoritarian breakdown. Most recently, Miller has shown that past experience with authoritarian elections makes democratization a more likely outcome following an authoritarian breakdown (Miller 2015).

The literature on authoritarianism often has a slightly different vantage point. Setting aside the democratizing potential of non-democratic elections, researchers have asked whether elections stabilize or destabilize an autocracy. But there are no clear indications of a stabilizing or a destabilizing effect of elections. Brownlee (2009) finds that although competitive regimes are more likely to democratize, the holding of competitive or hegemonic elections does not significantly affect a regime's likelihood of breaking down. Similarly, Gandhi (2008, 175–6) demonstrates that the presence or absence of a multi-party legislature does not affect dictators' rates of survival in office. Hadenius and Teorell (2007, 150) find that multi-party authoritarian regimes have the shortest average life span of all authoritarian regime types, but Magaloni (2008) identifies the survival probability of hegemonic autocracies to be greater than that of military regimes. Under all circumstances, it is not clear whether these survival rates and life spans are an effect of holding multi-party elections. Thus, the question of the effect of authoritarian elections remains unsettled.

A conditional effect

The discrepancies in the literature on authoritarian elections have not gone unnoticed. In recent years, work has emerged that addresses the paradoxical effect of elections in various ways (see, for instance, Schedler 2013; Flores and Nooruddin 2016; Knutsen, Nygård, and Wig 2017; van Ham and Seim 2017). All of the approaches give valuable insights into the dynamics of authoritarian elections. However, most of them fall short of answering the fundamental question of when elections stabilize authoritarian rule.[5]

In his 2013 book on the topic, Schedler takes an actor-centered approach to understanding the paradox of authoritarian elections. He acknowledges the evidence for regime-sustaining, regime-subverting, and democratizing elections and states that autocrats may perceive elections as a potential tool for stability, but they face a dilemma because, "Unless political institutions are granted minimal margins of power and autonomy, they cannot make an independent contribution to authoritarian governance and survival; and as soon as political institutions are granted minimal margins of power and autonomy, they can turn against the dictator" (Schedler 2013, 73). According to Schedler, elections are arenas of struggle between regime and opposition actors. The effect of elections depends on the outcome of that struggle. Where the incumbents win, elections may stabilize their rule. If the opposition is successful, elections bode change. This game is complicated by its two-level character – actors fight both over electoral rules and electoral outcomes – and by the immense uncertainty that is political reality in authoritarian regimes. This leads Schedler to draw a conclusion that is essentially voluntarist: "At each election, authoritarian success is the rule (the probable outcome), opposition success the exception (the possible outcome)" (Schedler 2013, 141). However, Schedler cannot explain under what conditions we may expect breakdown or stabilization.

A second approach to the seemingly paradoxical effect of authoritarian elections is taken by Knutsen and collaborators, who stress the temporal aspects of the effect (Knutsen, Nygård, and Wig 2017). They argue that we have witnessed a diverse effect of elections because the potentially regime-subverting effect of elections varies over time. They show that whereas elections increase the risk of authoritarian regime breakdown in the short term, there are indications that the holding of elections correlates with regime stability after the post-election period (Knutsen, Nygård, and Wig 2017). Their findings match the studies that find that post-electoral protests may unravel autocracies (Bunce and Wolchik 2011; Tucker 2007; Thompson and Kuntz 2004) as well as research on the long-term stabilizing effect of elections (Magaloni 2006; Greene 2007; Malesky and Schuler 2010). However, it does not explain why the dramatic scenarios of post-electoral breakdown unfold in some autocracies and not in others. How do rulers of stable electoral autocracies survive the imminently dangerous period following an electoral event?

A third strain of research enquires specifically into the conditions under which elections have certain effects but focuses on the determinants of democratization by elections. Researchers have focused on a subsection of regimes holding elections and asked why only some of these elections are democratizing.

Howard and Roessler (2006) identify the forming of an opposition coalition as the most important factor for making "liberalizing outcomes" more likely during an authoritarian election. Similarly, Bunce and Wolchik deliver qualitative evidence that authoritarian elections in post-communist regimes have contributed to democratization but only in some cases, an outcome they ascribe to the strategies pursued by opposition activists (2011, 332–4). In line with this, Donno (2013) finds competitive authoritarian regimes to be more likely to democratize than hegemonic regimes and argues that this effect is in itself dependent on international pressure or the existence of an opposition coalition.

Flores and Nourrudin focus less on opposition strategies and more on the autocrat's ability to win elections without manipulation. They argue that where autocrats have sufficient levels of legitimacy – performance and institutional – to win clean elections, they are less likely to manipulate them, and elections are thus more likely to turn democratic (Flores and Nooruddin 2016).

Levitsky and Way's extensive study of 35 competitive authoritarian regimes explores the conditions under which authoritarian elections are democratizing. They find that linkage to the Western world, exemplified by trade flows, immigration, and Western-educated domestic elites, increases the likelihood that competitive authoritarian regimes democratize. When such international linkage to the West is limited, the strength of the state and the ruling party, along with the leverage that Western powers hold over rulers, decides whether regimes remain stable or evolve into unstable, electoral autocracies (Levitsky and Way 2010).

Thus, theoretical and empirical accounts document that whether competitive or hegemonic authoritarian regimes democratize depends on a number of factors related to the opposition, the ruling group, and the international environment. But there are two important caveats. First, since these studies only find results for the competitive subgroup, it is unclear whether the effect is driven by what I in the previous chapter termed minimalist democracies. And second, since most of the studies only include electoral authoritarian regimes (or even competitive regimes), it remains unknown whether the elections (as opposed to no elections) actually positively affect democratization processes. We may know that electoral regimes are more likely to democratize under some circumstances than others, but we do not know whether they are more likely than non-electoral regimes to do so. In other words, we know very little about the causal effect of elections.

In the following, I develop a theory of the conditions under which elections may contribute to authoritarian domination and when they may spiral into regime breakdown. These conditions are not deterministic, but they do affect the probabilities of elections being regime stabilizing or regime subverting.

The theoretical approach follows Levitsky and Way, but my approach differs from the existing literature in a number of ways. First, I focus on the factors that affect authoritarian stability or breakdown through elections rather than democratization. Second, I present a theoretical argument that links the micro-level choices of the actor groups involved in authoritarian elections, elites, opposition, and citizens, to the macro-level outcomes. I argue that the choices made by authoritarian elites, opposition actors, and citizens are partly shaped by the capacities available to rulers. By using and abusing their capacities, autocrats can influence individual-level decisions within the key actor groups. Thus, the effect of elections due to actors' choices on the micro level is conditioned by authoritarian capacities. Third, I test the argument relying on both global large-N analyses and case studies. Furthermore, I do not limit the analysis to electoral autocracies but explicitly compare autocracies with and without elections to correctly estimate the effect of elections on regime stability.

The argument: authoritarian capacities and the conditional effect of elections

The paradox of authoritarian elections (see also Seeberg 2014) is summarized in Table 2.1. On the one hand, elections are viewed as a tool to promote regime stability: they may create legitimacy and contribute to co-optation of elites (both internal and opposition) or even whole segments of the voting population through rent distribution. On the other hand, elections can change the playing field in favor of the opposition. They may serve not only to de-legitimate the regime but also to provide voters and opposition with a tool to gain visibility and demonstrate dissatisfaction.

What determines whether the authoritarian leadership succeeds in abusing elections to entrench its own rule? When might elections spin out of control and produce regime breakdown rather than promote endurance? In the following sections, I theorize how central capacities of an authoritarian regime condition the effect of elections on regime stability. I argue that the likelihood of a stabilizing effect of elections increases with higher levels of administrative capacity and economic control, and thus elections are associated with regime stability in autocracies with strong bureaucracies or extensive control over the economy. Where administrative capacity and economic control are limited, autocrats may still survive elections by relying on their coercive capacity. Where all of these central capacities are lacking, elections are associated with regime breakdown.

The argument proceeds in five steps. First, I argue that choices made by the three main actor groups of the authoritarian regime – elites, opposition, and the population – are crucial in shaping the effect of authoritarian elections, and I spell out the factors that affect each of these choices on the individual level. Second, I present the concepts of state capacity and economic control and briefly relate them to the existing literature. Third, I introduce eight strategies through which autocrats may control elections. Each strategy is targeted at affecting the choices made by at least one of the actor groups so as to increase the likelihood of stabilization by election. Furthermore, for each strategy, I discuss how it is dependent on either administrative or coercive (state) capacity or control over the economy. Fourth, this synthesis of the micro and macro levels leads to six hypotheses on the overall relationship between elections, authoritarian capacities, and stability that are put to the test in the cross-national analyses of Chapters 3–4. Fifth, I sketch a number of observable implications of the theoretical mechanisms to guide the case studies of Chapters 5–6.

Voting choices, elite defections, opposition mobilization, and voter protests

To clarify how the effect of elections plays out, I focus on important choices made by the main actor groups of an authoritarian regime: (1) the choice of the *populace* acting in the role of voters of whether to support the rulers in elections; (2) the choice of (a) *elites* of whether to stay loyal to the leadership or defect, and of (b) defected regime *elites* and *opposition* politicians to run for elections on the opposition slate or be co-opted into the ruling front; and (3) the choice of the *populace* of whether to protest fraudulent elections (see Table 2.1).

The first choice, voters' decisions whether or not to support the ruling front on election day, is important because it affects the likelihood of the rulers winning elections with supermajority victories. An autocrat of course has other strategies to create supermajority victories absent the actual votes needed, as shall be discussed in detail later. But convincing or manipulating voters into supporting the ruling front at the ballot box is an integral part of such strategies. Furthermore, as spelled out previously, supermajority victories are an important feature of stabilizing elections, as these victories signal the autocrat's invincibility and thus affect the likelihood of elite loyalty (rather than defections) and opposition co-optation (rather than mobilization).

The choices made by *elites* of whether to go with the ruling front or actively support the *opposition* form the second set of choices discussed in the following. As spelled out previously, avoiding elite defections and successfully co-opting the opposition are vital strategies for stabilizing a regime through elections.

The third choice is that of citizens deciding whether to protest a (perceived) fraudulent election. Such protests are a crucial mechanism through which elections may destabilize an authoritarian regime, and have been argued to play an important part in convincing central regime elites to defect (Beissinger 2009, 75). The dynamics are illustrated in Figure 2.1. Importantly, all three actor groups may affect regime stability during elections both positively and negatively depending on how their actions turn out (i.e., loyalty versus defection or apathy versus protest).

The main claim of this book is that central capacities available to autocrats shape the likelihood that elections either support or subvert the regime on the macro level

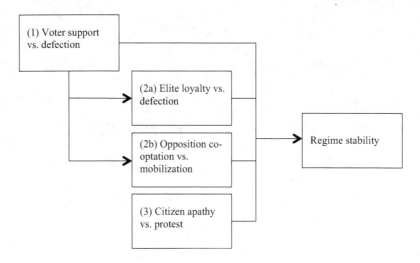

Figure 2.1 Actors' choices and regime stability

because they affect the three sets of choices made on the micro level. To illustrate this argument, I spell out the three sets of choices and the factors influencing them on the individual level. The aim is not to develop a full model of the whole range of factors that affect these choices but more humbly to sketch simplified versions. Against this background I illustrate how state capacity and economic control may alter these micro-level choices, potentially allowing elections to have differing effects.

(1) Voter choice

Models of voting behavior in multi-party electoral authoritarian regimes generally agree that a voter deciding whether to support the incumbent or the opposition will primarily consider three factors: ideological congruence with the respective parties, the benefits one might receive as a function of voting, and the costs of voting (Pfutze 2014; Greene 2007, chap. 2; Magaloni 2006, chap. 1). These factors are relevant because they also represent factors that the incumbent may try to manipulate in order to secure votes and in return derive the potential benefits of authoritarian elections

Ideological congruence or match with the respective parties is not dependent on the existence of party competition on, for instance, economic policy. Ideological congruence may just as well refer to the individual voter's attitudes toward, for instance, democratization or regime change. Some voters may experience a higher degree of ideological congruence with the incumbents while others find that their preferences match those of the opposition better.

The benefits or material spoils that one derives from voting for a specific party will often differ quite dramatically between the incumbent and the opposition party. Common spoils associated with a vote for the incumbents include economic transfers given to the individual in direct forms of vote buying, or goods – whether welfare benefits, a new clinic, or tractors – delivered to an entire village or district based on the ruling party's performance there. Although opposition parties may also hand out spoils in return for votes, these are likely to be much less significant given the limited resources available to the opposition in authoritarian systems – a factor discussed intensively later.

The costs of voting also vary across incumbent and opposition parties. Voting for the incumbent may only involve the costs of transporting oneself to the nearest ballot box and casting the vote. Voting for the opposition, on the other hand, may involve the risk of physical and economic harassment that rulers may target at suspected opposition voters.

Obviously, numerous other factors could also be said to influence a person's party choice, yet this basic model captures the general components that most voters consider before casting their vote in an authoritarian election. Before discussing the effect of state capacity and economic control on these utility calculations, I turn to the choices made by potential candidates and protesters.

(2) Candidate choice

To understand the choice of the individual politician whether to run under the ruling party banner or to participate as an opposition candidate,[6] a simplifying assumption is in order. Here, I assume that candidates gain utility only if their front wins the election.[7] The candidate's expected utility from running either for the opposition or the incumbent will depend on the material and ideological gains the candidate expects from the respective party, the probability that the party will win (which I assume is necessary in order for these benefits to materialize), and the costs of running for the party (incurred regardless of whether it wins) (see also Magaloni 2006, 44–6).

Just like for voters, the costs typically differ dramatically between opposition and incumbent candidates: for incumbent candidates, they usually amount to material costs such as paying for posters, rallies, and employees. In some cases, this may indeed be quite an investment. But whereas these same costs also apply to opposition candidates (and sometimes in greater measure), the opposition candidate may also expect physical costs as they are often physically harassed in authoritarian elections – a strategy discussed later.

Both opposition and incumbent candidates may obtain ideological benefits from running for a certain party and these will vary depending on the individual candidates' ideological match with the parties. Material spoils, on the other hand, are often much greater for incumbent candidates, who may be able to deliver spoils to family and friends in the home region or have lucrative access to government contracts as a result of a successful election.

But the overall benefit that a candidate can expect depends not only on her party choice but also on the probability that that party will win the election. Whereas an opposition candidate may incur the costs of running regardless of an eventual and unexpected opposition win (much harassment of opposition candidates occurs prior to the election in order to prevent them from running), the material gains (for both incumbent and opposition candidates) depend on a party victory. Thus, the incumbent may try to manipulate the candidate's choice directly (for instance, through harassment) but also indirectly by making an opposition victory less likely (for instance, through various forms of electoral manipulation). These tricks will be discussed in detail later. Thus, voters' choices (discussed previously) affect elite and opposition choices: the more voters who vote for the incumbent, the more attractive it is for the elites to run for the incumbent. This relationship is expressed in Figure 2.1 where vote choice affects regime stability not only directly but also indirectly through its effect on the choices of the internal elites and the opposition candidates.

Later, I unfold how authoritarian capacities may affect this choice made by the individual candidate. But first, I turn to the choice of citizens on whether to protest fraudulent elections.

(3) Protester choice

The individual's choice to engage in protests has been described and modeled in various ways over the years (see, for instance, Oliver 1993; Kuran 1989, 1991; Lichbach 1998; Lohmann 1994; Tucker 2007; Lorentzen 2013). But protesting is commonly recognized as a collective action problem with high incentives to free ride, as the individual citizen's participation is unlikely to change results and the achieved goods if protests are successful are public and non-excludable (Tullock 1971). Citizens who abstain from protesting receive the same goods as those who partake but without paying the costs (Acemoglu and Robinson 2005, 123).

However, protests have occurred throughout history, and numerous factors that can potentially solve the collective action problems of protesting or rebelling – such as ideologically motivating people to partake or attempting to exclude non-participators from the benefits of the new political order – have been highlighted (for a short summary see Acemoglu and Robinson 2005, 126–8).

In general, the individual citizen's choice to engage in anti-regime protests is expected to depend on "the costs of participation, the benefits of the goal being sought, and beliefs about the likelihood that the goal can be achieved" (Tucker 2007, 540). Still, models are often complex, and disagreement prevails over the importance of both the individual's expected utility derived from a changed social order as well as the importance of the individual's personal sentiments toward the rulers (Kuran 1991, 47). A common extension of the basic model is the argument of a "tipping logic"; the assumption that the number of other people taking to the streets matters greatly to the individual's decision to protest because higher numbers of protesters lower the costs incurred by the individual protester (Kuran 1991, 17–18), because an increasing number of dissatisfied protesters affects the evaluations of the regime made by other citizens (Lohmann 1994, 51), or because an increasing number of protesters signal that enough opposition exists to make regime change likely (Kricheli, Livne, and Magaloni 2011, 8–9).

To avoid engaging in the overly complex models needed to formalize the choice to protest, I present citizens' choices about whether to participate in protests along simpler lines. I expect the individual citizen's choice to engage in protest to be affected positively by the probability of regime change following the protests and her expected net utility of regime change, which expresses the level of spoils the individual citizen receives from the incumbent relative to those expected from a new regime, and the citizen's ideological congruence with the existing rulers relative to that expected with a new regime (see, for instance, Kricheli, Livne, and Magaloni 2011, 10). Thus, the net utility will be positive for regime supporters and negative for regime opponents. The probability of regime change depends in large part on the number of protesters, as described by Kricheli, Livne, and Magaloni (2011); Lohmann (1994); and Kuran (1991), but also on the capability of the regime to crush protests, as shall be discussed later.

The choice to engage in protest will be affected negatively by the costs the individual citizen expects to incur, such as the risk of imprisonment, death, or deprival of economic benefits associated with being caught in anti-regime protests. These costs can in part be argued to depend on the number of fellow protesters (Kuran 1991), but as argued later, they also depend on the capacities of the autocrat to impose physical and economic costs on protesters (see also Lorentzen 2013).

Given the goal of staying in power, the ruler will seek to minimize elite defections and maximize the potential for opposition co-optation. This requires maximizing the expected utility of voting for the incumbent in relation to voting for the opposition in order to enforce supermajority victories, and simultaneously maximizing the expected utility of running for the ruling front relative to the expected value of running for the opposition. Finally, the ruler will minimize the likelihood of voter protests by minimizing the individual voter's expected utility of protesting. The remainder of this chapter theorizes how administrative and coercive capacity along with economic control enable a ruler to carry out these tasks, and thus increase the likelihood of elections becoming a regime-stabilizing tool.

Authoritarian capacities and electoral strategies

I argue that the choices made by authoritarian elites, opposition actors, and citizens are partly shaped by the capacities available to rulers. By using and abusing their capacities, autocrats can influence individual-level decisions within the key actor groups. Thus, the effect of elections due to actors' choices on the micro level is conditioned by authoritarian capacities. I analyze the effect of the two most prominent authoritarian capacities on the effect of elections: state capacity (both the administrative and the coercive apparatus) and incumbent control over the economy. This is not to say that the ideological power of the autocrat or other factors such as party strength (Magaloni 2006; Brownlee 2007; Levitsky and Way 2010) or international factors (Donno 2013; Levitsky and Way 2010) do not affect the role of elections. Rather, the argument is that we have severely overlooked how power constellations relating to the state and the market influence the degree to which autocrats may abuse institutions such as elections, and this neglect has

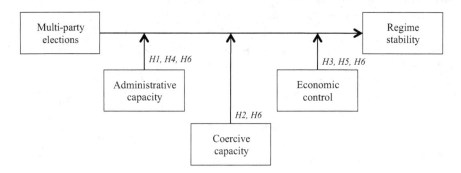

Figure 2.2 The conditioning effect of state capacity and incumbent economic control

Note: Hypotheses in italics are developed below

caused confusion over the effect of elections. In the following, I introduce the concepts of state capacity and economic control before proceeding to theorize how they condition the effect of elections on regime stability both at the macro and micro level. The overall model is depicted in Figure 2.2.

State capacity

State capacity – administrative and coercive – has long been identified as vital in determining authoritarian regime stability (Skocpol 1979; Bellin 2004; Crystal 1994; Slater 2003; Herbst 2001). An authoritarian regime can endure even in the face of widespread protests if the state is sufficiently strong (Skocpol 1979, 32; Way and Levitsky 2006, 389–90). Authoritarian rulers depend on their state apparatuses to coerce opposition, extract resources from society, survey citizens, and make them dependent on the ruling coalition (Slater and Fenner 2011). In his analysis of post-Soviet regime developments, Way argues that in the absence of true democrats, pluralism may still occur "by default" if the regime lacks the capacity to prevent it (Way 2015).

Nevertheless, state capacity not only affects regime stability directly. It is also likely to affect the outcome and effects of authoritarian elections. Although Levitsky and Way stress the importance of the international environment, they also highlight that "Authoritarian governments vary considerably in their ability to control civil society, co-opt or divide oppositions, repress protest, and/or steal elections" (2010, 54). In other words, when autocrats perform their strategies of coercion, co-optation, and legitimization, they do so based on their capacity in each discipline. Likewise, Schedler, in spite of his rather voluntarist approach, states that autocrats are endowed with varying levels of state, economic, and ideological capacity on which they may draw (Schedler 2013, 56–7). But how does the state matter during authoritarian elections? The connection still needs to be established both theoretically and empirically. In the following sections, I present an argument for how state capacity may condition the relationship between multi-party elections and authoritarian regime stability. Importantly, I distinguish between two different types of state capacity, administrative and coercive, and stress their differing roles in sustaining authoritarian regimes through elections.

The definition of state capacity employed here is Migdal's notion of a state's "capacities to penetrate society, regulate social relations, extract resources, and appropriate or use resources in determined ways" (1988, 4). This concept of state capacity does not depend on the rule of law or other traits of liberal democracy; rather, it is "about the performance of agents in carrying out the wishes of principals" (Fukuyama 2013, 350). It covers both the capabilities of the state apparatus and the ability of the rulers to use and control this apparatus. A strong state is unlikely to support an authoritarian system unless the autocrat controls the state. Thus, most autocrats with highly capable states at their disposal also display high degrees of control over the state apparatus as they are otherwise likely to lose power to exactly those elites who control the state.

To spell out the role of state capacity in the context of authoritarian elections, I split the concept into two dimensions: administrative capacity and coercive capacity (Skocpol 1979, 29). Administrative capacity is the territorial reach of the bureaucracy, its competences, and the autocrat's degree of control over it; that is, the ability and will to effectively implement the orders of the rulers. While a positive relationship may exist, competences should not be equated with professionalism of the bureaucracy in a Weberian sense but rather with the mere ability to implement policies, regardless of the means (Soifer and Hau 2008, 223). Coercive capacity is the reach as well as the ability and will to implement the rulers' orders within units such as the army, the police, or a presidential security guard.

I argue that state capacity, administrative as well as coercive, affects the authoritarian leader's ability to remain in power not only in general but, in particular, in a context of authoritarian elections. It does so because it allows the ruler to affect voters', regime elites', opposition candidates', and citizens' calculations of whether to support the ruling front, defect, mobilize, and protest, respectively. Administrative and coercive capacities are often but not always aligned. The two types of state capacities can, to some extent, be seen as substitutable in the game of electoral control. An autocrat lacking in one capacity may still control elections by relying on the other capacity, as shall be explicated later. Before unfolding the theoretical argument, I turn to another important authoritarian capacity.

Economic control

Control over the economy has been shown in case studies to supplement – or even substitute for – state capacity (see, for instance, Greene 2007; McMann 2006; Magaloni 2006). It should not be confused with administrative capacity. In his discussion of the importance of "administrative resources" in post-communist politics, Wilson stresses that "money helps, but it is not essential" (Wilson 2005, 74). Control over a large bureaucracy is a capacity in its own right. But controlling the economy is another and equally important capacity.

The link between economic factors, including modernization, growth, and economic crises, and regime developments has preoccupied researchers for decades (see, for instance, Lipset 1959; Haggard and Kaufman 1997; Bermeo 1990; Przeworski and Limongi 1997; Geddes 2003; Reuter and Gandhi 2011). But the effect of economic performance on authoritarian regime stability is complex, as captured by Magaloni: "Autocratic ruling parties are helped by economic growth but hurt by economic development" (2006, 70). Whereas growth initially supports authoritarian rule as voters are more inclined to support the incumbent, sustained growth creates wealth and thus "liberates voters from their dependence on the state" (Magaloni 2006, 70). In recent years, the literature on electoral authoritarian regimes has started to look into the concept of incumbent economic monopoly (Greene 2007, 2010) or the degree to which the economy is autonomous from the rulers (McMann 2006).[8]

Hence, it might not be the overall level of economic growth but rather the degree of incumbent control over the economy that affects the role of authoritarian elections in promoting regime stability. I extend this argument and propose that where autocrats lack the administrative capacity necessary to subtly control elections, control over the economy may substitute for bureaucratic capacity and be employed to dominate elections. Whereas several studies have pointed to the importance of an incumbent resource advantage for controlling elections (Levitsky and Way 2010; Lust 2009b; Greene 2007, 2010), none have systematically tested the claim on cross-national data.[9]

According to Greene, the incumbent's resource advantage or control of the economy hinges on two factors: a large public sector and a politicized bureaucracy (Greene 2007, 28). Taking this as the definition of incumbent economic control, however, would let the concept overlap with the earlier definition of administrative capacity. Indeed, when the bureaucracy is controlled by the ruler, as entailed in the concept of high administrative capacity in an authoritarian regime, a large public sector contributes directly to the incumbent's degree of economic control. But incumbent economic control is here defined more broadly as the ruler's domination of economic resources, including natural resource revenues, land, and employment opportunities. Thus, a large public sector clearly allows for some degree of control over employment opportunities, particularly when combined with a weak private sector or an economic crisis. And a politicized bureaucracy can leave the incumbent in control of import and export licenses, and thus international trade. But underlying economic structures, such as holding natural resources under government control – in democratization studies known as the "resource curse" (Ross 2001, 328) – may also contribute to an incumbent economic monopoly (Levitsky and Way 2010, 66). Importantly, economic control is literally about the control of whatever resources are there, rather than about an abundance of resources in the first place.

I argue that control of the economy affects the authoritarian leader's ability to remain in power not only in general but in particular in a context of authoritarian elections. A high degree of incumbent economic control may supplement administrative capacity in conditioning the effect of elections, or it may substitute for administrative capacity.

The following sections theorize how administrative capacity, coercive capacity, and economic control condition the relationship between elections and regime stability by enabling eight strategies of electoral control. These strategies affect the

Table 2.2 Strategies of electoral control and their effects

Strategies	Micro-level effects	Macro-level effects	Capacities	Character
Systemic manipulation	Increased utility of running for the incumbent relative to the opposition (choice 2)	Elite defections less likely Opposition mobilization less likely Opposition co-optation more likely Opposition splits more likely	Administrative capacity	Subtle
Manipulation of voters' preference formation	Increased utility of voting for the incumbent relative to the opposition (choice 1)		Administrative capacity, economic control	Subtle
Manipulation of voters' preference expression			Coercive capacity, economic control	Overt
Restricting access to the vote	Increased utility of running for the incumbent relative to the opposition (choice 2)		Administrative capacity	Subtle
Manipulation of vote counting			Administrative capacity	Overt
Legal and economic harassment of opposition	Decreased utility of running for the opposition (choice 2)	Opposition mobilization less likely Elite defections less likely	Administrative capacity, economic control	Subtle
Physical harassment of opposition			Coercive capacity	Overt
Violent crackdown on protesters	Decreased utility of protesting (choice 3)	Voter protests less likely	Coercive capacity	Overt

choices of the three central actor groups: citizens' vote choice and thus the probability of supermajority victories; ruling elites' and opposition choices of running for the incumbent party or the opposition; and citizens' choice of whether to protest. The capacities, strategies, and attempted effects are summarized in Table 2.2.

Authoritarian capacities, vote choice, supermajority victories, and the effect on candidate choice

In this section, I present the theoretical mechanisms through which authoritarian capacities affect voters' choice of whom to vote for (choice 1) and the chances of a supermajority victory. Thereby, they also indirectly shape candidates' choices of whether to run for the regime (choice 2). In turn, these dynamics affect regime stability. In the following section, I carry out the same exercise but focus on the mechanisms through which authoritarian capacities affect the costs of being in opposition (choice 2b) and protesting (choice 3) and thus regime stability.

As discussed previously, supermajority victories signal invincibility, deter elites from defecting, and lure the opposition into the ruling front, in turn making multi-party elections more likely to stabilize the regime (Magaloni 2006, 16–19; Geddes 2005, 11–12). But how are such supermajorities attainable? In authoritarian regimes, vote shares are a function of both citizen preferences and electoral manipulation (Schedler 2013, 124). The regime can thus target voters' preference formation, their ability to express their preferences, and the counting and weighting of votes when trying to secure a supermajority. In the following, I discuss five strategies aimed at generating supermajority victories and in turn controlling opposition and elites, and spell out how these strategies depend on state capacity and economic control. The strategies are: *systemic manipulation, manipulation of voters' preference formation, manipulation of voters' preference expression, restricting access to the vote*, and *manipulation of vote counting*. Not all autocrats apply these strategies in equal measure, but few have generated supermajority victories without employing at least one and typically more than one of these strategies. Furthermore, some of these strategies are also employed in more modest forms in democracies. According to Birch, there are both legitimate and illegitimate forms of electoral manipulation, and the boundary between them is not crystal clear (2011, 26–7). Here, however, I consider the illegitimate forms. By enabling these strategies, authoritarian capacities increase the likelihood that elections stabilize the regime.

Systemic manipulation is defined as the use and abuse of legal provisions to distort electoral outcomes (Vickery and Shein 2012, 2). It includes tactics such as gerrymandering of electoral districts, restrictions on candidates and parties registering for elections, and restrictions on campaigning. It does not directly affect individual voters' preferences but rather the weights given to individual votes and the possible alternatives among which voters can choose. Systemic manipulation increases the chances of a supermajority victory. Where systemic manipulation is extensive, the chances of the opposition winning are small, and the elites will thus tend to run for the incumbent (choice 2).

Electoral gerrymandering is employed to various degrees both by authoritarian and more democratic regimes. An example from the authoritarian camp is contemporary Malaysia, where the ruling party has systematically abused its ability to construct districts with unequal numbers of voters. Predominantly Malay districts have been much smaller than non-Malay districts, allowing the dominant party, United Malays National Organization (UMNO), to secure a dominant role in government as long as it was the most popular party among ethnic Malays (Hing and Ong 1987, 122; Crouch 1996b, 117–18; Rachagan 1987, 217–19). Legal barriers to entering the electoral race are common in the post-Soviet world and in present-day Russia; banning opposition candidates from entering the race due to technicalities or ordering parties to reregister through complicated legal procedures is common (Wilson 2005, 82–3).

Although such gerrymandering and legal meddling do not require great capacity once in place, the construction of a biased system necessitates detailed knowledge of the voter composition in various areas of the country as well as expert knowledge on electoral laws. An effective bureaucracy is key. Thus, whereas economic control and coercive capacity will not influence the success rate of this strategy, administrative capacity will heighten the likelihood that it succeeds.

Manipulation of voters' preference formation (Birch 2011, 31–4, 89–90) is the attempt to alter the individual voter's generic preference and make a vote for the incumbent more attractive (choice 1). Examples include the use of propaganda, abuse of state spending, or preventing the opposition from campaigning.

There are huge incumbent advantages in conducting these tasks (Birch 2011, 92) and administrative capacity is again key. Few autocrats can rely solely on the ruling party machine when they campaign, distribute patronage, create propaganda and slander, obstruct opposition candidates from bringing their message to the people, and gather information on potential opposition voters to urge them to cast their votes for the incumbent. High administrative capacity enables the autocrat to manipulate preference formation by abusing access to state personnel and facilities. Already embedded in the community and often enjoying the respect of the locals, public employees can deliver information to the ruling front, target spoils at supporters, and target propaganda at potential opposition voters and the population at large.

In the aftermath of the 2004 presidential election in Ukraine, Office for Democratic Institutions and Human Rights of the Organization for Security and Cooperation in Europe the OSCE/ODIHR election observation mission reported that local officials had campaigned for the incumbent in 22 regions (Birch 2011, 125). Similarly, during the 1995 Zimbabwean election campaign, the Minister of Agriculture claimed that "No one should say I work for the government and not for the party" (quoted in Kriger 2005, 23). Privileged access to state facilities may allow the incumbents to hold large campaign rallies, and printing facilities may be exclusively available to the rulers (Schedler 2013, 68), again allowing the incumbent's message to reach voters more effectively than that of the opposition.

However, in carrying out manipulation of voters' preference formation, administrative capacity is supplemented by – or potentially substituted by – incumbent control over the economy. An incumbent economic monopoly comes in handy when attempting to manipulate preference formation because it offers a number of campaigning advantages to the ruling front's candidates. Above all, it provides the rulers with the funds necessary to campaign. Money can be generated from state-owned enterprises, public money can be funneled to incumbents directly from the budget, and candidates may receive contributions from private businesses with links to the state (Greene 2007, 40–1).

Prior to the 1994 elections in Mexico, for instance, a newspaper revealed that a private reception had been hosted at which prominent businesspeople, many of whom also happened to profit from the government's privatization program, had been asked to donate millions of US dollars to the ruling PRI's election campaign (Lawson 2002, 143). An economic monopoly is also an effective way to put pressure on opposition-friendly media outlets: McMann describes how private businesses in the Russian province of Ul'ianovsk, in order to stay on friendly terms with the local government (which they depend on for licenses, etc.), avoid advertising in independent newspapers, thus depriving the independent media of essential sources of finance (McMann 2006, 74). All these tactics serve to promote the ruling party and alter individual voters' intrinsic preferences.

By reducing voters' perceived ideological costs of voting for the ruling party (choice 1), incumbent control of the economy and administrative capacity increase the probability of an incumbent victory. At the same time, they lower the costs of campaigning under the ruling party's banner, which will make the elites even more likely to stay loyal to the ruling front (choice 2).

Manipulation of voters' preference expression on election day is a less subtle form of voter manipulation. It could be targeted at raising the spoils attained by voting for the ruling party by offering particularistic benefits, for instance, through vote buying (choice 1). Or it could be aimed at increasing the costs of voting for the opposition by intimidation or coercion (choice 1). Whereas administrative capacity is a central capacity for autocrats carrying out more subtle forms of voter manipulation such as systemic manipulation and manipulation of preference formation, the more obvious manipulation of voters' expressed preferences – the party they actually vote for on election day – hinges on coercive capacity and extensive control over the economy.

First, the coercive apparatus can be employed to harass voters into altering their vote choice in favor of the ruling party on election day. The threat of beatings and arrests and the presence of military officers at voting stations raise the costs of voting for the opposition.

Second, extensive control over the economy is essential for buying votes or pressuring voters into voting for the ruling party. An important way of containing both voters and incumbent elites is by turning elections into exercises in competitive clientelism (Lust 2009b, 123–5). In studies of North Africa and the Middle East, Lust argues that voters recognize that elections are not about politics and support candidates that can deliver spoils, jobs, and goods. Candidates in turn support the ruling front, as this is the only way to satisfy voters' demands for patronage (Lust 2009b, 127–9). Without relying heavily on repression, the incumbent maintains control of both the elite and the voters (Lust 2009b, 130). But since the rulers are dependent on handing out spoils, control over a vast amount of resources is vital (Lust 2009b, 133).

The examples of autocrats' abuse of state money to secure votes are many. Unity in Russia has benefited from doling out money to public sector workers at election time (Colton and McFaul 2003, 57). Blaydes has demonstrated the existence of budget cycles and their connection to the centralized economy in Mubarak's Egypt (Blaydes 2011, chap. 5), and Magaloni presents convincing evidence of the Mexican PRI's abuse of state funds through the PRONASOL, a poverty-relief program, to reward swing municipalities that did not elect an opposition candidate (Magaloni 2006, chap. 4). Thus, the mechanism of rent distribution forms part of a strategy to construct supermajority victories. Rent distribution affects not only the probability of incumbent victory but also the spoils associated with supporting the incumbent. Thus, if citizens are tied to the ruling front through patronage networks, the spoils associated with the incumbent are higher, and the net utility of regime change is lower, leaving the individual citizen less likely to protest (choice 3).

Finally, a large public sector and few options of employment outside the reach of the ruling group provide rulers with a final tool to pressure voters into compliance by manipulating their preference expression. Both UMNO in Malaysia and ZANU(PF) in Zimbabwe have traditionally made sure to inform public sector workers that a vote for the opposition could entail job loss or a transfer to the outskirts of the country (Crouch 1996a, 127; Kriger 2005, 23). In this way, incumbent control over the economy may not only increase the material spoils associated with voting for the incumbent but also raise the costs of voting for the opposition (choice 1).

Restricting access to the vote involves technical maneuvers such as manipulation of voter registration and limiting access to the ballot. It does not affect the utility calculation of the individual voters but prevents entire groups of voters deemed likely to support the opposition from voting; it thus increases the likelihood of a supermajority victory and, in turn, decreases the likelihood of elite defections (choice 2). Restricting access to the vote is here distinguished from other forms of fraud that take place on election day. Restricting access to the vote is usually a carefully planned strategy, whereas the stealing of votes on or after election day, for instance, through manipulation of vote counting (discussed later), is often an emergency measure applied by autocrats who are surprised by a strong oppositional performance.

Restricting access to the vote by legal maneuvers is a more subtle measure that requires high administrative capacity. In Cameroon in 2007, the ruling party controlled voter registration on the ground in local districts through mayors' offices, police stations, and local chiefs, and the government thus severely restricted the access to voter identity cards in opposition strongholds (Albaugh 2011, 399–402). In the 1999 elections for the Russian Duma, the Central Electoral Committee (of which one-third of members were appointed by the President, the rest by the houses of government) restricted access to the ballot for parts of the opposition (Colton and McFaul 2003, 19–21). Here, economic control or coercive capacity is not necessary as long as the ruling party has the knowledge and administrative infrastructure to limit access to the vote for selected parts of the population – namely the opposition.

Manipulation of vote counting includes ballot-stuffing and all types of deliberate, incorrect counting and tabulating of votes. This strategy is a more overt form of fraud as it often involves visible ballot-stuffing at voting stations or delays in the announcement of results. When successful, it increases the likelihood of incumbent victory and thus of elite loyalty (choice 2). In the 2008 parliamentary and presidential elections in Zimbabwe, the opposition performed surprisingly well in elections for the House, upon which the announcement of presidential election results was postponed for five weeks, leading to massive accusations of fraud in the counting and tabulating process (ZESN 2013). Like the strategy of restricting access to the vote, this strategy primarily hinges on an efficient administrative infrastructure.

The five election manipulation strategies carried out by autocrats are all aimed at generating supermajority victories, enticing and pressuring voters into voting for the incumbent (choice 1), and encouraging elite loyalty (choice 2). Furthermore, they all depend on either administrative capacity or a certain degree of control over the economy. Only more overt manipulation of voters' ability to express their true preferences on election day depends specifically on the autocrats' coercive capacity (see the overview in Table 2.2). The five strategies thus form part of the explanation for how state capacity and economic control condition the effect of elections: by enabling manipulative strategies, such capacities allow the autocrat to control elections and use them to her own advantage.

Authoritarian capacities and increased costs of being in opposition and protesting

The aforementioned strategies are all targeted at controlling the vote, and many autocrats have relied on these strategies to ensure supermajority victories and sustain the regime. But as discussed previously, an authoritarian election may also cause opposition mobilization or provoke post-electoral protests that can spiral until the regime falls. To prevent elites from defecting and opponents from mobilizing (choice 2), and to avoid post-electoral protests (choice 3), autocrats may – on top of the strategies described to secure a supermajority victory – employ their capacities to harass the opposition and potential protesters using various degrees of outright repression. Here the coercive apparatus plays a more direct role. In the following, I present three additional authoritarian strategies aimed at increasing the costs of being in opposition and of protesting.

Legal and economic harassment of opposition candidates is the non-violent aspect of what Levitsky and Way term low-intensity coercion. The strategy is simply to increase the costs of being in opposition (choice 2). This more subtle type of repression relies primarily on administrative capacity and economic control. To legally harass opposition members, autocrats rely on their administrative capacity. Opposition candidates may be surveyed, have licenses revoked, and be harassed by public officials in various ways (Levitsky and Way 2010, 58). Especially in the post-Soviet space, tax officers and even fire inspectors are employed to harass the opposition by closing down establishments or demanding excessive paperwork (Wilson 2005, 84).

Economic harassment, on the other hand, is dependent upon control over the economy. In her investigation of differing degrees of democracy on the subnational level in Kyrgyzstan and Russia, McMann explains how "The ability to make a living independent of the state is critical to the practice of democracy; otherwise, citizens will avoid activism for fear of economic reprisals by the government" (McMann 2006, 4; see also Levitsky and Way 2010, 66–7; Allina-Pisano 2010). The explanation is simply that the individual will not risk her livelihood for political activism. Thus in order for the opposition to thrive in electoral authoritarian regimes, there must be a sufficient supply of jobs outside of the public sphere and hence outside of incumbent control. Where citizens have economic autonomy, McMann finds them more prone to oppositional activities (2006, 4).

Thus, an incumbent economic monopoly will prevent elites from defecting and limit potential opposition candidates.[10] In Belarus, the authoritarian government of Lukashenka limited employment at state-owned enterprises to one-year contracts that could be extended at the will of the management and declared that academic degrees could be withdrawn based on opposition activism (Silitski 2005, 91–2).

Physical harassment of opposition candidates corresponds to Levitsky and Way's category of high-intensity coercion. It is aimed at increasing the costs of being in opposition and thus decreases the risks of opposition mobilization and elite defections (choice 2). It necessitates a strong coercive apparatus. Fear of the rulers' coercive capacity may in itself have a preventive effect on dissent. If not, active coercion such as assassinations of key opposition politicians, disappearances, and long prison sentences for opposition activity is often employed (Way and Levitsky 2006, 392). Such tactics have been witnessed across electoral authoritarian regimes from Russia to the Philippines to Zimbabwe. The assassination of one prominent opposition figure does not require a full coercive apparatus but often only a few loyal troops. However, in order to run a full terror regime aimed at repressing the entire opposition violently, the state must control a coercive apparatus able and willing to commit such atrocities.

Violent crackdown on protesters is a strategy employed to prevent or stop post-electoral protests (choice 3). Contrary to the previous two strategies, it does not target opposition candidates but protesters. It is a last resort but one that is regularly employed nonetheless, as demonstrated in Iran following the 2009 elections, where riot police and the ruler's paramilitary force, the Basij, quelled post-electoral protests with violence, causing between 37 and 200 deaths (US Department of State 2010). Display of brute force – and the willingness to use it – increases citizens' perceived costs of protesting, reducing the expected utility of protesting, and thus decreasing the likelihood of large-scale post-electoral protests.

In cases where such capacity does not exist and incumbents lack the tools to keep the people off the streets, the regime may break down following mass public displays of dissatisfaction. In Georgia during the 2003 "Rose Revolution," president Shevardnadze lacked the necessary control of the military and security forces to repress the post-electoral demonstrations (Mitchell 2004, 348; Wilson 2005, 87) that led to the breakdown of the authoritarian regime. The strategies, the required capacities, and their intended effects on the micro and macro levels are summed up in Table 2.2.

Hypotheses

Together, these eight strategies, dependent on the regime's degree of administrative capacity, coercive capacity, and economic control, link authoritarian capacities, elections, and regime stability. On the macro level, the theory results in the following hypotheses:

> H1: The effect of authoritarian multi-party elections on the likelihood of regime breakdown will decrease with higher levels of *administrative capacity*.

H2: The effect of authoritarian multi-party elections on the likelihood of regime breakdown will decrease with higher levels of *coercive capacity*.

H3: The effect of authoritarian multi-party elections on the likelihood of regime breakdown will decrease with higher levels of *economic control*.

Hypotheses 1–3 summarize the theoretical solution to the paradox of authoritarian elections. Administrative capacity, coercive capacity, and economic control are expected to sharpen an autocrat's ability to create supermajority victories (and thus deter elites from defecting and promote opposition co-optation), hinder opposition mobilization, co-opt and split the opposition, prevent voter protests, and effectively silence these protests where they do arise. This should make high-capacity authoritarian regimes more stable and, in turn, breakdown less likely to occur. However, not all strategies of electoral control are equally attractive to a dictator, and the implications of this hierarchy of strategies will be discussed later. The discussion leads to another three hypotheses on the differing effects of the three types of capacities.

The costs of violence and fraud

The strategies summarized in Table 2.2 should be available to a dictator who presides over a highly capable state and controls the economy. However, the strategies vary both in terms of their costs and effectiveness, and from the viewpoint of an office-seeking dictator, some strategies are thus preferable to others.

Birch argues that the manipulation of the legal system (here termed *systemic manipulation*) will be preferable to most dictators as "this strategy carries a relatively low level of risk" (Birch 2011, 60). This less obvious type of fraud is not as likely to provoke rage and condemnation either nationally or internationally. In this category, I also include *restriction of access to the vote*, as this strategy includes various measures of disenfranchising the opposition by use of the administration and the legal apparatus rather than by stationing soldiers at the polls. However, in only a few cases are these strategies sufficient to ensure electoral victory, and they are thus often combined with the other measures.

According to Birch, among the strategies of manipulation that directly concern the electoral process, the second most attractive strategy is the subtle manipulation of vote choice (and in Birch's typology, this actually includes what I have termed *legal and economic harassment of the opposition*). I argue that subtlety is only a trait of the *manipulation of voters' intrinsic preferences* – the stationing of soldiers at voting stations and the direct buying of votes (*manipulation of voters' preference expression*) are more overt strategies that have a higher risk of sparking protests after the elections and of being condemned by international observers.

While the more subtle types of manipulation of the legal framework, of voters' intrinsic preferences, and of discreet harassment of the opposition and potential protesters are often preferable to dictators, they are not always attainable. An autocrat may thus be forced to rely on cruder strategies, such as blatant fraud on election day or violence toward voters or the opposition. But these strategies are more costly. Rather than strengthening the regime, a stolen election may increase grievances in the populace, with the potential for raising dissent (Kuntz and Thompson 2009, 257–8; Magaloni 2006, chap. 6; Birch 2011, 110; Tucker 2007, 542–3; Lehoucq 2003). This happened following blatant fraud in the counting process of the 2003 Azerbaijani presidential election, forcing the president to "brutally suppress[ed]" the resulting protests (Wilson 2005, 86). But open repression is also a costly endeavor that may compel elites to defect and the opposition to mobilize (Haber 2006, 699; Mason and Krane 1989; Bellin 2004). Both obvious fraud and intimidation are also more likely to catch the eye of the international community and lead to condemnation (Kelley 2009).

If the presence of security services at voting stations, violent crackdowns, and blatant electoral manipulation increase the costs of elite defections, opposition mobilization, and voter protests but also alienate voters and elites, it can be expected to affect the strategies of the rulers. They will be urged to employ blatant manipulation of the administration of elections and violent crackdowns on opposition and voters only when no other options are available. These dynamics were exemplified in the 1985 Zimbabwean presidential race, when – in the midst of extensive pro-regime violence – incumbent President Mugabe encouraged his supporters to refrain from blatant acts of violence (Kriger 2005, 8–9). "We don't want the supporters of the minority parties to have any excuse to call the elections unfair when they lose . . . Do not force them to join ZANU-PF because after the election they will have no option but to join ZANU-PF as it is the majority and all their parties will have lost" was the official statement from the secretary of administration of the ruling party, Nyagumbo, at a rally in 1985 (quoted in Kriger 2005, 9). Although violence continued on a lower scale, the Mugabe leadership clearly preferred to base its victory on less costly arrangements, such as systemic manipulation and vote buying, as was seen in 1985 and subsequent elections (Kriger 2005).

The hierarchy of strategies to some extent translates into a hierarchy of capacities. I argue that if the more subtle strategies of *systemic manipulation, manipulation of voters' intrinsic preferences, restriction of access to the ballot,* and *legal and economic harassment of the opposition* are successfully carried out, they should be enough to produce supermajority victories and prevent elite defections and opposition mobilization. Furthermore, they are seldom sufficient to trigger massive post-electoral protests and thus raise the need for a violent crackdown after elections. These strategies are primarily dependent on administrative capacity or economic control, and each capacity in and of itself should thus increase the likelihood that elections are stabilizing. If the ruler is able to exploit fully either a strong administrative force or an extensive control over the economy, coercive capacity will seldom be necessary. Thus,

> H4: The effect of authoritarian multi-party elections on regime breakdown will be negative for high levels of administrative capacity irrespective of the levels of coercive capacity and economic control.
> H5: The effect of authoritarian multi-party elections on regime breakdown will be negative for high levels of economic control irrespective of the levels of administrative and coercive capacity.

That is, regimes with high levels of administrative capacity and/or economic control will be more likely to stabilize through elections. In this case, elections – as opposed to no elections – will be associated with lower risks of regime breakdown.

The expectations with regard to the effect of coercive capacity are different. Coercive capacity is essential where the more subtle forms of manipulation have failed. It is an emergency measure employed where the autocrat otherwise runs the risk of losing power either at the ballot or during post-electoral protests. I believe autocrats may win an election by relying on their repressive apparatus but I do not expect high levels of coercive capacity on their own to be sufficient to secure a stabilizing effect of elections in the longer run. However, autocrats who lack all capacities are not even able to carry out the emergency measures, such as violent crackdowns or large-scale fraud. In these cases, elections will be destabilizing:

H6: The effect of authoritarian multi-party elections on regime breakdown will be positive when levels of administrative capacity, coercive capacity, and economic control are all low.

Table 2.3 summarizes the hypotheses that are put to the test in the following chapters.

Table 2.3 Hypotheses

State capacity			
Administrative	H1		The effect of authoritarian multi-party elections on the likelihood of regime breakdown will decrease with higher levels of administrative capacity.
	H4		The effect of authoritarian multi-party elections on regime breakdown will be negative for high levels of administrative capacity irrespective of coercive capacity and economic control.
Coercive	H2		The effect of authoritarian multi-party elections on the likelihood of regime breakdown will decrease with higher levels of coercive capacity.
Economic control			
	H3		The effect of authoritarian multi-party elections on the likelihood of regime breakdown will decrease with higher degrees of incumbent control over the economy.
	H5		The effect of authoritarian multi-party elections on regime breakdown will be negative for high levels of economic control irrespective of administrative and coercive capacity.
Joint effects			
	H6		The effect of authoritarian multi-party elections on regime breakdown will be positive when levels of administrative capacity, coercive capacity, and economic control are all low.

Typical cases and observable implications

The following chapters test the theoretical argument in global, quantitative analyses and case studies. The hypotheses are the main focus of the quantitative analyses of Chapters 3–4. However, the quantitative tests focus on the overall relationships and do not delve into the mechanisms: the ways in which authoritarian capacities enable various electoral strategies, in turn impacting the effect of elections.

Thus, I also turn to four cases in Chapters 5–6: the Philippines in 1986, Malaysia in 1990, and Zimbabwe in 2008 and 2013. The selection of cases is discussed in Chapters 5 and 6. The goal of the case studies is twofold. First, whereas the quantitative analyses test the correlations between elections, capacities, and stability, the case studies assess other aspects of the theoretical apparatus, particularly the interaction between capacities and strategies. The research strategy resembles what Mahoney, building on Campbell (1975), terms pattern-matching: "evaluating whether patterns derived from cross-case analysis can be matched with observations from within specific cases" (Mahoney 2003, 361). If the observable implications of the theory expected to lie behind the cross-case findings are detected in specific cases, the within-case analysis increases our belief in the theory (Campbell 1975, 182). Thus, both the research strategy and its goal resemble that of process-tracing: a thorough within-case analysis is performed to further assess the causal argument. But unlike process-tracing, the case studies do not trace the causal mechanism understood as a system of interlocking entities (see Beach and Pedersen 2013, 23–45). Instead, they assess evidence of whether various indications of the underlying theoretical mechanisms are present in the four cases. To enable this strategy, the following section sketches the observable implications of the theoretical argument for various combinations of authoritarian capacities. Chapters 5–6 attempt to identify these implications in selected cases.

Another advantage of the case studies is that they allow for more nuanced measurement of the conditioning variables (Gerring 2007, 49). Thus, an assessment of coercive capacity in a single case may take into account the police force and government-sponsored militias rather than simply relying on cross-nationally available measures of military expenditure. Similarly, looking into economic control within a single case may reveal information on informal ways that dictators can control the economy of their country – information that is not evident from publicly available statistics. The case studies may thus capture aspects of authoritarian capacities that are not measurable across a large number of countries over time.

Three scenarios of authoritarian capacities

There are two opposing effects of authoritarian elections that I should be able to detect in case studies. One scenario, *stabilization by election*, is more likely when either administrative capacity or economic control is high (H4 and H5). Another, *breakdown by election*, is theorized as more likely where all capacities are low (H6). However, as discussed in the section on the costs of the more overt strategies of electoral fraud and violence, cases are not necessarily high or low on all three capacities. Where levels of administrative capacity and economic control are low but coercive capacity is high, elections may be won by emergency measures, but due to the costs of the more overt strategies supported by coercive capacity, such a victory will not result in long-term, stabilizing effects. This combination of capacities is thus more likely to result in what could be termed *electoral survival*.

In the following, I go through the three theorized combinations of authoritarian capacities and derive the observable implications of the theory that should be detectable in each of these cases in order to lend support to the theoretical argument. These scenarios and the observable implications are derived directly from the theoretical framework. They are in correspondence with all hypotheses tested in Chapters 3–4. They are meant to flesh out the logic to enable a systematic application of the theory to qualitative data in order to assess not only the general relationship between elections, capacities, and regime stability, but also the underlying mechanisms that may drive this relationship. However, the three scenarios are ideal types. Not all authoritarian elections will fall clearly into one of these categories. Nonetheless, the degree to which selected cases conform to these observable implications can help assess the theoretical framework. The theory is tested in the case studies of Chapters 5–6.

Stabilization by election: high administrative capacity and/or economic control

As specified in H4 and H5, high levels of administrative capacity or incumbent economic control should in themselves increase the likelihood of authoritarian control through elections, independent of the levels of the other capacities. A high-capacity case that complies with the theory should display the following characteristics: first, the autocrat should have extensive control over a strong administrative apparatus and/ or extensive control over the economy. The level of coercive capacity could be high or low, but the coercive apparatus should not play a very visible role in elections.

Second, the rulers should rely on a range of the more subtle strategies of electoral manipulation, namely *systemic manipulation, manipulation of voters' intrinsic preferences, restrictions on access to the ballot*, and *economic and legal harassment of the opposition*. Third, these strategies should be directed from above, carried out by agents of the ruling front, and draw on the ruling group's resources or capacities. Fourth, they should lead to an incumbent victory in elections. And fifth, the electoral victory should have at least some of the stabilizing effects suggested by the literature on authoritarian elections, namely preventing elite defections and opposition mobilization, provoking opposition splits and causing opposition co-optation into the ruling front, preventing post-electoral protests, and creating domestic and international legitimacy.

Breakdown by election: limited capacities

As explicated in H6, autocrats are expected to be more likely to experience breakdown following elections if they have low levels of both administrative and coercive capacity and are unable to yield control over the economy. The first implication of the theory in these cases is thus low levels of both administrative and coercive capacity and limited economic control. Second, these autocrats are not expected to carry out any of the subtle strategies of electoral manipulation, although there may be sporadic fraud or violence against the opposition and voters. Third, the opposition will mobilize, the elite will defect, elections will not generate legitimacy, and voter protests may arise if the rulers do not lose the election outright. Fourth, rulers will either lose elections outright or succumb to domestic or international pressure afterward, with regime breakdown as the result. Fifth, if domestic protests arise, rulers are not expected to successfully quell them.

Electoral survival: high coercive capacity but limited administrative capacity and economic control

The previous two scenarios were the ideal cases of what presents us with the "paradox" of authoritarian elections. Different levels of authoritarian capacities may solve this paradox. But what happens if the autocrat does not have high administrative capacity and/or economic control but does not lack all capacities either? I have theorized that administrative capacity and economic control both have a positive effect on the relationship between elections and regime stability independent of the other capacities. But coercive capacity is not without use. It plays an important part in enabling the regime-sustaining strategies of authoritarian elections summed up in Table 2.1. However, as discussed previously, there is a hierarchy among electoral strategies, and the ones that are solely dependent on coercive capacity happen to be the least attractive strategies in the long run (see Table 2.2).

The observable implications of the theory for these cases are as follows. First, these regimes have high levels of coercive capacity without corresponding high levels of administrative capacity or economic control. An extensive coercive machinery may win the autocrat an election by orchestrating large-scale fraud, pressuring voters and opposition into compliance through violence, and quelling popular protests. Thus, the second observable implication of the theory in these cases should be the extensive use of one or more of these strategies. Third, the strategies should be directed from above and carried out by agents of the coercive apparatus. Fourth, they should lead to an incumbent victory in elections. Fifth, the election should have some but not all of the desired effects. Whereas elite defections and opposition mobilization should indeed be deterred through violence, and popular protests should either be prevented or quelled once they appear, legitimacy should not follow. The regime may have survived but not necessarily stabilized – it should not be able to survive on these strategies in consecutive elections.

Table 2.4 outlines the observable implications of the theory that will structure the case studies. In Chapters 5–6, I select cases that conform to these scenarios and test whether the observable implications are present in the cases, thus lending support to the theoretical apparatus presented here. Before we proceed to the case studies, the following chapters assess the hypotheses in time-series, cross-sectional analyses.

66 *Stabilization through elections*

Table 2.4 Observable implications of the theory for each combination of capacities

	Stabilization by election	Breakdown by election	Electoral survival
Authoritarian capacities	High administrative capacity and/or economic control	Low administrative capacity, coercive capacity, and economic control	High coercive capacity, low administrative capacity and economic control
Observable implications	Employment of subtle manipulation strategies	No use of subtle strategies, potential use of limited versions of overt strategies	Extensive use of one or more of the overt strategies
	Directed from above and carried out by government agents	Destabilizing effect of elections such as: • Elite defections • Opposition mobilization • Legitimacy loss • Voter protests	Directed from above and carried out by agents of the coercive apparatus
	Incumbent victory in elections	No successful quelling of protests if they arise	Incumbent victory in elections
	Stabilizing effect of elections such as: • Preventing elite defections and opposition mobilization • Provoking opposition splits and causing opposition co-optation into the ruling front • Preventing post-electoral protests • Creating domestic and international legitimacy	Regime breakdown	Some but not all of the stabilizing effects: • Preventing elite defections and opposition mobilization • Popular protests should either be prevented or quelled • But loss of legitimacy

Notes

1 Threats from external actors have become increasingly important in recent years but are not considered here. According to data from (Geddes, Wright, and Frantz 2014), breakdowns following foreign interventions have accounted for 4% of regime breakdowns in authoritarian regimes since 1946.
2 "Unconstitutionally" refers to transfers of power that do not follow an officially endorsed process (Svolik 2012, 40).
3 Indeed, embedded in the very notion of the succession dilemma is the idea that dictators need strong allies, but these allies are also their biggest rival: having established a second in command who is destined to take over power might free the regime of elite splits should the leader fall ill, but dictators often shy away from appointing such a successor because: "If a man occupies a clear second place, every opponent of the top

man will tend to rally around him, and he will then become a serious rival to the man on top" (Burling 1974, 256).
4 Elections are also argued to provide rulers with information on opposition strength, allowing them to judge the level of concessions necessary to co-opt and successfully quell dissent (Gandhi 2008, 167–8).
5 An exception is van Ham and Seim (2017), who have recently argued that authoritarian elections are more likely to lead to turnover where authoritarian state capacity is low but that low state capacity in turn inhibits democratization. The argument that strong states support stabilization by elections is unfolded later.
6 Here, the choice is presented in the form of a potential candidate deciding which party to run for. But assuming that elites, regardless of whether they run for Parliament or not, are forced to make clear their commitment (or lack thereof) to the incumbent regime, the model may easily be extended to also depict the choice made by those elites who do not run for Parliament but are known regime or opposition supporters.
7 In the case of regime change, I find it plausible that candidates of the previous dictatorship do not harvest many benefits from a regime-changing election, even if they personally gain a seat in spite of their party's overall losses. In the more common case of ruling party victory, it is more problematic to assume that an opposition candidate does not derive utility from gaining a seat unless the opposition as a whole wins the elections. Many personal benefits could be assumed to follow from being an opposition member of Parliament. Furthermore, it may also be problematic to expect a candidate's benefits to be tied strictly to that of the party, as a party may win elections without all individual candidates gaining seats. However, for simplicity, I have disregarded these potential benefits and assume that opposition candidates are driven by the benefits they expect to gain, whether ideological or material, from opposition takeover. The simplifying assumption does not affect the conclusions as the purpose is not to explain candidate motivation as a whole but to track the effect of the capacities available to rulers on individual-level decisions to run for the opposition or the incumbent.
8 Although Blaydes argues that the Egyptian regime under Mubarak depended less on "state largesse" (Blaydes 2011, 10–11), the ample opportunities for corruption among parliamentarians still depended on a certain state dominance over the economy.
9 The exception is Greene (2010), who tests the general effect of economic control on regime stability in a sample of eight dominant party regimes but does not test how economic control conditions the effect of elections.
10 According to Greene, this does not mean that there are no opposition candidates left. But due to the opportunity costs – combined with the risks of intimidation – of joining the opposition, only individuals who strongly disagree with the status quo, and are not strictly office seeking, join the opposition (Greene 2007, 5). As a result, policy-seeking opposition parties become niche parties typically placed on either side of the dominant party on the political spectrum – a structure that discourages opposition unity and alienates many voters (Greene 2007, 5–6).

References

Acemoglu, Daron, and James A. Robinson. 2005. *Economic Origins of Dictatorship and Democracy*. New York: Cambridge University Press.

Albaugh, Ericka A. 2011. "An Autocrat's Toolkit: Adaptation and Manipulation in 'Democratic' Cameroon." *Democratization* 18 (2): 388–414.

Allina-Pisano, Jessica. 2010. "Social Contracts and Authoritarian Projects in Post-Soviet Space: The Use of Administrative Resource." *Communist and Post-Communist Studies* 43 (4): 373–82.

Beach, Derek, and Rasmus Brun Pedersen. 2013. *Process-Tracing Methods: Foundations and Guidelines*. Ann Arbor: University of Michigan Press.

Beissinger, Mark R. 2009. "An Interrelated Wave." *Journal of Democracy* 20 (1): 74–7.
Bellin, Eva. 2004. "The Robustness of Authoritarianism in the Middle East: Exceptionalism in Comparative Perspective." *Comparative Politics* 36 (2): 139–57.
Bermeo, Nancy. 1990. "Rethinking Regime Change." *Comparative Politics* 22 (3): 359–77.
Birch, Sarah. 2011. *Electoral Malpractice*. Oxford and New York: Oxford University Press.
Blaydes, Lisa. 2011. *Elections and Distributive Politics in Mubarak's Egypt*. New York: Cambridge University Press.
Bogaards, Matthijs. 2013. "Reexamining African Elections." *Journal of Democracy* 24 (4): 151–60.
Bratton, Michael, and Nicolas van de Walle. 1997. *Democratic Experiments in Africa: Regime Transitions in Comparative Perspective*. New York: Cambridge University Press.
Brownlee, Jason. 2007. *Authoritarianism in an Age of Democratization*. New York: Cambridge University Press.
———. 2009. "Portents of Pluralism: How Hybrid Regimes Affect Democratic Transitions." *American Journal of Political Science* 55 (3): 515–32.
Bueno de Mesquita, Bruce, Alastair Smith, Randolph M. Siverson, and James D. Morrow. 2003. *The Logic of Political Survival*. Cambridge, MA: The MIT Press.
Bunce, Valerie, and Sharon Wolchik. 2011. *Defeating Authoritarian Leaders in Postcommunist Countries*. New York: Cambridge University Press.
Burling, Robbins. 1974. *The Passage of Power: Studies in Political Succession*. New York: Academic Press.
Campbell, Donald T. 1975. "III. 'Degrees of Freedom' and the Case Study." *Comparative Political Studies* 8 (2): 178–93.
Colton, Timothy J., and Michael McFaul. 2003. *Popular Choice and Managed Democracy: The Russian Elections of 1999 and 2000*. Washington D.C.: Brookings Institution Press.
Crouch, Harold. 1996a. *Government and Society in Malaysia*. Ithaca: Cornell University Press.
———. 1996b. "Malaysia: Do Elections Make a Difference?" In *The Politics of Elections in Southeast Asia*, edited by R. H. Taylor, 114–35. Cambridge: Cambridge University Press.
Crystal, Jill. 1994. "Authoritarianism and Its Adversaries in the Arab World." *World Politics* 46 (2): 262–89.
Diamond, Larry. 1994. "Toward Democratic Consolidation." *Journal of Democracy* 5 (3): 4–17.
Donno, Daniela. 2013. "Elections and Democratization in Authoritarian Regimes." *American Journal of Political Science* 57 (3): 703–16.
Downs, Anthony. 1957. *An Economic Theory of Democracy*. New York: Harper.
Flores, Thomas Edward, and Irfan Nooruddin. 2016. *Elections in Hard Times: Building Stronger Democracies in the 21st Century*. Cambridge, NY: Cambridge University Press.
Fukuyama, Francis. 2013. "What Is Governance?" *Governance* 26 (3): 347–68.
Gandhi, Jennifer. 2008. *Political Institutions under Dictatorship*. New York: Cambridge University Press.
Gandhi, Jennifer, and Ellen Lust-Okar. 2009. "Elections under Authoritarianism." *Annual Review of Political Science* 12: 403–22.
Gandhi, Jennifer, and Adam Przeworski. 2006. "Cooperation, Cooptation, and Rebellion under Dictatorships." *Economics & Politics* 18 (1): 1–26.

Geddes, Barbara. 2003. *Paradigms and Sand Castles: Theory Building and Research Design in Comparative Politics*. Ann Arbor: University of Michigan Press.

———. 2005. "Why Parties and Elections in Authoritarian Regimes?" Paper presented for presentation at the annual meeting of the American Political Science Association. Washington, DC.

Geddes, Barbara, Joseph Wright, and Erica Frantz. 2014. "Autocratic Breakdown and Regime Transitions: A New Data Set." *Perspectives on Politics* 12 (2): 313–31.

Gerring, John. 2007. *Case Study Research: Principles and Practices*. Cambridge, NY: Cambridge University Press.

Goemans, Henk E. 2008. "Which Way Out? The Manner and Consequences of Losing Office." *Journal of Conflict Resolution* 52 (6): 771–94.

Goldstone, Jack. 2001. "Toward a Fourth Generation of Revolutionary Theory." *Annual Review of Political Science* 4: 139–87.

Greene, Kenneth. 2007. *Why Dominant Parties Lose: Mexico's Democratization in Comparative Perspective*. Cambridge: Cambridge University Press.

———. 2010. "The Political Economy of Authoritarian Single-Party Dominance." *Comparative Political Studies* 43 (7): 807–34.

Haber, Stephen. 2006. "Authoritarian Government." In *The Oxford Handbook of Political Economy*, edited by Barry Weingast and Donald Wittman, 693–707. New York: Oxford University Press.

Hadenius, Axel, and Jan Teorell. 2007. "Pathways from Authoritarianism." *Journal of Democracy* 18 (1): 143–56.

———. 2009. "Elections as Levers of Democratization: A Global Inquiry." In *Democratization by Elections: A New Mode of Transition*, 77–100. Baltimore: The Johns Hopkins University Press.

Haggard, Stephan, and Robert R. Kaufman. 1997. "The Political Economy of Democratic Transitions." *Comparative Politics*, 263–83.

Herbst, Jeffrey. 2001. "Political Liberalization in Africa after Ten Years." *Comparative Politics* 33 (3): 357–75.

Hermet, Guy. 1978. "State-Controlled Elections: A Framework." In *Elections without Choice*, edited by Guy Hermet, Richard Rose, and Alain Rouquié, 1–18. London and Basingstoke: The MacMillan Press LTD.

Hing, Lee Kam, and Michael Ong. 1987. "Malaysia." In *Competitive Elections in Developing Countries*, edited by Myron Weiner and Erun Özbudun, 112–46. Durham, NC: Duke University Press.

Howard, Marc, and Philip Roessler. 2006. "Liberalizing Electoral Outcomes in Competitive Authoritarian Regimes." *American Journal of Political Science* 50 (2): 365–81.

Kaya, Ruchan, and Michael Bernhard. 2013. "Are Elections Mechanisms of Authoritarian Stability or Democratization? Evidence from Postcommunist Eurasia." *Perspectives on Politics* 11 (3): 734–52.

Kelley, Judith. 2009. "D-Minus Elections: The Politics and Norms of International Elections Observation." *International Organization* 63 (4): 765–87.

Knutsen, Carl Henrik, Håvard Mokleiv Nygård, and Tore Wig. 2017. "Autocratic Elections: Stabilizing Tool or Force for Change?" *World Politics* 69 (1): 98–143.

Kricheli, Ruth and Livne, Yair and Magaloni, Beatriz. 2011. *Taking to the Streets: Theory and Evidence on Protests under Authoritarianism*. APSA 2010 Annual Meeting Paper. Available at SSRN: https://ssrn.com/abstract=1642040

Kriger, Norma. 2005. "ZANU(PF) Strategies in General Elections, 1980–2000: Discourse and Coercion." *African Affairs* 104 (414): 1–34.

Kuntz, Philipp, and Mark Thompson. 2009. "More Than Just the Final Straw: Stolen Elections as Revolutionary Triggers." *Comparative Politics* 41 (3): 253–72.

Kuran, Timur. 1989. "Sparks and Prairie Fires: A Theory of Unanticipated Political Revolution." *Public Choice* 61 (1): 41–74.

———. 1991. "Now Out of Never: The Element of Surprise in the East European Revolution of 1989." *World Politics* 44 (1): 7–48.

Lawson, Chappell. 2002. *Building the Fourth Estate: Democratization and the Rise of a Free Press in Mexico*. Berkeley: University of California Press.

Lee, Julian C.H. 2007. "Barisan Nasional – Political Dominance and the General Elections of 2004 in Malaysia". In *Südostasien aktuell : journal of current Southeast Asian affairs* 26 (2): 38–65. URN: http://nbn-resolving.de/urn:nbn:de:0168-ssoar-336605

Lehoucq, Fabrice. 2003. "Electoral Fraud: Causes, Types, and Consequences." *Annual Review of Political Science* 6 (1): 233–56.

Levitsky, Steven, and Lucan Way. 2010. *Competitive Authoritarianism: Hybrid Regimes after the Cold War*. Cambridge: Cambridge University Press.

Lichbach, Mark Irving. 1998. *The Rebel's Dilemma*. Ann Arbor: University of Michigan Press.

Lindberg, Staffan. 2006. *Democracy and Elections in Africa*. Baltimore: The Johns Hopkins University Press.

Linz, Juan J. 1978. "Non-Competitive Elections in Europe." In *Elections without Choice*, edited by Guy Hermet, Richard Rose, and Alain Rouquié, 36–65. London and Basingstoke: The MacMillan Press LTD.

Lipset, Seymour Martin. 1959. "Some Social Requisites of Democracy: Economic Development and Political Legitimacy." *The American Political Science Review* 53 (1): 69–105.

Lohmann, Susanne. 1994. "The Dynamics of Informational Cascades: The Monday Demonstrations in Leipzig, East Germany, 1989–91." *World Politics* 47 (1): 42–101.

Lorentzen, Peter L. 2013. "Regularizing Rioting: Permitting Public Protest in an Authoritarian Regime." *Quarterly Journal of Political Science* 8 (2): 127–58.

Lust, Ellen. 2009a. "Competitive Clientelism in the Middle East." *Journal of Democracy* 20 (3): 122–35.

———. 2009b. "Democratization by Elections? Competitive Clientelism in the Middle East." *Journal of Democracy* 20 (3): 122–35.

Magaloni, Beatriz. 2006. *Voting for Autocracy*. New York: Cambridge University Press.

———. 2008. "Credible Power-Sharing and the Longevity of Authoritarian Rule." *Comparative Political Studies* 41 (4/5): 715–41.

Mahoney, James. 2003. "Strategies of Causal Assessment in Comparative Historical Analysis." In *Comparative Historical Analysis in the Social Sciences*, edited by James Mahoney and Dietrich Rueschemeyer, 337–72. New York: Cambridge University Press.

Malesky, Edmund, and Paul Schuler. 2010. "Nodding or Needling: Analyzing Delegate Responsiveness in an Authoritarian Parliament." *American Political Science Review* 104 (3): 482–502.

———. 2011. "The Single-Party Dictator's Dilemma: Information in Elections without Opposition." *Legislative Studies Quarterly* 46 (4): 491–530.

Mason, T. David, and Dale A. Krane. 1989. "The Political Economy of Death Squads: Toward a Theory of the Impact of State-Sanctioned Terror." *International Studies Quarterly* 33 (2): 175–98.

McCoy, Jennifer, and Jonathan Hartlyn. 2009. "The Relative Powerlessness of Elections in Latin America." In *Democratization by Elections: A New Mode of Transition*, edited by Staffan Lindberg, 47–76. Baltimore: The Johns Hopkins University Press.

McMann, Kelly. 2006. *Economic Autonomy and Democracy: Hybrid Regimes in Russia and Kyrgyzstan*. Cambridge and New York: Cambridge University Press.
Migdal, Joel. 1988. *State-Society Relations and State Capabilities in the Third World*. Princeton: Princeton University Press.
Miller, Michael K. 2015. "Democratic Pieces: Autocratic Elections and Democratic Development since 1815." *British Journal of Political Science* 45 (3): 501–30.
Mitchell, Lincoln. 2004. "Georgia's Rose Revolution." *Current History* 103 (675): 342–8.
O'Donnell, Guillermo, Philippe C. Schmitter, and Laurence Whitehead. 1986. *Transitions from Authoritarian Rule: Comparative Perspectives*. Baltimore and London: The Johns Hopkins University Press.
Oliver, Pamela E. 1993. "Formal Models of Collective Action." *Annual Review of Sociology* 19 (1): 271–300.
Pfutze, Tobias. 2014. "Clientelism versus Social Learning: The Electoral Effects of International Migration." *International Studies Quarterly* 8 (2): 295–307.
Pop-Eleches, G., and Robertson, G. B. 2009. *Elections, information and liberalization in the post-cold war era* (Unpublished manuscript). Princeton University, Princeton, NJ; the University of North Carolina, Chapel Hill, NC.
Przeworski, Adam. 1991. *Democracy and the Market: Political and Economic Reforms in Eastern Europe and Latin America*. Cambridge and New York: Cambridge University Press.
Przeworski, Adam, and Fernando Limongi. 1997. "Modernization: Theories and Facts." *World Politics* 49 (2): 155–83.
Rachagan, Sothi. 1987. "The 1986 Parliamentary Elections in Peninsular Malaysia." *Southeast Asian Affairs* 14 (1): 217–35.
Rakner, Lise, and Nicolas van de Walle. 2009. "Opposition Parties and Incumbent Presidents." In *Democratization by Elections: A New Mode of Transition*, edited by Staffan Lindberg, 202–25. Baltimore: The Johns Hopkins University Press.
Reuter, Ora John, and Jennifer Gandhi. 2011. "Economic Performance and Elite Defection from Hegemonic Parties." *British Journal of Political Science* 41 (1): 83–110.
Ross, Michael. 2001. "Does Oil Hinder Democracy?" *World Politics* 53 (3): 325–61.
Schedler, Andreas. 2002a. "The Menu of Manipulation." *Journal of Democracy* 13 (2): 26–50.
———. 2002b. "The Nested Game of Democratization by Elections." *International Political Science Review* 23 (1): 103–22.
———, ed. 2006. *Electoral Authoritarianism: The Dynamics of Unfree Competition*. Boulder: Lynne Rienner Publishers.
———. 2009. "The Contingent Power of Authoritarian Elections: A New Mode of Transition." In *Democratization by Elections: A New Mode of Transition*, edited by Staffan Lindberg, 291–313. Baltimore: The Johns Hopkins University Press.
———. 2013. *The Politics of Uncertainty: Sustaining and Subverting Electoral Authoritarianism*. Oxford: Oxford University Press.
Seeberg, Merete Bech. 2014. "State Capacity and the Paradox of Authoritarian Elections." *Democratization* 21 (7): 1265–85.
Silitski, Vitali. 2005. "Preempting Democracy: The Case of Belarus." *Journal of Democracy* 16 (4): 83–97.
Skocpol, Theda. 1979. *States and Social Revolutions: A Comparative Analysis of France, Russia, and China*. Cambridge: Cambridge University Press.
Slater, Dan. 2003. "Iron Cage in an Iron Fist: Authoritarian Institutions and the Personalization of Power in Malaysia." *Comparative Politics* 36 (1): 81–101.

Slater, Dan, and Sofia Fenner. 2011. "State Power and Staying Power: Infrastructural Mechanisms and Authoritarian Durability." *Journal of International Affairs* 65 (1): 15–29.

Soifer, Hillel, and Matthias vom Hau. 2008. "Unpacking the Strength of the State: The Utility of State Infrastructural Power." *Studies in Comparative International Development* 43 (3/4): 219–30.

Svolik, Milan W. 2012. *The Politics of Authoritarian Rule*. New York: Cambridge University Press.

Thompson, Mark, and Philipp Kuntz. 2004. "Stolen Elections: The Case of the Serbian October." *Journal of Democracy* 15 (4): 160–72.

Tucker, Joshua A. 2007. "Enough! Electoral Fraud, Collective Action Problems, and Post-Communist Colored Revolutions." *Perspectives on Politics* 5 (3): 535–51.

Tullock, Gordon. 1971. "The Paradox of Revolution." *Public Choice* 11 (1): 89–99.

———. 1987. *Autocracy*. Dordrecht: Springer.

Ulfelder, Jay. 2005. "Contentious Collective Action and the Breakdown of Authoritarian Regimes." *International Political Science Review* 26 (3): 311–34.

US Department of State. 2010. "2009 Human Rights Report: Iran." Washington, DC: Bureau of Democracy, Human Rights, and Labor. www.state.gov/j/drl/rls/hrrpt/2009/nea/136068.htm.

van Ham, Carolien, and Brigitte Seim. 2018. "Strong States, Weak Elections? How State Capacity in Authoritarian Regimes Conditions the Democratizing Power of Elections". *International Political Science Review* 39 (1): 49–66.

Vickery, Chad, and Erica Shein. 2012. *Assessing Electoral Fraud in New Democracies: Refining the Vocabulary*. International Foundation for Electoral Systems, Washington D.C.: White Paper Series.

Way, Lucan. 2015. *Pluralism by Default: Weak Autocrats and the Rise of Competitive Politics*. Baltimore: The Johns Hopkins University Press.

Way, Lucan, and Steven Levitsky. 2006. "The Dynamics of Autocratic Coercion after the Cold War." *Communist and Post-Communist Studies* 39 (3): 387–410.

Welsh, Bridget. 2005. "Malaysia in 2004: Out of Mahathir's Shadow?" *Asian Survey* 45 (1): 153–60.

Wilson, Andrew. 2005. *Virtual Politics: Faking Democracy in the Post-Soviet World*. New Haven: Yale University Press.

ZESN, Zimbabwe Election Support Network. 2013. "Report on the Zimbabwe 31 July 2013 Harmonised Elections." Available at: http://www.zesn.org.zw/wp-content/uploads/2016/04/ZESN-2013-harmonised-election-report.pdf. Harare.

3 State capacity and the effect of elections in authoritarian regimes

In Singapore, the People's Action Party (PAP) has ruled since independence. Whereas impressive economic performance has arguably contributed to the regime's durability (Chua 1997), studies show that its strong state exemplified by the highly efficient bureaucracy has allowed the ruling party to apply a number of strategies to dominate elections (Slater 2012). PAP draws on extensive security laws, and the police have regularly detained opposition members and activists (Nasir and Turner 2012). Throughout the years, the opposition has been harassed to the extent that until the 2000s, PAP ran uncontested in more than half of all districts (Slater 2012, 28–9).

Where the opposition does run, systemic manipulation is subtly applied through gerrymandering of districts, ethnic quotas, limits to fund-raising, and restrictions on rallies – all designed to limit the opposition's chances to campaign and be elected (Tan 2013; Li and Elklit 1999). In the 1997 elections, decentralized counting of votes was introduced, allowing the ruling party full information on which precincts supported its candidates, and the prime minister promised to distribute public resources, such as upgrading of public housing, accordingly (Li and Elklit 1999; Ong and Tim 2014). As a result, PAP continues to win more than 60% of votes translating into an even larger seat share. This chapter asks whether this observed relationship between state capacity, elections, and regime stability is a more general phenomenon. Does state capacity condition the relationship between elections and authoritarian regime breakdown?

The analyses rely on quantitative data of all authoritarian regimes from 1960–2006, and the first section presents the data. Second, I test whether administrative capacity conditions the relationship between elections and regime breakdown. Third, I conduct similar tests of the hypotheses pertaining to coercive capacity. The following chapter tunes in on the effect of economic control.

Method and data

The *dependent* variable is regime breakdown.[1] It is operationalized using the GWF data. Thus, breakdown is identified where the rules for accessing power are changed, where someone outside the ruling front wins elections and is allowed to take power, where a coup puts in place a new ruling group that changes the rules for accessing power, or where the leadership themselves change these rules, for instance, by changing the group from which the members of its inner circle are drawn (Geddes, Wright, and Frantz 2014b, 7–8). The variable captures both transitions from authoritarian rule to democracy and transitions from one autocracy to the next. I thus do not analyze the democratizing power of elections but the stabilizing or destabilizing power of elections. As the measure captures power transfers between autocratic ruling groups, it is ideal for investigating the advantages or disadvantages for regime stabilization that elections present an authoritarian leader. The dependent variable is scored 1 if one or more regime breakdowns occurred in the given year: 221 of the 4,587 observed authoritarian country-years saw at least one regime breakdown according to the GWF coding rules. These breakdowns were illustrated by a grey box in Figure 1.1, which also plotted authoritarian elections and spells of authoritarian rule.

The *independent* variable is multi-party elections. As described in Chapter 1, I use NELDA data to identify elections (Hyde and Marinov 2012) and data from the CGV dataset to determine whether an election featured multiple parties including parties from outside the ruling front. In the theoretical argument presented in Chapter 2, it is the occurrence of elections, and not the number of times such elections have been conducted, that matters. But in contrast to analyses that test the effect of whether regimes are "electoral" or not (e.g., Brownlee 2009a), the theoretical argument here makes clear that certain time dynamics are likely to be at play: some of the potentially regime-destabilizing effects, such as the threat of post-electoral protests, are likely to have consequences for regime stability within a year or so of the election. Other mechanisms, stabilizing and destabilizing, including the spread of democratic norms in society, the potential for generating legitimacy, and the avoidance of elite defections by demonstrating electoral superiority, will likely last for a few years after the election. However, an autocrat is unlikely to reap benefits of legitimacy or supremacy from an electoral outcome that is, say, eight years old, as the electorate will likely be expecting a new electoral contest (see also Flores and Nooruddin 2016) and the democratic learning thesis also assumes some regularity of elections. There is thus also an upper time limit to the effect of elections.

To accommodate the varying time horizons of the different theoretical mechanisms, I work with a three-year time horizon in the main models: the dependent variable is scored 1 if at least one de facto multi-party election has been held within the past three years under the current regime. Otherwise, it is scored 0. In alternative specifications, I also test for the effect of elections being held within the past year, the past five years, and the past seven years but expect the effect to be weaker after the five-year mark.

The effect of two *conditioning variables* – administrative and coercive state capacity – is tested in this chapter. Administrative capacity was defined as the territorial reach of the bureaucracy, its competences, and the autocrat's degree of control over it. It is a distinctly authoritarian version of administrative capacity and, as discussed in Chapter 2, should not be equated with a Weberian understanding of a capable state. I proxy administrative capacity by an authoritarian regime's tax extraction rates. The logic for employing tax extraction to proxy state capacity is that "the development of state power, or the state's authority over society and the market economy, is usefully examined by highlighting its ability to get citizens to do something that they would rather not do – namely, pay taxes" (Lieberman 2002, 92). This perspective also underlies Besley and Persson's concept of fiscal capacity, where the actual tax rate upheld is expected to correlate strongly with the underlying ability to administer, monitor, and enforce tax payments (2013, 6, 91–2; see also Thies 2005). Furthermore, the taxes extracted should themselves contribute positively to the level of state capacity (Fukuyama 2013, 353; Slater 2010).

The measure has the distinct advantage that it does not increase with elements associated with a democratic state such as the rule of law, low corruption levels, or an independent bureaucracy. As spelled out in the previous chapter, authoritarian state capacity should not be equated with a Weberian understanding of the bureaucracy in which public servants operate independently of the rulers and shy away from corruption. Such qualities do not enhance autocrats' control over their bureaucracy, and high state capacity in the Weberian understanding of the term would not have the stabilizing electoral effects theorized in Chapter 2. For the purpose of this analysis, I thus reject the various measures of government effectiveness and bureaucratic quality that increase with administrative independence and lower levels of corruption (i.e., the Worldwide governance indicators from World Bank 2014; the Bureaucratic Quality indicator from Political Risk Services 2013), as this would typically also imply that the autocrat had limited control of the bureaucracy.

I also refrain from employing performance-based proxies of state capacity, including public goods provisions such as primary school enrolment or infrastructure. In an authoritarian context, where rulers' continued stay in power is dependent on a smaller section of the population, the distribution of private rather than public goods is often sufficient for survival in office (Bueno de Mesquita et al. 2003). It is not guaranteed that leaders will provide public goods just because they can, when private goods may be a less costly alternative. The provision of public goods will thus indicate the presence of administrative capacity, but the absence of public goods provisions may simply reflect a policy choice. The rulers may have the capacity to provide goods but choose to survive on the basis of private goods, which leaves more resources for the leadership.

To proxy administrative capacity, I thus use a measure of the tax-to-GDP ratio scaled from 0 to 1. Data are from Kugler and Tammen (2012) and available through Andersen et al. (2014) for the period 1960–2006. As the election variable indicates whether elections were held within the past three years, I construct a three-year running average of administrative capacity.

Proxying administrative capacity by the tax extraction rate may be seen as problematic because actual extraction rates do not necessarily accurately proxy the state's capacity to extract, as extraction also depends on willingness to extract. However, this argument is often employed with respect to advanced democracies that may have ideological preferences for low extraction rates (Fukuyama 2013, 353). Whereas autocrats may be viewed as unlikely to invest in public goods as they are less dependent on these as a survival strategy, they are commonly viewed as more likely to extract as many resources as possible for their own benefit as long as it does not endanger their position in power (Bueno de Mesquita et al. 2003; Svolik

2012). Studying autocracies, it seems valid to assume that the state will extract to the maximum degree that its capacity allows, and extractive capacity will thus more closely reflect administrative capacity in authoritarian than in democratic regimes.[2]

I conduct robustness checks with an alternative measure of administrative capacity. The measure of "relative political extraction" (RPE) (Kugler and Tammen 2012) captures a country's actual tax extraction in relation to the predicted tax extraction (scaled 0–1). A country's predicted tax extraction is assessed for every year using an algorithm that takes into account the country's agricultural revenues, mining, and exports relative to GDP and OECD membership (Trans-Research Consortium 2013, 11).

Furthermore, there are no tax extraction data available on the post-communist countries or a few other authoritarian regimes including Cuba. To avoid excluding these cases, I run alternative models where I perform multiple imputation in an attempt to construct time-series of tax data on all the countries that are missing from the original data. Analyses based on imputed data are often less biased than those excluding cases due to missing data (King et al. 2001). However, as countries are not missing at random and as there are no observations of the tax-to-GDP ratio for any of the countries for which I impute tax data, the results should be interpreted with caution. I thus only rely on the imputed data for robustness checks.

In the qualitative analyses in Chapters 5–6, I rely on other types of evidence to assess both the strength and the loyalty of the administrative force and thus perform a fuller evaluation of administrative capacity in the selected cases.

Relying on the tax-to-GDP ratio to classify authoritarian regimes according to their administrative capacity, countries including Kuwait, Nigeria, and Uganda in the 1960s-1980s are at the very bottom. At the very top are Saudi Arabia and Libya in the 1970s and 1980s. Around the mean of 0.15 are a host of countries including Egypt in the early 2000s, Jordan in the 1990s, and South Korea in the 1970s. When data are restricted to the 2000s, Myanmar, Sudan, and the DRC are found at the bottom of the range and Angola, Namibia, and the UAE are at the top, with Malaysia and Tunisia, among others, around the mean.

The other aspect of state capacity, coercive capacity, was defined as the reach as well as the ability and will to implement the rulers' orders of units such as the army, the police, or a presidential security guard. To capture a state's degree of coercive capacity, I use a measure of military spending per capita (measured in thousands of current-year USD) from the National Material Capabilities v.40. Dataset of the Correlates of War Project (COW) (Singer et al. 1972). I take the logarithm of military spending per capita to normalize its distribution. As for administrative capacity, I construct a three-year running average.

The measure has two drawbacks. First, high levels of spending on the military do not necessarily reflect the incumbent's degree of control over the armed forces. We do not know if they will obey her if worst comes to worst. As for administrative capacity, the issue of control will be discussed in the qualitative analyses. Second, the measure captures military capacity but not spending on security services, police, militias, paramilitary troops, presidential security guards, etc. These groups are often the backbone of low-intensity coercion in authoritarian regimes, and the

State capacity and the effect of elections 77

measure may thus be biased. On the other hand, the military is often the only force large enough to deal with potentially regime-toppling mass protests like the ones that can occur after fraudulent elections (Svolik 2012, 127; Albertus and Menaldo 2012). From Tiananmen Square in China's capital to Hama in Syria, the armed forces of authoritarian regimes have been employed to suppress public protests. Thus, this measure of coercive capacity should affect regime stability through one of the most important mechanisms of elections discussed in the previous chapter. As there are no cross-national measures of the size of the police or other arms of the repressive apparatus, I rely on military spending in all main analyses and run robustness checks with data on military personnel, also from COW (Singer et al. 1972). I use the logarithm of military personnel (in thousands) per capita. But it should be noted that the cases in which strong coercive apparatuses exist outside the armed forces, the Iranian Basij militia that quelled the post-electoral protests of 2009 being one example, will not be captured by this measure.

Using the logarithm of military spending to proxy coercive capacity puts newly independent African states with no military spending, such as Lesotho and Botswana in the 1960s–1970s, at the bottom of the range. At the top are UAE and Kuwait in recent years, but also countries such as Singapore. Hovering around the mean of 9.55 are a large group of countries including Senegal in the 1990s and Indonesia and Guatemala in the 1980s. Table 3.1 summarizes the measures employed, including indicators for economic control, which will be discussed in the following chapter.

To test the effect of elections on regime stability conditioned by administrative and coercive capacity, I use logistic regression models. I include in the analyses all

Table 3.1 Operationalizations

Concept	Indicator	Source	Coverage
Authoritarianism	Regime type	Geddes, Wright, and Frantz (2014a)	1946–2010
Stability	Absence of breakdown	Geddes, Wright, and Frantz (2014a)	1946–2010
Multi-party election	Elections with competitors from outside the ruling front	Hyde and Marinov (2012) and Cheibub, Gandhi, and Vreeland (2010)	1946–2010
Administrative capacity	Tax-to-GDP ratio	(Kugler and Tammen 2012)	1960–2006
	Relative political extraction	(Kugler and Tammen 2012)	1960–2006
Coercive capacity	Military spending	Singer et al. (1972)	1816–2007
	Military personnel	Singer et al. (1972)	1816–2007
Economic control	Government share of GDP	Penn World Table (2013)	1950–2010
	Index of regulations	Gwartney, Lawson, and Hall (2013)	1970–2010
	Income from natural resources	Haber and Menaldo (2011)	1900–2006

authoritarian country-years from 1960 to 2006 (the period in which the measure for administrative capacity is available), whether they have elections or not, in order to assess the effect of having elections (as opposed to not having elections) given different levels of authoritarian capacities.

In this study, two types of bias could potentially follow from the relationship between institutions, regime stability, and a number of potential confounders related to the country, the regime, or the strength of the autocrat. One type of bias would arise if certain countries or regions were more (or less) likely to hold elections and at the same time more (or less) likely to see regime breakdown without elections themselves affecting regime stability. To deal with the risk of omitted variable bias, I run robustness checks relying on country fixed effects models. Fixed effects models estimate effects solely based on variation within countries and are consistent even if countries display certain un-modeled generic features (Cameron and Trivedi 2009, 257–9).

A second type of bias arises if autocrats can introduce and abandon elections at will and their choice to hold elections correlates with the risk of regime breakdown – what could be termed self-selection bias. The risk of selection bias in the study of authoritarian institutions has recently been pointed out by Pepinsky (2014). He stresses that institutions, including elections, may be mere epiphenomena, affected by the very same factors that also influence the downstream outcomes that institutions are theorized to create.

Autocrats do have a say over the holding of multi-party elections. President Ferdinand Marcos of the Philippines abandoned elections and declared martial law from 1972 to 1981, and Pepinsky stresses the emergency measures put in place by the Malaysian ruling party, UMNO, after the opposition's gain in the 1969 election. But autocrats are less free than what is often assumed. Indeed, they may manipulate elections to their own advantage – this is exactly the argument unfolded in Chapter 2 – but as this book explicates, the ability to do so depends on other factors.

Although autocrats may manipulate electoral administration and outcomes, they are rarely completely free to introduce and abandon elections at will. President Marcos was under pressure to reintroduce multi-party competition and ended up losing power in the aftermath of the 1986 elections in spite of his formal victory. In Malaysia, Parliament reconvened only two years after the 1969 elections, and regular elections have been held ever since. Despite the electoral threat facing the ruling coalition when the opposition *Reformasi* movement appeared in the late 1990s and the eventual loss of their supermajority, it was unthinkable that the BN should have called off Malaysian multi-party elections. Multi-party elections may be introduced by dictators, but they are often inherited from the previous democratic, authoritarian, or colonial regimes and their abandonment is likely to spark a domestic and international outcry. Authoritarian elections, although heavily manipulated, are thus an entrenched institution both in countries where they support the current rulers and in those where they ultimately lead to their downfall. Figure 3.1 illustrates that a clear pattern of self-selection is not evident. Authoritarian elections are not primarily held by autocrats with weak bureaucracies, low coercive capacity, or low levels of economic control (operationalized in the following chapter) unable to resist public pressure or by strong autocrats

Panel A: Administrative capacity

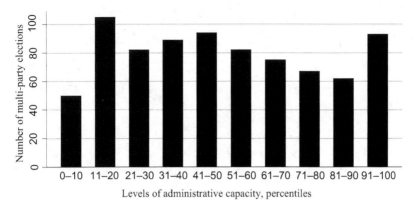

Panel B: Coercive capacity

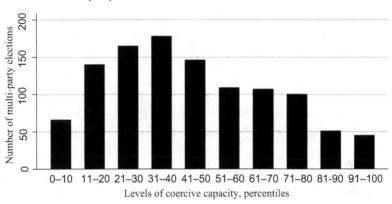

Panel C: Economic control

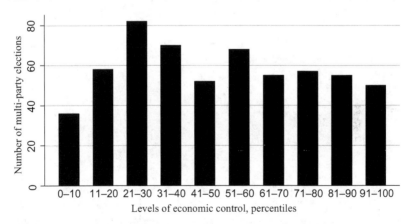

Figure 3.1 The spread of elections across levels of capacities

Note: Number of elections across levels of authoritarian capacities. Columns represent percentiles on administrative capacity, coercive capacity, and economic control respectively – i.e., the first column in Panel A illustrates that in the group of countries with levels of administrative capacity corresponding to the bottom 10% of the sample 45 elections were held in the investigated time period.

expecting to win them. Rather, they are common across all levels of administrative and coercive capacity and economic control.

Nonetheless, I take into account the risk of selection bias in the empirical analyses. An instrument that correlates with the timing of elections within countries but is independent of the risk of regime breakdown is not available. Instead, I control for a number of factors that could affect the dictator's choice to hold elections state capacity, economic control, and regime breakdown. All models thus include controls for wealth, growth, and income from natural resources (data from Haber and Menaldo 2011) (unless economic control is also included in the model). In the models assessing the effect of coercive capacity, a control for engagement in interstate war is introduced as an increase in military expenditure due to war activity is not expected to reflect a stronger coercive apparatus available for domestic repression.

I also introduce a cubed version of *time* (with 1960 as baseline) to ensure that the relationship between elections, capacities, and breakdown is not driven simply by time trends (Carter and Signorino 2010; Beck, Katz, and Tucker 1998).[3] Finally, the *age of the regime* (including regime age squared and regime age cubed) is often included in time-series cross-sectional studies of regime breakdown as regimes are expected to be more likely to break down in the very early years and after prolonged rule (Geddes 2003; Svolik 2012).

In alternative specifications, I control for changes in the levels of protests, which could arguably influence a potential choice to hold elections along with the risk of breakdown (data from Banks and Wilson 2012); levels of media freedom and constraints on the executive (to test whether a potential relationship between elections and regime breakdown is driven by underlying processes of political opening) (data from Whitten-Woodring and Belle 2014; Marshall, Jaggers, and Gurr 2011); aid as percentage of GNI (data from World Bank 2014); authoritarian regime type (Geddes, Wright, and Frantz 2014a); and the post-Cold War era.

Finally, I control for the first multi-party election held by every authoritarian ruling group. Once elections are in place, the autocrat's ability to abandon them at will is restricted. But an autocrat may choose to only introduce elections into a regime once she expects to win them (or alternatively, be forced to allow elections when her regime is already weak). The control for first multi-party election under a given regime should reduce the risk of this type of bias affecting the results.

Administrative capacity, elections, and regime breakdown

I first test the two hypotheses on the macro-level relationship between administrative capacity, authoritarian elections, and regime breakdown:

H1: The effect of authoritarian multi-party elections on the likelihood of regime breakdown will decrease with higher levels of administrative capacity.
H4: The effect of authoritarian multi-party elections on regime breakdown will be negative for high levels of administrative capacity irrespective of levels of coercive capacity and economic control.

Table 3.2 Multi-party elections, administrative capacity, and regime breakdown

	1	2	3	4	5
	RE	RE	RE	FE	RE
Multi-party elections	0.455* (0.239)	0.460* (0.275)	1.700*** (0.540)	1.859** (0.764)	1.548** (0.669)
Tax-to-GDP ratio		−3.100** (1.319)	−1.065 (1.304)	1.678 (2.344)	−2.753 (1.868)
Elections* Tax ratio			−9.755*** (3.487)	−12.150** (5.400)	−8.317* (4.330)
Military expenditure		−0.024 (0.068)	−0.014 (0.067)	0.077 (0.210)	−0.312** (0.135)
Economic control (reduced index)					−0.103 (0.279)
GDP/cap	−0.310** (0.139)	−0.244 (0.151)	−0.292* (0.153)	0.649 (0.666)	0.067 (0.236)
Growth	−0.036*** (0.013)	−0.038** (0.015)	−0.038** (0.015)	−0.037** (0.017)	−0.052** (0.023)
Natural resource income	−0.034 (0.023)	−0.030 (0.025)	−0.026 (0.025)	−0.100* (0.059)	
t	−0.218** (0.097)	−0.201** (0.101)	−0.199* (0.103)	−0.336*** (0.117)	−0.470 (0.535)
t^2	0.010** (0.005)	0.010** (0.005)	0.010** (0.005)	0.014*** (0.006)	0.021 (0.019)
t^3	−0.000** (0.000)	−0.000** (0.000)	−0.000** (0.000)	−0.000** (0.000)	−0.000 (0.000)
Regime duration	−0.026 (0.024)	−0.022 (0.022)	−0.020 (0.022)	0.109 (0.069)	0.006 (0.028)
Regime duration^2	0.001 (0.000)	0.001 (0.000)	0.000 (0.000)	−0.007 (0.005)	−0.000 (0.001)
Regime duration^3	−0.000 (0.000)	−0.000* (0.000)	−0.000 (0.000)	0.000** (0.000)	−0.000 (0.000)
Constant	2.997 (1.945)	2.429 (1.800)	2.689 (1.812)		1.914 (5.317)
N	2520	2520	2520	1737	1410
Breakdowns	109	109	109	109	59

Note: Dependent variable is regime breakdown. Logistic regression models with robust standard errors clustered on country in parentheses. RE denotes random effects models and FE fixed effects models. Multi-party elections note whether at least one election was held in the past five years. Tax ratio, military expenditure, and economic control are three-year running averages. All covariates except time trends are lagged one year.

* $p < 0.10$, ** $p < 0.05$, *** $p < 0.01$

Table 3.2, Model 1, is a logistic regression model that tests the effect of having held at least one multi-party election over the course of the past three years on the likelihood of regime breakdown. The effect is controlled for time trends as well as wealth, growth, and natural resource income. According to this model, holding authoritarian elections increases the risk of breakdown in the following years. This finding supports the notion that elections are potentially threatening to authoritarian rulers (Schedler 2013; Bunce and Wolchik 2011; Kuntz and Thompson 2009). Unlike in previous cross-national studies (Brownlee 2009b), I do find that holding multi-party elections – all else equal – destabilizes authoritarian regimes. Furthermore, unlike elections, both wealth and growth contribute to regime stability. When controls for state capacity – administrative and coercive – are added (Model 2), the positive effect of elections on breakdown remains. While coercive capacity, measured through military expenditure, has no significant effect on regime stability, higher levels of administrative capacity (proxied through tax extraction rates) reduce the risk of breakdown. There is thus no immediate support for a positive effect of coercive capacity on authoritarian stability although this effect is documented in previous work (Bellin 2004; Albertus and Menaldo 2012). In line with previous research, however, I do find that administrative capacity strengthens authoritarian rule (Slater and Fenner 2011; Andersen et al. 2014).

Model 3 in Table 3.2 tests the conditional effect of administrative capacity (H1) by interacting the tax-to-GDP ratio with the holding of multi-party elections. The interaction term between multi-party elections and administrative capacity is negative and statistically significant ($p < 0.01$). This indicates that the positive effect of elections on regime breakdown is reduced as administrative capacity increases. This finding supports H1: authoritarian elections may be potentially regime-subverting but this effect is reduced as administrative capacity increases. The effect remains if we only look at changes to levels of administrative capacity within the same countries over time (the fixed effects estimation in Model 4) and when a control for the incumbents' degree of control over the economy is included (which also reduces the number of observations due to data limitations on this variable) (Model 5).

In the interaction models (Models 3–5), the direct effect of elections on regime breakdown remains positive and statistically significant and increases in magnitude. The regression coefficient on elections in these models refers to the effect of elections where administrative capacity (the tax-to-GDP ratio) is 0 – a case that is not represented in the data and would equal extremely low levels of administrative capacity.

The finding supports not only the theory of a conditional effect of authoritarian elections. It is also in sync with the mixed findings in the literature on the effect of authoritarian elections (Lindberg 2006; McCoy and Hartlyn 2009; Hadenius and Teorell 2009; Magaloni 2008; Donno 2013; Brownlee 2009b). The results indicate that administrative state capacity may help explain why elections in some cases strengthen and in others undermine authoritarian rule.

The findings are scrutinized in Tables 3.3 and 3.4. First, a number of alternative controls are introduced in Table 3.3. The support for H1 is remarkably robust. Thus, the conditional effect of administrative capacity on the effect of elections holds across different authoritarian regime types. Even though party regimes, military regimes, monarchies, and personalist dictatorships have different propensities to break down (Geddes 2003) and are not equally likely to hold elections (Chapter 1), the interaction effect of administrative capacity remains negative and

Table 3.3 Multi-party elections, administrative capacity, and regime breakdown – alternative controls

	1	2	3	4	5	6	7
Multi-party elections	1.462*** (0.539)	1.657*** (0.557)	1.835*** (0.555)	1.350** (0.608)	1.844*** (0.539)	1.714*** (0.562)	1.674*** (0.544)
Tax-to-GDP ratio	−0.091 (1.360)	−1.082 (1.317)	−1.128 (1.381)	−1.252 (1.365)	−0.509 (1.475)	−1.262 (1.341)	−1.077 (1.307)
Military expenditure	−0.059 (0.073)	0.009 (0.068)	0.003 (0.069)	−0.009 (0.070)	−0.052 (0.070)	−0.016 (0.067)	−0.014 (0.067)
Elections* Tax ratio	−8.667** (3.534)	−9.789*** (3.553)	−11.722*** (3.667)	−7.438* (3.883)	−11.115*** (3.693)	−10.039*** (3.624)	−9.659*** (3.534)
GDP/cap	−0.221 (0.159)	−0.308** (0.150)	−0.337* (0.185)	−0.381** (0.181)	−0.233 (0.167)	−0.281* (0.146)	−0.291* (0.154)
Growth	−0.042** (0.017)	−0.038** (0.015)	−0.035** (0.016)	−0.033* (0.018)	−0.038** (0.017)	-0.039*** (0.015)	−0.038** (0.015)
Natural resource income	−0.029 (0.024)	−0.027 (0.026)	−0.015 (0.027)	−0.017 (0.026)	−0.008 (0.026)	−0.026 (0.025)	−0.026 (0.025)
Military	1.254*** (0.314)						
Monarchy	−0.266 (0.489)						
Personalist	0.929*** (0.231)						
Media freedom		0.213 (0.323)					
Executive constraints			0.178* (0.102)				
Foreign aid				−0.003 (0.003)			
Protests					0.270* (0.163)		
Post-Cold War						0.222 (0.294)	
First election							0.086 (0.554)
Constant	1.351 (1.942)	2.506 (1.883)	2.494 (2.253)	3.074 (2.423)	1.611 (2.064)	1.551 (1.795)	2.665 (1.817)
N	2520	2520	2428	2174	2293	2520	2520
Breakdowns	109	109	97	89	92	109	109

Note: Dependent variable is regime breakdown. Logistic regression models with random effects and robust standard errors clustered on country in parentheses. Multi-party elections note whether at least one election was held in the past three years. Tax ratio and military expenditure are three-year running averages. Controls for time and regime age (cubed) are included (except Model 6) but not shown in the table. All covariates except time trends are lagged one year.

*$p < 0.10$, **$p < 0.05$, ***$p < 0.01$

Table 3.4 Multi-party elections, administrative capacity, and regime breakdown – varying time horizons

	1	2	3	4	5	6
	RE	FE	RE	FE	RE	FE
	1 year		5 years		7 years	
Multi-party elections	1.814*** (0.494)	1.489*** (0.565)	1.467*** (0.549)	1.431* (0.840)	1.439 (1.091)	1.068 (0.855)
Tax-to-GDP ratio	−1.629 (1.253)	1.207 (2.080)	−1.141 (1.478)	1.415 (2.759)	−1.133 (2.958)	0.629 (3.292)
Elections* Tax ratio	−5.457* (3.217)	−4.200 (4.115)	−7.961** (3.586)	−10.050 (6.518)	−6.860 (5.634)	−3.132 (6.511)
Military expenditure	0.026 (0.057)	0.173 (0.147)	−0.017 (0.070)	0.214 (0.282)	−0.041 (0.218)	−0.010 (0.233)
GDP/cap	−0.347** (0.151)	0.071 (0.668)	−0.265 (0.163)	0.668 (0.800)	−0.265 (0.247)	1.249 (0.766)
Growth	−0.011 (0.008)	−0.011 (0.010)	−0.036** (0.016)	−0.037** (0.017)	−0.025 (0.020)	−0.028 (0.024)
Natural resource income	−0.033 (0.027)	−0.127** (0.060)	−0.026 (0.026)	−0.101 (0.063)	−0.017 (0.061)	−0.069 (0.072)
Constant	2.544 (1.801)		2.855 (2.009)		2.319 (4.141)	
N	2652	1910	2347	1528	2167	1401
Breakdowns	114	114	98	98	86	86

Note: Dependent variable is regime breakdown. Logistic regression models with robust standard errors clustered on country in parentheses. RE denotes random effects models and FE fixed effects models. Multi-party elections note whether at least one election was held in the past year (Models 1–2), the past five years (Models 3–4), and the past seven years (Models 5–6). Tax ratio and military expenditure are one-, five-, and seven-year running averages respectively. Controls for time and regime age (cubed) are included but not shown in the table. All covariates except time trends are lagged one year.

*$p < 0.10$, **$p < 0.05$, ***$p < 0.01$

statistically significant ($p < 0.05$) when I control for authoritarian regime type (Model 1). Furthermore, in line with existing research, the model also shows that controlling for the holding of elections, both military regimes and personalist regimes are more likely to break down than are party regimes (Geddes 2003). To take into account the possibility that an increased risk of breakdown following authoritarian elections may not be due to elections but to an underlying process of democratization that is causing elections to be held and the dictatorship to break down, Models 2–3 control for underlying processes of democratization through indicators of media freedom and executive constraints respectively. The interaction effect of administrative capacity on the relationship between elections and breakdown remains negative and statistically significant ($p < 0.01$) in both models. Furthermore, autocracies with higher levels of constraints on the executive are more likely to break down irrespective of the holding of elections.

The findings are also robust to controls for aid inflows (Model 4) even though high levels of aid could be expected to affect the holding of elections, the risk of breakdown, and the level of tax extraction. Similarly, controlling for levels of protest, which could likely affect both the timing of elections and the risk of breakdown, does not affect results even though protests do increase the risk of breakdown (Model 5). Chapter 1 showed that the propensity for autocracies to hold elections has changed dramatically after the end of the Cold War, but Model 6 reveals that the post-Cold War period is not driving results. Finally, the coefficient on the interaction term remains negative and statistically significant ($p < 0.01$) when I exclude the first multi-party elections held under an authoritarian regime (Model 7). Dictators arguably hold more power over the decision to hold or block the first multi-party elections than they do over institutionalized elections. Excluding first multi-party elections held under the ruling front should thus reduce the risk of bias that may exist if elections are only introduced by weak dictators who face extreme risks of breakdown – or by strong dictators who estimate that they will win them (Pepinsky 2014). Thus, the conditional effect of administrative capacity on the relationship between elections and regime breakdown is robust to a number of controls.

The support found for H1 pertains to elections held within the past three years. This is an interval within which both stabilizing and destabilizing effects of elections are expected to play out (see also Knutsen, Nygård, and Wig 2017). Table 3.4 expands the analysis and tests the conditional effect of elections immediately after they are held, within a five-year period and over a seven-year time horizon. It shows that the conditional effect of administrative capacity is strongest when an election has been held within the past three years. But although the effect is substantially smaller, the risk of breakdown following an authoritarian election that has been held within the past year also decreases as administrative capacity increases (Model 1). The effect is statistically significant when it is estimated across countries ($p < 0.1$). Similarly, the effect of elections held in the past five years is also significantly conditioned by administrative capacity (Model 3) when the effect is estimated across countries. In the longer time frame, however, the effect is washed out. Administrative capacity does not significantly alter the effect of an election held within the prior seven years. This is likely because the effect of an election wears out after the first few years (note that the direct effects of elections on breakdown are no longer statistically significant in the seven-year models). The destabilizing effects are often immediate, such as the risk of post-electoral protests (see also Knutsen, Nygård, and Wig 2017), and the stabilizing effects of elections (such as legitimation) do not last forever; at some point, voters and elites will demand a new election (see also Flores and Nooruddin 2016).

There is evidence that administrative capacity conditions the effect of elections – as it increases, it contains the potentially regime-subverting effect of elections. But does that mean that elections are stabilizing under high levels of administrative capacity? H4 is tested in the following section.

The marginal effects of elections on regime stability for increasing levels of administrative capacity are displayed in Figure 3.2, Panel A. The marginal effect

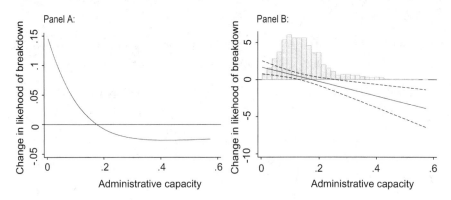

Figure 3.2 Marginal effect of elections for increasing levels of administrative capacity

Note: Marginal effect of multi-party elections (versus no multi-party elections) on likelihood of regime breakdown for various levels of administrative capacity based on Table 3.2, Model 3. For each observation, the covariates are held at their observed values and the marginal effects are calculated and then averaged across observations (observed-value approach; see Hanmer and Kalkan 2013). Panel A provides the substantially meaningful marginal effect (probability scale). Panel B provides 90% confidence intervals (logit scale) and distribution of included observations across the tax-to-GDP ratio.

of elections is the difference between having held at least one multi-party election within the past three years and not having held a multi-party election. Panel A shows that where administrative capacity is low, elections are associated with regime breakdown (the marginal effect is positive) and this effect is statistically significant for the bottom half of the sample (Panel B, which is plotted on the logit scale, provides correct confidence intervals). That is, for countries with tax-to-GDP ratios below 0.13, elections destabilize autocracies. This part of the sample includes countries such as the DRC in the early 2000s. But as administrative capacity increases above the 50th percentile, the marginal effect changes. For tax extraction rates above 0.26 (the 90th percentile of the sample), holding multi-party elections *reduces* the risk of breakdown, and the effect is again statistically significant. In these 10% of countries that have the highest levels of administrative capacity proxied by tax extraction ratios, including South Africa in the early 1990s and Algeria, elections correlate significantly with regime stability. There is thus support for H4. Only where administrative capacity is high do elections serve to stabilize authoritarian rule. In fact, where administrative capacity is low, holding elections increases the risk of regime breakdown independent of the rulers' coercive capacity and economic control.

Figure 3.3 further substantiates the results by presenting the predicted probabilities of breakdown for two fictive regimes. In Panel A, administrative capacity is held at its 5th percentile (a tax ratio of 0.04 corresponding to that of Haiti in the 1990s or Pakistan in the 1960s). The likelihood of regime breakdown for a low-capacity regime is 4.3% if it does not hold elections. If an election had been held under the same regime, the risk of breakdown would increase to 13.5% (and this

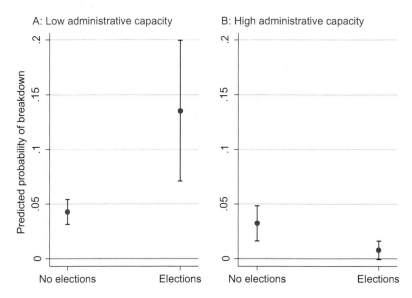

Figure 3.3 Predicted probability of breakdown for low and high administrative capacity

Note: Based on Table 3.2, Model 3. Low administrative capacity is a tax ratio of 0.04 (5th percentile). High administrative capacity is a tax ratio of 0.32 (95th percentile). "Election" indicates whether a multi-party election has been held in the past three years. 90% confidence intervals. For each observation, the covariates are held at their observed values and the marginal effects are calculated and then averaged across observations (observed-value approach; see Hanmer and Kalkan 2013).

difference is statistically significant according to Panel B, Figure 3.2). The scenario is different if the regime were to increase its administrative capacity to the 95th percentile of the sample, corresponding to a tax ratio of 0.32, such as Algeria in 2002 (Panel B). In this case, the electoral regime's risk of breakdown would decrease from 13.5% to 0.8%. But had a multi-party election not been held within the past three years, the regime would have a significantly higher predicted probability of breakdown (3.2%). In other words, high administrative capacity lowers the risk of breakdown for electoral regimes, while there is no significant effect of increasing administrative capacity for regimes that have not recently held a multi-party election. Holding elections, on the other hand, only lowers the risk of breakdown where administrative capacity is high (H4). In fact, where administrative capacity is low, breakdown propensities are higher for electoral than for non-electoral regimes.

In comparison, a similar increase in levels of economic growth, a common predictor of authoritarian regime breakdown, from the 5th to the 95th percentile, would reduce the risk of breakdown far less. Whereas this increase in administrative capacity would lead to a reduction in breakdown propensity for electoral regimes of almost 12 percentage points, the increase in growth levels would only decrease the risk of breakdown by 4.4 percentage points. Thus, in support of H1 and H4, the effect of changes to administrative capacity on the risk of breakdown

88 State capacity and the effect of elections

following authoritarian elections is substantial. It may very well be that the differing effects of elections in countries such as Malaysia and Singapore on the one hand and Georgia and Serbia on the other come down to differences in levels of administrative capacity.

As a final test of the hypotheses on administrative capacity, I run two robustness checks. First, as the tax extraction rate is not available for post-communist countries, I rely on multiple imputation to include these countries in the analysis (see Table 3.5, Model 1). The negative and statistically significant interaction term ($p < 0.1$) implies that the results also hold for the post-communist world even though the tax extraction data has been imputed for this part of the world.[6]

Table 3.5 Multi-party elections, administrative capacity, and regime breakdown – robustness checks

	1	2
Multi-party elections	1.499***	1.371**
	(0.534)	(0.593)
Tax-to-GDP ratio	−1.835	
	(1.466)	
Elections* Tax ratio	−5.902*	
	(3.326)	
Relative political extraction		−0.233
		(0.272)
Elections* Relative political extraction		−1.138**
		(0.561)
Military expenditure	−0.029	−0.062
	(0.063)	(0.066)
GDP/cap	−0.188	−0.180
	(0.146)	(0.151)
Growth	−0.048***	−0.039***
	(0.014)	(0.015)
Natural resource income	−0.039	−0.032
	(0.029)	(0.021)
Constant	0.053	1.812
	(1.780)	(1.935)
Observations	3340	2709
Breakdowns	131	113

Note: Dependent variable is regime breakdown. Logistic regression models with random effects and robust standard errors clustered on country in parentheses. Multi-party elections note whether at least one election was held in the past three years. Tax ratio, relative political extraction, and military expenditure are three-year running averages. Controls for time and regime age (cubed) are included but not shown in the table. All covariates except time trends are lagged one year.

*$p < 0.10$, **$p < 0.05$, ***$p < 0.01$

Second, I test the effect of an alternative measure of administrative capacity. In Table 3.5, Model 2, administrative capacity is proxied by a country's relative political extraction, that is, actual extraction rates relative to predicted extraction rates (calculated based on agricultural revenues, mining, and exports relative to GDP, and OECD membership) (Kugler and Tammen 2012; data available from Andersen et al. 2014). The interaction effect is again negative and statistically significant ($p < 0.1$). If administrative capacity is proxied by a country's relative levels of extraction, elections still become more likely to stabilize an authoritarian regime as administrative capacity increases ($p < 0.05$).

In sum, the results are robust when I rely on measures of extraction as a proxy for administrative capacity. The findings support the claim that where administrative capacity is low, recent multi-party elections are associated with instability. As capacity increases, elections become more likely to stabilize the regime, and for high levels of administrative capacity, autocracies with multi-party elections are more stable than autocracies without such contests. The diverse effect of authoritarian elections both across countries and over time is not entirely surprising considering dictators' ability to manipulate elections by abusing an effective administrative apparatus. The results provide cross-national support to Slater and collaborators' argument that administrative capacity may support authoritarian rule (Slater 2010; Slater and Fenner 2011) and suggest an explanation for why the effect of elections on authoritarian regime stability remains disputed. The following section tests the effect of another important part of the state apparatus – the coercive branch – on the effect of elections.

Coercive capacity, elections, and regime breakdown

In addition to the claim that administrative capacity conditions the effect of elections, the theoretical framework includes a hypothesis on the effect of coercive capacity:

> H2: The effect of authoritarian multi-party elections on the likelihood of regime breakdown will decrease with higher levels of coercive capacity.

Authoritarian regimes may be more likely to stabilize through elections if the autocrat disposes over a strong administrative apparatus. But the same may be true for the coercive force. However, applying the state's coercive capacity to win an election is often an emergency measure that is not – on its own – likely to generate regime stability in the longer term. I thus expect coercive capacity to reduce the risk of breakdown following elections. However, I do not necessarily expect that elections are stabilizing at high levels of coercive capacity where administrative capacity and economic control are limited. In this case, subtle electoral manipulation on a large scale cannot be carried out and elections are unlikely to be stabilizing in the longer term.

The following section tests the claim that coercive capacity reduces the risk of regime breakdown following authoritarian elections. Models 1–2 in Table 3.6 are

Table 3.6 Multi-party elections, coercive capacity, and regime breakdown

	1	2	3	4	5
	RE	RE	RE	FE	RE
Multi-party elections	0.488** (0.242)	0.501* (0.284)	0.051 (1.003)	1.895 (2.515)	0.276 (2.320)
Military expenditure		−0.011 (0.070)	−0.032 (0.081)	0.103 (0.205)	−0.332** (0.144)
Elections* Military expenditure			0.050 (0.099)	−0.164 (0.274)	0.024 (0.233)
Tax-to-GDP ratio		−3.108** (1.346)	−3.149** (1.357)	−0.163 (2.512)	−5.090*** (1.812)
Economic control (reduced index)					−0.126 (0.294)
GDP/cap	−0.326** (0.142)	−0.273* (0.152)	−0.267* (0.152)	0.500 (0.723)	0.064 (0.238)
Growth	−0.037*** (0.013)	−0.038** (0.015)	−0.039** (0.015)	−0.035** (0.016)	−0.053** (0.022)
Natural resource income	−0.030 (0.024)	−0.025 (0.025)	−0.024 (0.026)	−0.104* (0.062)	
War	−0.585 (0.742)	−0.647 (0.954)	−0.625 (0.954)	−0.651 (1.148)	0.226 (1.246)
t	−0.221** (0.100)	−0.203* (0.105)	−0.199* (0.106)	−0.357*** (0.121)	−0.499 (0.576)
t^2	0.010** (0.005)	0.010* (0.005)	0.010* (0.005)	0.016*** (0.006)	0.022 (0.021)
t^3	−0.000** (0.000)	−0.000* (0.000)	−0.000* (0.000)	−0.000** (0.000)	−0.000 (0.000)
Regime duration	−0.021 (0.025)	−0.019 (0.022)	−0.019 (0.022)	0.114 (0.080)	0.008 (0.025)
Regime duration^2	0.000 (0.000)	0.000 (0.000)	0.000 (0.000)	−0.007 (0.005)	−0.000 (0.000)
Regime duration^3	−0.000 (0.000)	−0.000* (0.000)	−0.000* (0.000)	0.000** (0.000)	−0.000 (0.000)
Constant	3.183 (1.987)	2.722 (1.811)	2.786 (1.800)		2.617 (5.429)
Observations	2479	2479	2479	1718	1376
Breakdowns	108	108	108	108	58

Note: Dependent variable is regime breakdown. Logistic regression models with robust standard errors clustered on country in parentheses. RE denotes random effects models and FE fixed effects models. Multi-party elections note whether at least one election was held in the past three years. Tax ratio, military expenditure, and economic control are three-year running averages. All covariates except time trends are lagged one year.

*$p < 0.10$, **$p < 0.05$, ***$p < 0.01$

logistic regression models similar to those in Table 3.2 and assess the relationship between multi-party elections and regime breakdown. In addition to controls for wealth, growth resource income, and time trends, a control for engagement in interstate war is introduced as an increase in military expenditure due to war activity is not expected to reflect a stronger coercive apparatus available for domestic repression.[4] As in Table 3.2, elections significantly increase the risk of regime breakdown even when controlling for the administrative and coercive capacity at the regime's disposal (Model 2). But unlike administrative capacity, coercive capacity – proxied by military expenditure – has no direct effect on regime stability (Model 2).

The conditional effect of coercive capacity is tested in Model 3 where the election-dummy is multiplied by coercive capacity (proxied by a three-year running average of the logarithm of military expenditures lagged by one year). The coefficient of elections now represents the effect of holding elections in cases with no military expenditure and the effect turns insignificant. More importantly, there is no support for H2: coercive capacity does not significantly condition the effect of elections. Furthermore, the insignificant effect is slightly positive rather than negative as expected. This result does not change when the economic control variable is included in the model (Model 5). When we compare changes within countries over time (Model 4), the conditioning effect of coercive capacity is in the expected direction but remains insignificant. The only sign that coercive capacity affects authoritarian regime dynamics is in Model 5 where increasing levels of military expenditure significantly reduce the risk of breakdown. There is thus some indication of a direct effect of coercive capacity on regime stability, but only in non-electoral cases (in the interaction model, the coefficient on coercive capacity indicates its effect where the election variable is 0). The finding cannot be confirmed in the other models, however, and the interaction effect remains insignificant.

The findings do not change when controls for regime type, ongoing liberalization processes (proxied through executive constraints and media freedom), protests, aid levels, the post-Cold War period, or the ruling group's first multi-party elections are introduced (Table A, Appendix). The results also remain insignificant when coercive capacity is proxied by number of military personnel rather than expenditure (Table B, Appendix).

The results not only reject H2, which states that high levels of coercive capacity reduce the risk of authoritarian breakdown following elections. They also question findings from previous studies stating that coercive capacity strengthens authoritarian rule (Albertus and Menaldo 2012; Bellin 2004). However, it is plausible that the findings are an artefact of the available measures of coercive capacity. Although the military has indeed been employed against – or failed to clamp down on – post-electoral protests in countries as different as Georgia, the Philippines, and Cambodia, it is clear that other arms of the coercive apparatus are likely to have a tremendous effect. In Venezuela, late President Chavez made a point of stressing that should the army dessert him, he had a loyal, private militia numbering hundreds of thousands of men and women to which he might turn (Romero 2010). The case study in Chapter 6 investigates the role of other arms of the coercive force, including the police, youth militias, and war veterans, in Zimbabwean elections. The case study thus nuances the quantitative (non-)findings that are limited to the effect of military capacity.

As a final test, Table 3.7 presents the conditioning effect of coercive capacity when elections have been held within shorter and longer time horizons. H2 is again rejected when the effect of coercive capacity on elections held within the past five and seven years is estimated. In Models 2–6, the coefficient on the interaction term remains insignificant. In the short term, however, coercive capacity does seem to significantly condition the effect of elections on regime breakdown

Table 3.7 Multi-party elections, coercive capacity, and regime breakdown – varying time horizons

	1	2	3	4	5	6
	RE	FE	RE	FE	RE	FE
	1 year		5 years		7 years	
Multi-party elections	−0.860 (1.093)	−3.148 (2.127)	−0.613 (1.086)	−0.668 (2.721)	−0.674 (1.071)	−0.322 (2.801)
Military expenditure	−0.010 (0.057)	0.123 (0.130)	−0.070 (0.097)	0.210 (0.262)	−0.112 (0.095)	0.016 (0.226)
Elections* Military expenditure	0.217** (0.107)	0.460** (0.223)	0.121 (0.114)	0.121 (0.300)	0.139 (0.114)	0.138 (0.310)
Tax-to-GDP ratio	−2.541** (1.203)	0.890 (2.129)	−3.741*** (1.440)	−0.725 (3.133)	−3.827** (1.549)	−0.445 (3.556)
GDP/cap	−0.356** (0.151)	−0.134 (0.725)	−0.234 (0.162)	0.338 (0.833)	−0.234 (0.181)	1.012 (0.750)
Growth	−0.012 (0.008)	−0.010 (0.010)	−0.038** (0.017)	−0.034** (0.016)	−0.027 (0.020)	−0.026 (0.023)
Natural resource income	−0.029 (0.026)	−0.130** (0.063)	−0.023 (0.026)	−0.107 (0.067)	−0.012 (0.025)	−0.072 (0.078)
War	−0.526 (0.687)	−0.407 (0.726)	−0.313 (0.927)	−0.573 (1.384)	−0.380 (1.020)	−1.209 (1.264)
Constant	3.032 (1.857)		3.057 (1.990)		2.575 (2.491)	
N	2611	1889	2306	1512	2126	1385
Breakdowns	113	113	97	97	85	85

Note: Dependent variable is regime breakdown. Logistic regression models with robust standard errors clustered on country in parentheses. RE denotes random effects models and FE fixed effects models. Multi-party elections note whether at least one election was held in the past year (Models 1–2), the past five years (Models 3–4), and the past seven years (Models 5–6). Tax ratio, military expenditure, and economic control are one-, five-, and seven-year running averages respectively. Controls for time and regime age (cubed) are included but not shown in the table. All covariates except time trends are lagged one year.

*$p < 0.10$, **$p < 0.05$, ***$p < 0.01$

($p < 0.05$), but the effect is positive rather than negative. For elections held within the past year, elections are *more* likely to increase the risk of breakdown as military expenditure increases.

This curious effect of military expenditure on breakdown following elections held within the past year is explored further in Figure 3.4. Figure 3.4 clearly illustrates that as coercive capacity increases, the marginal effect of elections on the likelihood of breakdown increases as well. That is, as military expenditure increases, breakdown following elections becomes *more* likely. The marginal effect is positive and statistically significant for the top 90% of the sample. Excluding the countries with low military expenditure, having held an election within the past year makes regime breakdown more likely than if the country had not held a recent election.

The counterintuitive result may also follow from the less than ideal measure of coercive capacity. It is plausible that rather than breakdown becoming more likely when coercive capacity increases, military expenditures are likely to rise in cases where elections provoke post-electoral protests and autocrats use their coercive apparatus to repress them. In his role as president of a country previously plagued by military coups and public protests, and amid dropping popularity rates and soaring inflation, Venezuelan President Maduro announced a 45% pay raise for the armed forces in October 2014 (BBC News 2014). According to this logic, military spending would increase with the dictator's perceived risk of regime breakdown. This could lead to a positive correlation between military spending and breakdown. Such a relationship could explain why the risk of breakdown only correlates with high levels of coercive capacity immediately following elections and not a few years after the electoral contest.

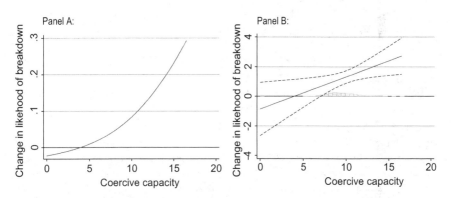

Figure 3.4 Marginal effect of elections (held within the past year) for increasing levels of coercive capacity

Note: Marginal effect of multi-party elections held within the past year (versus no multi-party elections) on likelihood of regime breakdown for increasing levels of coercive capacity based on Table 3.7, Model 1. For each observation, the covariates are held at their observed values and the marginal effects are calculated and then averaged across observations (observed-value approach; see Hanmer and Kalkan 2013). Panel A provides the substantially meaningful marginal effect (probability scale). Panel B provides 90% confidence intervals (logit scale) and distribution of included observations across military expenditure.

Conclusion

Chapter 2 pointed to the markedly different contexts in which authoritarian elections take place and suggested that perhaps the paradox of authoritarian elections is not so paradoxical after all. The analyses in this chapter have lent credence to this argument. The results suggest that administrative capacity – proxied by tax extraction rates – conditions the effect of multi-party elections on the likelihood of authoritarian regime breakdown. In regimes where tax extraction rates are above 0.26, corresponding to the top 10% of the sample, holding elections decreases the likelihood of breakdown and more so the more tax extraction rates increase. For the 50% of the countries that have the lowest tax-to-GDP ratios, on the other hand, having held an election within the past three years significantly increases the risk of breakdown. Identical effects of administrative capacity are visible when we look at elections held within the past year and the past five years, indicating that administrative capacity affects the role of elections both in the short and the long term. Seven years after elections have been held, however, there is no longer a visible conditioning effect of administrative capacity (nor a direct effect of elections).

The statistical relationship is not driven by fluctuations in wealth, growth, or control over the economy, nor by political conflicts, prior levels of liberalization, authoritarian regime type, changes to the international environment, or the age of the regime. The results are robust to proxying administrative capacity by an adjusted taxation measure and to the inclusion of imputed tax data for the post-communist countries.

The relationship between administrative capacity, proxied by tax extraction rates, elections, and regime breakdown corroborates the theoretical claims. There is evidence that the variation in the effect of elections that has puzzled the literature on electoral authoritarianism can be explained when administrative capacity is taken into account. However, whereas one arm of the state, the administrative, seems to influence the effect of elections, no such effect of the coercive arm of the state was found.

Coercive capacity, proxied either by military expenditure or military personnel, does not affect the effect of authoritarian elections. The rejection of H2 is robust to the inclusion of alternative controls and to exploring the effect of elections over various time horizons. The only exception is for elections held within the past year where high levels of military expenditure – counter to theoretical expectations – correlate with a higher risk of breakdown. Rather than high levels of coercive capacity increasing the risk of breakdown, however, it is plausible that an increase in the perceived risk of breakdown – for instance, because of post-electoral protests – causes dictators to increase spending on coercive capacity, including the military.

Returning to the example of Singapore, given its high levels of administrative capacity (a tax-to-GDP ratio averaging 0.18 in the past decade), it is unsurprising that Singapore remains stable in the face of regular, authoritarian, multi-party elections.[5] In fact, based on the results presented here, were Singapore to experience a significant blow to its administrative apparatus (without a corresponding increase in levels of economic control), resulting in a markedly lower extractive capacity, the regime would be more likely to destabilize following the holding of elections. On the other hand, if Singapore were to continue with similar levels of administrative capacity but abandon elections, this would also be expected to increase the likelihood of regime breakdown. But there is no evidence from the quantitative studies that Singapore's coercive capacity would also have contributed to this regime-stabilizing effect of elections.

That coercive capacity does not reduce the risk of breakdown by elections is perhaps not surprising in cases such as Singapore, where the rulers can rely on other capacities to control elections. Yet two questions remain. First, an important caveat to the rejection of H2 is the available measures of coercive capacity. These only include the army. Thus, it remains possible that a more full proxy for coercive capacity, including information on police, paramilitary forces, and private militias, would yield different results. Second, the analyses have demonstrated a general pattern linking administrative capacity to authoritarian regime stability. But the question remains whether it is indeed a capable bureaucracy that allows authoritarian leaders in cases such as Singapore to control elections through the various strategies spelled out in Chapter 2. Does administrative capacity allow autocrats to rely on more subtle measures of electoral manipulation? And do these strategies ensure legitimacy and elite loyalty while preventing opposition mobilization and mass protests? The case studies in Chapters 5–6 focus on these two issues. The main purpose is to assess the degree to which selected, typical cases conform to the patterns laid out in the theoretical framework. But they also contribute to nuancing the findings on coercive capacity. By focusing on the two most recent elections in Zimbabwe, Chapter 6 analyzes a case where both the military and the non-military arms of the coercive force have played an important role in elections. But before the book turns to the underlying mechanisms of the conditioning relationships, Chapter 4 analyzes the effect of economic control.

Notes

1. In Chapter 1, regime stability was defined as the absence of breakdown.
2. In the same vein, the tax-to-GDP ratio is also dependent on the level of GDP. Thus, countries with high GDPs will have lower extraction rates than low-GDP countries if they extract the same amount of taxes (Saylor 2013, 20–1). But if we again assume that autocrats extract as many resources as possible without endangering their position in power, richer autocrats should extract more resources, all else being equal, and the tax ratio should thus still capture administrative capacity.
3. In alternative specifications, year-dummies are included.
4. As coercive capacity is measured as a three-year running average of military expenses lagged one year, this is also the case for the war variable.
5. Note, however, that highly stable countries such as Singapore are not driving results. In the fixed effects estimations where highly stable countries are not included (fixed effect estimators are based on changes in key variables and thus exclude countries that do not experience breakdown), the interaction effect of administrative capacity remains significant.

References

Albertus, Michael, and Victor Menaldo. 2012. "Coercive Capacity and the Prospects for Democratization." *Comparative Politics* 44 (2): 151–69.
Andersen, David, Jørgen Møller, Lasse Lykke Rørbæk, and Svend-Erik Skaaning. 2014. "State Capacity and Political Regime Stability." *Democratization* 21 (7): 1305–25.
Banks, Arthus, and Kenneth Wilson. 2012. "Cross-National Time-Series Data Archive." Jerusalem: Databanks International. www.databanksinternational.com.
BBC News. 2014. "Venezuela to Raise Minimum Wage." Accessed November 13. www.bbc.com/news/world-latin-america-29894940.
Beck, Nathaniel, Jonathan Katz, and Richard Tucker. 1998. "Taking Time Seriously: Time-Series-Cross-Section Analysis with a Binary Dependent Variable." *American Journal of Political Science* 42 (4): 1260–88.
Bellin, Eva. 2004. "The Robustness of Authoritarianism in the Middle East: Exceptionalism in Comparative Perspective." *Comparative Politics* 36 (2): 139–57.
Besley, Timothy, and Torsten Persson. 2013. *Pillars of Prosperity: The Political Economics of Development Clusters*. Princeton, NJ: Princeton University Press.
Brownlee, Jason. 2009a. "Harbinger of Democracy: Competitive Elections before the End of Authoritarianism." In *Democratization by Elections: A New Mode of Transition*, edited by Staffan Lindberg, 128–47. Baltimore: The Johns Hopkins University Press.
———. 2009b. "Portents of Pluralism: How Hybrid Regimes Affect Democratic Transitions." *American Journal of Political Science* 55 (3): 515–32.
Bueno de Mesquita, Bruce, Alastair Smith, Randolph M. Siverson, and James D. Morrow. 2003. *The Logic of Political Survival*. Cambridge, MA: The MIT Press.
Bunce, Valerie, and Sharon Wolchik. 2011. *Defeating Authoritarian Leaders in Postcommunist Countries*. New York: Cambridge University Press.
Cameron, A. Colin, and Pravin K. Trivedi. 2009. *Microeconometrics Using Stata*. 1st edition. College Station, TX: Stata Press.
Carter, David, and Curtis S. Signorino. 2010. "Back to the Future: Modeling Time Dependence in Binary Data." *Political Analysis* 18 (3): 271–92.
Cheibub, Jose, Jennifer Gandhi, and James Vreeland. 2010. "Democracy and Dictatorship Revisited." *Public Choice* 143 (1): 67–101.
Chua, Beng-Huat. 1997. *Communitarian Ideology and Democracy in Singapore*. 1st edition. London: Routledge.
Donno, Daniela. 2013. "Elections and Democratization in Authoritarian Regimes." *American Journal of Political Science* 57 (3): 703–16.
Flores, Thomas Edward, and Irfan Nooruddin. 2016. *Elections in Hard Times: Building Stronger Democracies in the 21st Century*. Cambridge, New York, NY and Washington, DC: Cambridge University Press.
Fukuyama, Francis. 2013. "What Is Governance?" *Governance* 26 (3): 347–68.
Geddes, Barbara. 2003. *Paradigms and Sand Castles: Theory Building and Research Design in Comparative Politics*. Ann Arbor: University of Michigan Press.
Geddes, Barbara, Joseph Wright, and Erica Frantz. 2014a. "Autocratic Breakdown and Regime Transitions: A New Data Set." *Perspectives on Politics* 12 (2): 313–31.
———. 2014b. "Autocratic Regimes Code Book: Version 1.2." http://sites.psu.edu/dictators/.
Gwartney, James, Robert Lawson, and Joshua Hall. 2013. "2013 Economic Freedom Dataset." Economic Freedom of the World: 2013 Annual Report. Fraser Institute. www.freetheworld.com/datasets_efw.html.

Haber, Stephen, and Victor Menaldo. 2011. "Do Natural Resources Fuel Authoritarianism? A Reappraisal of the Resource Curse." *American Political Science Review* 105 (1): 1–26.

Hadenius, Axel, and Jan Teorell. 2009. "Elections as Levers of Democratization: A Global Inquiry." In *Democratization by Elections: A New Mode of Transition*, 77–100. Baltimore: The Johns Hopkins University Press.

Hanmer, Michael J., and Kerem Ozan Kalkan. 2013. "Behind the Curve: Clarifying the Best Approach to Calculating Predicted Probabilities and Marginal Effects from Limited Dependent Variable Models." *American Journal of Political Science* 57 (1): 263–77.

Hyde, Susan, and Nikolay Marinov. 2012. "Which Elections Can Be Lost?" *Political Analysis* 20 (2): 191–210.

King, Gary, James Honaker, Anne Joseph, and Kenneth Scheve. 2001. "Analyzing Incomplete Political Science Data: An Alternative Algorithm for Multiple Imputation." *The American Political Science Review* 95 (1): 49–69.

Knutsen, Carl Henrik, Håvard Mokleiv Nygård, and Tore Wig. 2017. "Autocratic Elections: Stabilizing Tool or Force for Change?" *World Politics* 69 (1): 98–143.

Kugler, Jacek, and Ronald L. Tammen. 2012. *The Performance of Nations*. 1st edition. Lanham: Rowman & Littlefield Publishers.

Kuntz, Philipp, and Mark Thompson. 2009. "More Than Just the Final Straw: Stolen Elections as Revolutionary Triggers." *Comparative Politics* 41 (3): 253–72.

Li, Jinshan and Jørgen Elklit. 1999. "The Singapore General Election 1997: Campaigning Strategy, Results, and Analysis." *Electoral Studies* 18 (2): 199–216.

Lieberman, Evan S. 2002. "Taxation Data as Indicators of State-Society Relations: Possibilities and Pitfalls in Cross-National Research." *Studies in Comparative International Development* 36 (4): 89–115.

Lindberg, Staffan. 2006. *Democracy and Elections in Africa*. Baltimore: The Johns Hopkins University Press.

Magaloni, Beatriz. 2008. "Credible Power-Sharing and the Longevity of Authoritarian Rule." *Comparative Political Studies* 41 (4/5): 715–41.

Marshall, Monty, Keith Jaggers, and Ted Gurr. 2011. "Polity IV Project." Center for Systemic Peace. www.systemicpeace.org/polity/polity4.htm.

McCoy, Jennifer, and Jonathan Hartlyn. 2009. "The Relative Powerlessness of Elections in Latin America." In *Democratization by Elections: A New Mode of Transition*, edited by Staffan Lindberg, 47–76. Baltimore: The Johns Hopkins University Press.

Nasir, Kamaludeen M., and Bryan S. Turner. 2012. "Governing as Gardening: Reflections on Soft Authoritarianism in Singapore." *Citizenship Studies* 17 (3/4): 339–52.

Ong, Elvin, and Mou Hui Tim. 2014. "Singapore's 2011 General Elections and Beyond: Beating the PAP at Its Own Game." *Asian Survey* 54 (4): 749–72.

Penn World Table. 2013. "Penn World Table." https://pwt.sas.upenn.edu/php_site/pwt_index.php.

Pepinsky, Thomas. 2014. "The Institutional Turn in Comparative Authoritarianism." *British Journal of Political Science* 44 (3): 631–53.

Political Risk Services. 2013. "International Crisis Research Group." The PRS Group. www.prsgroup.com/about-us/our-two-methodologies/icrg.

Romero, Simon. 2010. "Venezuela's Military Ties with Cuba Stir Concerns." *The New York Times*, June 14, sec. World/Americas. www.nytimes.com/2010/06/15/world/americas/15venez.html.

Saylor, Ryan. 2013. "Concepts, Measures, and Measuring Well: An Alternative Outlook." *Sociological Methods & Research* 42 (3): 354–91.

Schedler, Andreas. 2013. *The Politics of Uncertainty: Sustaining and Subverting Electoral Authoritarianism*. Oxford: Oxford University Press.

Singer, David, Stuart Bremer, John Stuckey, and Bruce Russett. 1972. "Capability Distribution, Uncertainty, and Major Power War, 1820–1965." In *Peace, War, and Numbers*, 19–48. Beverly Hills: Sage.

Slater, Dan. 2010. *Ordering Power: Contentious Politics and Authoritarian Leviathans in Southeast Asia*. New York: Cambridge University Press.

———. 2012. "Strong-State Democratization in Malaysia and Singapore." *Journal of Democracy* 23 (2): 19–33.

Slater, Dan, and Sofia Fenner. 2011. "State Power and Staying Power: Infrastructural Mechanisms and Authoritarian Durability." *Journal of International Affairs* 65 (1): 15–29.

Svolik, Milan W. 2012. *The Politics of Authoritarian Rule*. New York: Cambridge University Press.

Tan, Netina. 2013. "Manipulating Electoral Laws in Singapore." *Electoral Studies*, Special Symposium: The New Research Agenda on Electoral Integrity 32 (4): 632–43.

Thies, Cameron G. 2005. "War, Rivalry, and State Building in Latin America." *American Journal of Political Science* 49 (3): 451–65.

TransResearch Consortium. 2013. "Relative Political Performance Data Set Documentation: Version 2.1." http://thedata.harvard.edu/dvn/dv/rpc/faces/study/StudyPage.xhtml?globalId=hdl:1902.1/16845.

Whitten-Woodring, Jenifer, and Douglas A. Van Belle. 2014. *Historical Guide to Media Freedom*. Los Angeles: CQ Press.

World Bank. 2014. "World Development Indicators (WDI)." Washington, DC. http://data.worldbank.org/data-catalog/world-development-indicators.

4 Economic control and the effect of elections in authoritarian regimes

From 1929 to 2000, the leadership of the ruling Institutional Revolutionary Party (PRI) in authoritarian Mexico held regular elections without experiencing a transfer of power. The PRI repeatedly acquired more than 60% of votes until the opposition started gaining ground in the 1980s. To uphold electoral dominance, the ruling party pursued a number of strategies. Informal patron-client relationships pervaded politics, and candidates delivered infrastructure and electricity to neighborhoods in return for votes (Camp 1990; Langston and Morgenstern 2009). Early state-supported programs, including food stores and infrastructure development, were targeted at potential areas of insurgency to divert support from opposition movements to the PRI (Fox 1994). Loyalists were given jobs in the large bureaucracy – and were in turn expected to work for the party (Greene 2007, 98) – and government resources were employed in ruling party campaigns. When the PRI's popularity declined following the economic crisis of the early 1980s, the state-sponsored poverty relief program, PRONASOL, was targeted at potential swing states to avoid defection to the opposition and removed from opposition-supporting districts (Cornelius and Craig 1991; Magaloni 2006, chap. 4).

What these strategies have in common is their foundation in the ruling party's economic monopoly, built up through years of dominating the system. In the early 1980s, state-owned enterprises accounted for almost a quarter of GDP, and the federal government employed more than three million people (Greene 2007, 101–3; Magaloni 2006; Camp 1990). This chapter asks whether this dynamic of sustaining power by winning elections through economic domination extends beyond the Mexican case. Does economic control condition the relationship between elections and authoritarian regime breakdown?

The previous chapter demonstrated that conditioned on administrative capacity, measured as the ability to collect taxes, elections have a significant effect on regime breakdown. The more administrative capacity increases, the more likely authoritarian regimes are to remain stable following an election. For high levels of administrative capacity, electoral regimes are more stable than non-electoral regimes. In the first section, I operationalize economic control. I then test the claim that the effect of elections is conditioned not only by state capacity but also by economic control. Finally, I estimate the effect of elections in authoritarian regimes that are low on all types of capacities.

Method and data

As in the analyses in the previous chapter, the *dependent* variable is regime breakdown (data from Geddes, Wright, and Frantz 2014). The *independent* variable is a dummy taking the value of 1 if multi-party elections have been held within the past one, three, five, or seven years depending on the model (see Chapter 3). The *conditioning* variable is economic control defined as the rulers' domination of economic resources including natural resource revenues, land, and employment opportunities. Here, I break the concept down into three measurable dimensions.

First, the size of the public sector gauges citizens' dependence on the rulers both for jobs and benefits. There are no time-series cross-sectional measures available on public sector jobs, but if the public sector is larger, citizens will – all else equal – be more likely to earn their living in public jobs. Furthermore, money can be directed from the state budget to the rulers and be spent for partisan purposes (Greene 2007, 40–1). Alternative measures that would be highly relevant to capture this dimension of economic control are the number of state-owned enterprises or data on (lack of) privatization (Greene 2007). Again, such data are not available on a cross-national basis for authoritarian regimes. Furthermore, scholars have highlighted that privatization does not necessarily equal a broader distribution of resources. Rather, in cases such as Angola, privatization has caused ownership to shift hands from the state to loyalists of the ruling group, contributing to rather than reducing incumbent control (Messiant 2001). Instead, I use government spending as a share of GDP from the Penn World Table to capture government size (Penn World Table 2013). The measure is log transformed to normalize the distribution. Although data are missing for some authoritarian regimes, the measure has reasonable coverage dating back to 1950.

Second, regulations on private business indicate the degree to which the government controls private endeavors to earn a living. Where private business is heavily controlled – or can be bullied by the government – economic freedom is restricted, and citizens are more dependent on the government. To capture the degree of regulation, I use an index of regulation from the Economic Freedom in the World Dataset (Gwartney, Lawson, and Hall 2013). The index captures regulation on credit markets, labor markets, and business, including information on the costs of starting a business (including, for instance, bribery), licensing restrictions, and ownership of banks (Gwartney, Lawson, and Block 1996, 243–8). The aggregate measure of regulation is available for some regimes as early as 1970 and for other regimes much later. Until 2000, regimes are scored every five years, and after 2000, the measure is available on a yearly basis. The index is inversed so that a higher score equals higher levels of regulation.[1]

The index on regulation only provides data every five years from 1970 at the earliest (some authoritarian regimes only have data from later years onward) to 2000 and yearly measures thereafter. At the same time, measures for a number of the other main variables (including the tax ratio) are only available until the mid-2000s. Thus, relying only on observed regulation data will significantly restrict my ability to conduct analyses over time. Therefore, I interpolate the data on the regulation index: I generate average values for the missing data from the observed values of the same variable in the same country in the year before and after the missing observations.

Third, income from natural resources is a factor that is commonly stressed as one that increases leaders' control over the economy. Such resources can be extracted with little reliance on labor and often provide for rent windfalls to the dictator that can be distributed to loyal followers. Levitsky and Way rely on information on the mineral sector, among other measures, to code autocrats' organizational power (Levitsky and Way 2010, 378). Such resources have also been highlighted as easily captured by (or at least in various ways profitable for) rebels and thus potentially undermining to incumbent control (Ross 2003, 30–4). In that case, resources would actually lower incumbent control and potentially cause instability. This risk is partially circumvented as my analyses only include regimes in which most of the territory is in government hands (see Chapter 2), and thus assume that natural resources in most of the cases will contribute to the incumbent's degree of control. I use the logarithm of total income from natural resources per capita from Haber and Menaldo (2011).

In the analyses, I employ the individual dimensions as well as an index comprising public sector size, regulation, and income from natural resources. For comparability, I standardize all three dimensions to have mean 0 and variance 1.[2] I reverse the index on regulation so that for all three dimensions, high scores equal higher degrees of economic control. The dimensions are not necessarily expected to correlate, as an autocrat may control one dimension without the regime scoring highly on the others (indeed Pearson's correlations vary between –0.15 and 0.58). That is, resource-rich countries do not necessarily have heavy restrictions on business. Rather, the index is additive: taken together, the dimensions express an overall level of economic control. A ruling group that controls business and disposes over a large public sector and natural resources has very high degrees of economic control. But medium degrees of economic control may be attained both by scoring high on one or two dimensions and low on the others or by having mean values on all three. I construct the index by summing all three variables and dividing by three, letting each dimension have equal weight in the final index.

Based on the overall index, authoritarian regimes with high degrees of economic control include Syria, Iran, and China in the 1980s and 1990s. At the bottom are Singapore in recent years and Malawi in the 1980s and 1990s. Around the mean of 0.04 are Tunisia and Botswana.

The potential sources of bias discussed in the previous chapter also apply here. I take the same precautions in this chapter as in the previous. All models are logistical regression models with either random or fixed effects estimators and with robust standard errors clustered on country. The same control variables as in previous analyses are included, namely wealth, growth, time trends, and regime age (including its squared and cubed expression). Selected models also include controls for levels of protest, ongoing processes of democratization, foreign aid, the Cold War period, authoritarian regime type, and the first multi-party election held under each authoritarian regime (see Chapter 3).

Economic control, elections, and regime breakdown

This chapter tests H3 and H5 on the relationship between elections, economic control, and regime breakdown and H6 on the role of elections in regimes where rulers are low on all capacities. To recap:

> H3: The effect of authoritarian multi-party elections on the likelihood of regime breakdown will decrease with higher levels of economic control.
> H5: The effect of authoritarian multi-party elections on regime breakdown will be negative for high levels of economic control irrespective of the levels of administrative and coercive capacity.
> H6: The effect of authoritarian multi-party elections on regime breakdown will be positive when levels of administrative capacity, coercive capacity, and economic control are all low.

If the mechanisms presented in the theoretical framework hold, economic control should condition the relationship between elections and the likelihood of breakdown in authoritarian regimes. Some regimes may be more likely to stabilize through elections because the rulers can rely on an effective administrative apparatus to control numerous aspects of elections (e.g., Singapore). Other ruling coalitions may supplement, or possibly substitute, such administrative effectiveness with economic dominance, as was the case in 20th century Mexico.

Table 4.1 employs logistic regression models to test H3, which states that the likelihood of breakdown following an authoritarian election will decrease with higher levels of control over the economy. The election dummy indicates whether one or more multi-party elections were held within the previous three years, and the index of economic control is a three-year running average. The models include controls for administrative and coercive capacity, wealth, growth, and time trends.

In Model 1, the finding that elections increase the risk of breakdown all else equal (see Chapter 3) is not repeated, perhaps due to the reduced sample (the full index of economic control is available for a smaller time period than the measures for administrative and coercive capacity). As expected, however, both wealth and growth significantly reduce the risk of authoritarian regime breakdown. Model 2 adds the three authoritarian capacities: administrative, coercive, and economic. All types of capacities reduce the risk of authoritarian regime breakdown but the effect of economic control is statistically insignificant.[3]

The lack of a direct effect of economic control on authoritarian regime stability deserves mention. The existing literature has demonstrated a direct, negative effect of various aspects of economic control on authoritarian regime developments. Perhaps due to the difficulties of measuring other aspects of economic control, most quantitative studies have centered on the effect of generating rents from natural resources or other types of "windfall" including foreign aid. For instance, non-tax-based revenue, including revenue from natural resources, has been shown to stabilize authoritarian regimes (Morrison 2009). Including other aspects of economic control, such as regulation and government spending, may explain why the results differ from those findings. But case studies have also explored other

Table 4.1 Multi-party elections, economic control, and regime breakdown

	1	2	3	4	5
	RE	RE	RE	FE	RE
Multi-party elections	0.453 (0.319)	0.443 (0.350)	0.426 (0.359)	0.104 (0.524)	0.513 (0.360)
Economic control		−0.153 (0.283)	−0.009 (0.390)	1.431 (1.085)	−0.362 (0.403)
Elections* Economic control			−0.490 (0.758)	−1.198 (0.841)	0.485 (0.787)
Tax-to-GDP ratio		−5.104*** (1.777)	−4.788*** (1.832)	−5.412 (4.518)	
Military expenditure		−0.336** (0.134)	−0.354*** (0.135)	0.409 (0.530)	
GDP/cap	−0.406** (0.168)	0.087 (0.232)	0.097 (0.234)	0.592 (1.813)	−0.248 (0.159)
Growth	−0.049** (0.019)	−0.052** (0.023)	−0.053** (0.023)	−0.057** (0.025)	−0.053*** (0.020)
t	−0.661 (0.476)	−0.460 (0.526)	−0.435 (0.534)	−0.946 (0.927)	−0.573 (0.513)
t^2	0.026 (0.017)	0.020 (0.019)	0.019 (0.019)	0.035 (0.033)	0.024 (0.018)
t^3	−0.000 (0.000)	−0.000 (0.000)	−0.000 (0.000)	−0.000 (0.000)	−0.000 (0.000)
Regime duration	−0.014 (0.026)	0.003 (0.026)	0.001 (0.027)	0.100 (0.121)	−0.011 (0.041)
Regime duration^2	0.000 (0.000)	0.000 (0.000)	0.000 (0.000)	−0.005 (0.007)	0.000 (0.001)
Regime duration^3	−0.000 (0.000)	−0.000 (0.000)	−0.000 (0.000)	0.000* (0.000)	−0.000 (0.000)
Constant	7.748* (4.660)	2.053 (5.211)	1.797 (5.299)		4.221 (4.432)
Observations	1410	1410	1410	877	1653
Breakdowns	59	59	59	58	74

Note: Dependent variable is regime breakdown. Logistic regression models with robust standard errors clustered on country in parentheses. RE denotes random effects models and FE fixed effects models. Multi-party elections note whether at least one election was held in the past three years. Tax ratio, military expenditure, and economic control are three-year running averages. All covariates except time trends are lagged one year.

*p < 0.10, **p < 0.05, ***p < 0.01

aspects of economic control, for instance, McMann's study arguing that economic autonomy – the antithesis of economic control, exemplified by citizens' ability to make a living independent of the rulers – contributes to democratization on the sub-national level in Russia and Kyrgyzstan (McMann 2006). These findings do not find general support with the measures employed here.

Model 3 in Table 4.1 performs the first test of H3 as the election dummy is interacted with the index of economic control. As expected, the interaction effect is negative but it is not statistically significant. This result does not change when the effect is tested based on changes within countries over time (fixed effect estimators in Model 4) or when administrative and coercive state capacity is excluded from the equation (Model 5). The initial evidence does not lend support to H3 as economic control does not have a statistically significant effect on the relationship between elections held within the past three years and regime breakdown. The results do not change when controlling for authoritarian regime type, levels of protest, ongoing processes of democratization, foreign aid, the Cold War period, or first multi-party elections held under each authoritarian regime (Table C, Appendix).

In Table 4.2, the analysis is expanded to the effect of elections held within the past year, the past five years, and the past seven years. Curiously, although H3 is

Table 4.2 Multi-party elections, economic control, and regime breakdown – varying time horizons

	1	2	3	4	5	6
	RE	FE	RE	FE	RE	FE
	1 year		5 years		7 years	
Multi-party elections	1.465** (0.598)	1.387*** (0.385)	0.663* (0.397)	0.612 (1.008)	0.777* (0.405)	0.624 (1.073)
Economic control	0.203 (0.340)	1.128 (0.796)	0.221 (0.424)	2.776** (1.270)	0.291 (0.453)	3.046** (1.453)
Elections* Economic control	−0.842 (0.688)	−1.048* (0.609)	−1.076* (0.611)	−1.816 (1.342)	−1.135* (0.645)	−2.042 (1.502)
Tax-to-GDP ratio	−3.700 (3.421)	0.464 (3.533)	−3.225 (2.027)	−2.037 (6.294)	−3.456 (2.183)	−5.446 (8.401)
Military expenditure	−0.267* (0.154)	0.321 (0.464)	−0.424*** (0.156)	1.040 (0.797)	−0.498*** (0.189)	0.692 (1.085)
GDP/cap	−0.040 (0.485)	0.359 (1.583)	0.172 (0.271)	1.409 (2.909)	0.270 (0.294)	1.952 (3.397)
Growth	−0.051 (0.034)	−0.059** (0.024)	−0.052** (0.025)	−0.048 (0.034)	−0.038 (0.028)	−0.053 (0.044)
Constant	4.143 (6.726)		−1.515 (7.527)		−1.663 (10.402)	
Observations	1553	975	1267	761	1133	679
Breakdowns	66	66	51	49	47	46

Note: Dependent variable is regime breakdown. Logistic regression models with robust standard errors clustered on country in parentheses. RE denotes random effects models and FE fixed effects models. Multi-party elections note whether at least one election was held in the past year (Models 1–2), the past five years (Models 3–4), and the past seven years (Models 5–6). Tax ratio, military expenditure, and economic control are one-, five-, and seven-year running averages respectively. Controls for time and regime age (cubed) are included but not shown in the table. All covariates except time trends are lagged one year.

*$p < 0.10$, **$p < 0.05$, ***$p < 0.01$

not supported when we look at elections held within the past three years, it finds support in both the shorter and longer run. In terms of changes within countries over time, economic control significantly ($p < 0.1$) reduces the risk of breakdown when an election has been held within the past year (Model 2). The effect is not statistically significant for elections held within the past five years or more when we look at within-country differences. If the sample is expanded to look at differences both within and between countries (random effects), economic control significantly reduces the effect of elections held within the past five and seven years (Models 3 and 5). Furthermore, in these models, the direct effect of elections on regime breakdown is positive. This indicates that for countries with levels of economic control just below the mean (which is just above 0), such as the Philippines in the 1980s and Guatemala in the 1990s, having held an authoritarian election increases the risk of regime breakdown. This effect is reduced as economic control increases.

The conditioning effect of economic control on elections in the shorter and longer run is relatively robust to alternative controls. Table D in the Appendix illustrates the results for the five-year time span. Controlling for authoritarian regime type and the post-Cold War period, the coefficient on the interaction term remains negative and of roughly the same size, but p-levels are just above conventional levels of significance. The conditioning effect of economic control on electoral dynamics is robust to controls for ongoing processes of democratization (proxied by media freedom and executive constraints). Further, the reduced risk of breakdown when economic control increases is not driven by increasing levels of foreign aid or by a lower level of popular protests. Finally, controlling for the first multi-party elections held under each regime does not change results, which indicates that the effect is not an artefact of rulers with high levels of economic control and a lower risk of regime breakdown being more willing to introduce elections.

The conditioning effects of economic control in the short and long term are illustrated in Figure 4.1. It graphs the marginal effect of an election held within the past year and five years as economic control increases. The findings lend support to H3. The marginal effects are positive but decreasing. Both in the short and long term, the increased risk of breakdown following an authoritarian election decreases as economic control increases (Panel A1 and A2). As is also clear from the figure, the effects are statistically significant. For elections held within the past year, the conditioning effect of economic control is significant for 85% of the sample (Panel B1), and when elections have been held within the past five years, the effect is significant for 28% of the sample (Panel B2).

H3 is not supported when we look at the effect of elections held within the past three years. It is hard to theoretically explain the lack of an effect in the three-year models as the results change both when I limit and restrict the time horizon. Thus, the theoretical argument is supported when we look at shorter and longer time spans.

As H3 finds support for most time spans, I proceed to testing H5, which states that multi-party elections strengthen authoritarian stability where economic control is high. This hypothesis does not find support in the short or long run. The marginal effects clearly illustrate that for low levels of economic control, elections are

106 *Economic control and the effect of elections*

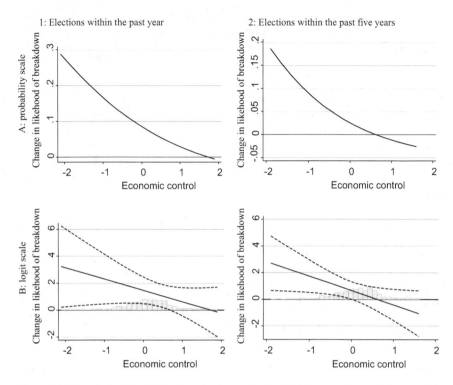

Figure 4.1 Marginal effect of elections for increasing levels of economic control – varying time horizons

Note: Marginal effect of multi-party elections (versus no multi-party elections) on likelihood of regime breakdown for increasing levels of economic control based on Table 4.2, Models 1 and 3. For each observation, the covariates are held at their observed values and the marginal effects are calculated and then averaged across observations (observed-value approach; see Hanmer and Kalkan 2013). Panel A provides the substantially meaningful marginal effect (probability scale). Panel B provides 90% confidence intervals (logit scale) and distribution of included observations across economic control.

destabilizing. For high levels of economic control, the marginal effect of holding elections (compared to not holding elections) is not statistically significant. There is no evidence that high-control regimes can use elections to stabilize their rule.

The predicted probabilities of breakdown for high- and low-control regimes with and without elections (held within the past five years) are illustrated in Figure 4.2. Autocrats with low economic control corresponding to the 5th percentile, such as Kenya in the early 1990s, face a much greater risk of regime breakdown if they have held an election within the past five years than if they have not (Panel A). Holding an election under these conditions increases the risk of breakdown from 2.5% to almost 10%. For low-control regimes, elections are regime

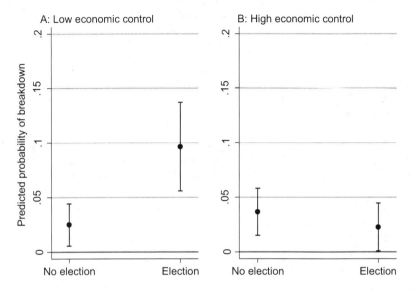

Figure 4.2 Predicted probability of breakdown for regime with high and low levels of economic control

Note: Based on Table 4.2, Model 3. Low administrative capacity is a tax ratio of 0.04 (5th percentile). High administrative capacity is a tax ratio of 0.32 (95th percentile). "Election" indicates whether a multi-party election has been held in the past five years. 90% confidence intervals. For each observation, the covariates are held at their observed values and the marginal effects are calculated and then averaged across observations (observed-value approach; see Hanmer and Kalkan 2013).

destabilizing. For high-control regimes such as China in the 1980s (corresponding to the 95th percentile; see Panel B), the risk of breakdown following elections is much smaller. In correspondence with H3, increasing levels of economic control reduce the risk of elections from almost 10% (Panel A) to 2.5% (Panel B). But for a high-control regime such as China, the risk of breakdown does not change when elections are held. Although the breakdown risk for an electoral regime is slightly smaller than for a non-electoral regime in Panel B, the confidence intervals overlap and there is no substantially or statistically significant difference.

Substantially, the rejection of H5 means that even though economic control conditions the effect of authoritarian elections, it cannot explain why some elections stabilize authoritarian rule. Rather, it can explain how some dictators reduce the risk of breakdown following elections. Thus, the cross-national patterns point to a greater risk of breakdown following an authoritarian election when control over the economy diminishes. This was witnessed in Mexico from the 1980s onward when the debt crisis sparked a turn toward neo-liberal policies, causing state-owned enterprises to be privatized and public sector employment to be reduced, in turn diminishing the PRI's control over elites and voters (Greene 2007, chap. 3; Collier 1992; Magaloni 2006). But there is no systematic, cross-national evidence that

The subcomponents of economic control

Not only administrative capacity but also economic control condition the effect of authoritarian elections. Although high levels of economic control cannot ensure autocrats stabilization through elections, increasing levels of control make dictatorships less likely to crumble following a multi-party election. But what aspects of economic control have this effect on authoritarian elections? Is the effect primarily driven by the world's resource-rich dictatorships or does it stem from policies such as regulation of business, labor, and credit markets or government spending? Table 4.3 shows the conditioning effect of the three subcomponents of economic control on the relationship between elections (held within the past year) and regime breakdown.

Surprisingly, natural resource dependence does not affect the relationship between elections and regime breakdown (Models 5–6). Although natural resource wealth has been shown to destabilize dictatorships and reduce chances of democratization (Morrison 2009; Ross 2013), it is not resource wealth that allows dictators to limit the risk of regime breakdown following authoritarian elections. Similarly, there is no evidence that dictators who heavily regulate business, labor, and credit are more likely to survive multi-party elections (Models 3–4). In all models, the interaction effect is statistically insignificant. Rather, the effect of economic control apparently runs through government spending as a percentage of GDP. Looking at changes within countries over time (Model 2) as well as changes between countries (Model 1), the coefficient on the interaction term between government spending and elections is negative and statistically significant. As government spending increases, the risk of breakdown following an election decreases. The results are robust to controls for regime type, the post-Cold War period, ongoing processes of liberalization, and the first multi-party elections held under an authoritarian regime but not to controls for levels of foreign aid (see Table E, Appendix).

The results are substantiated in Figure 4.3, which presents the marginal effect of a recent election for increasing levels of government spending. Panel A clearly illustrates that for lower levels of government spending, holding elections increases the risk of breakdown. For the 92% of countries that do not have very high levels of government spending, electoral regimes are more unstable than non-electoral regimes. However, the risk of breakdown decreases as government spending increases. With very high levels of government spending as a percentage of GDP, elections no longer provoke breakdown (although they do not stabilize the regime either).

The results indicate that when autocrats use their economic power to control elections, they do so by using and abusing a large public sector as was the case in 20th century Mexico. How autocrats use the public sector, however, remains unknown. Do they threaten public employees with job loss and use government

Table 4.3 Multi-party elections, subcomponents of economic control, and regime breakdown

	1	2	3	4	5	6
	RE	FE	RE	FE	RE	FE
Multi-party elections	3.293*** (1.190)	4.439*** (1.553)	1.608* (0.824)	2.153*** (0.376)	1.022** (0.465)	1.025** (0.487)
Government spending	0.121 (0.177)	0.643 (0.560)				
Elections* Government spending	−0.795* (0.424)	−1.298** (0.570)				
Regulations			−0.006 (0.158)	0.492* (0.256)		
Elections* Regulations			−0.498 (0.381)	−0.024 (0.411)		
Natural resource income					−0.038 (0.028)	−0.127** (0.060)
Elections* Natural resource income					0.011 (0.048)	−0.008 (0.055)
Tax-to-GDP ratio	−3.440*** (1.208)	0.029 (2.444)	−4.024 (5.334)	−1.787 (3.082)	−2.427** (1.166)	0.887 (2.116)
Military expenditure	0.012 (0.053)	0.297* (0.154)	−0.268* (0.148)	0.646 (0.399)	0.021 (0.057)	0.172 (0.147)
GDP/cap	−0.521*** (0.174)	−0.620 (0.733)	−0.071 (0.691)	−0.186 (1.496)	−0.326** (0.149)	0.052 (0.677)
Growth	−0.013* (0.007)	−0.013 (0.008)	−0.054 (0.055)	−0.046* (0.024)	−0.011 (0.008)	−0.011 (0.010)
Constant	4.567** (2.230)		4.317 (10.055)		2.403 (1.794)	
Observations	2550	1787	1591	1070	2652	1910
Breakdowns	109	109	67	86	114	114

Note: Dependent variable is regime breakdown. Logistic regression models with robust standard errors clustered on country in parentheses. RE denotes random effects models and FE fixed effects models. Multi-party elections note whether at least one election was held in the past year. Controls for time and regime age (cubed) are included but not shown in the table. All covariates except time trends are lagged one year.

*$p < 0.10$, **$p < 0.05$, ***$p < 0.01$

resources for partisan purposes as theorized in Chapter 3? The case studies of elections in the Philippines, Malaysia, and Zimbabwe in Chapters 5 and 6 test whether the relationship between elections, economic control, and breakdown can be explained by the mechanisms theorized in Chapter 3.

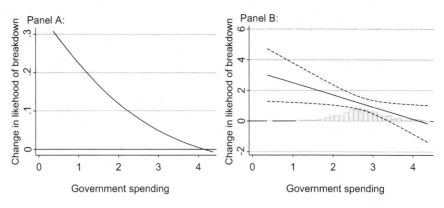

Figure 4.3 Marginal effect of elections for increasing levels of government spending

Note: Marginal effect of multi-party elections held in the past year (versus no multi-party elections) on likelihood of regime breakdown for increasing levels of government spending based on Table 4.3, Model 1. For each observation, the covariates are held at their observed values and the marginal effects are calculated and then averaged across observations (observed-value approach; see Hanmer and Kalkan 2013). Panel A provides the substantially meaningful marginal effect (probability scale). Panel B provides 90% confidence intervals (logit scale) and distribution of included observations across government spending.

Furthermore, the case evidence from Zimbabwe presented in Chapter 6 indicates that autocrats may also control the economy in informal ways and abuse this power to their advantage in elections. The cross-national analysis did not find support for a conditioning effect of natural resource rents on electoral dynamics. Often, however, autocrats' appropriation of natural resources is not recorded in public records. The cross-national results based on official statistics may thus underestimate the effect of natural resources on electoral dynamics in autocracies. Furthermore, dictators may not put regulation of private business into law but still heavily repress it, a pattern that is also hard to estimate in large-N studies. These dynamics are discussed in depth in Chapter 6. First, however, I test the final hypothesis (H6), which states that authoritarian multi-party elections are destabilizing where rulers lack state capacity and control over the economy.

Testing the effect of elections where all capacities are low

So far, the analyses have focused on the cases where rulers were high or low on a single capacity. Whereas coercive capacity has no conditioning effect on electoral dynamics, administrative capacity and economic control reduce the risk of breakdown following elections. Furthermore, elections are stabilizing at high levels of administrative capacity. However, H5, which states that elections should be stabilizing for high levels of economic control, did not find support. Instead, the cross-national data demonstrated that where economic control is low – or even at medium levels – holding multi-party elections increases the risk of authoritarian breakdown. Further, the analyses in Chapter 3 reveal that while elections are stabilizing at high levels of administrative capacity, they are destabilizing at low

Economic control and the effect of elections 111

levels. These findings indicate support for H6, which stated that where autocrats have limited state capacity and control over the economy, elections will destabilize their rule. If elections are destabilizing even where one of such capacities is limited, they are most likely also destabilizing where rulers lack both control over the economy and state capacity.

Nonetheless, the results of a formal test of H6 are shown in Figure 4.4. Again, the model is a logistic regression with regime breakdown as the dependent variable. The elections variable indicates whether multi-party elections were held in the past year, and controls for wealth, growth, and time trends are introduced. In the figure, administrative capacity, coercive capacity, and economic control are held at their 5th percentile. Thus, the figure presents the predicted probability of breakdown following an election where the ruler has limited capacities. The findings support H6. A low-capacity ruler who has not held an election within the past year faces a relatively high risk of breakdown of 6.4%. If that ruler holds an election, however, the risk of breakdown increases to a staggering 32.1%. Although the confidence interval around the breakdown risk following elections is high, the difference is statistically significant. Holding elections without controlling a capable state and commanding the economy increases the risk of authoritarian breakdown.

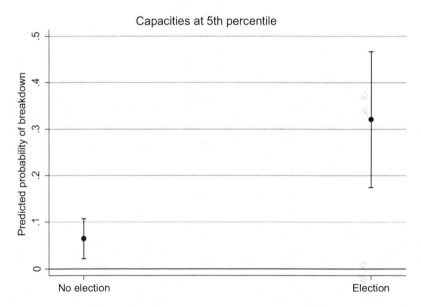

Figure 4.4 Predicted probability of regime breakdown where authoritarian capacities are low

Note: Logistic regression model (not reported). "Election" indicates whether a multi-party election was held in the past year. Administrative capacity, coercive capacity, and economic control (full index) are held at their 5th percentiles. All remaining covariates (wealth, growth, time trends) are held at their observed values. 90% confidence intervals. For each observation, the covariates are held at their observed values and the marginal effects are calculated and then averaged across observations (observed-value approach; see Hanmer and Kalkan 2013).

Conclusion

Extensive control over the economy through natural resources, business regulation, and a large public sector should allow an autocrat to subtly manipulate elections. Patronage may be distributed, votes may be bought, and potential opposition members may be kept at bay fearing economic ruin as a result of government punishment. Case studies have illustrated these dynamics at play across the world from Latin America to the post-Soviet space. This chapter has found some cross-national support for the claim that control over the economy helps dictators stabilize their rule through elections.

In support of H3, increasing levels of economic control reduce the risk of breakdown. Although the effect is not statistically significant for elections held within the past three years, economic control conditions the effects of elections after one, five, and seven years. H5 did not find support. Elections correlate with regime breakdown where economic control is at low or medium values, but even at extremely high values of economic control, elections are not stabilizing. Thus, economic control may explain how dictators avoid losing power following elections but cannot on its own explain how elections become regime stabilizing.

Furthermore, the effect of economic control runs through the indicator of government spending. Thus, the findings primarily support the theoretical mechanisms that state that a dictator controlling the economy through a large public sector may subtly manipulate elites, opposition, and citizens, for instance, by doling out public money or threatening public employees. There is no support for an effect of regulation of business or of natural resource wealth. The theoretical mechanisms are explored in the following chapters. In case studies of elections in the Philippines, Malaysia, and Zimbabwe, I ask whether it is indeed control over a large public sector that allows dictators to control elections – or the lack of such an apparatus that leads to election-related breakdown. I further discuss the possibility that business regulations and resource wealth may indeed affect electoral dynamics, but that autocrats often control businesses and amass resources in informal ways that are not easily captured in public statistics and are thus hard to test on a cross-national basis.

Finally, the chapter found support for H6. Elections are indeed destabilizing at low levels of state capacity and economic control. Low-capacity dictators who hold elections face markedly increasing risks of breakdown compared to dictators of non-electoral regimes. Thus, the cross-national analyses support the overall notion that authoritarian capacities may help explain the divergent effect of elections across cases.

Whether these general patterns can be attributed to the theoretical mechanisms presented in Chapter 2 is put to the test in the following chapters. I ask whether the breakdown that followed the authoritarian elections in the Philippines in 1986 can be attributed to the ruler's lack of capacities. Was there evidence that President Marcos was unable to carry out the necessary electoral strategies due to his lack of capacities? And I investigate whether the stabilizing effect of elections in Malaysia is related to the ruling coalition's effective administrative and coercive apparatus.

Did the ruling party, UMNO, employ its authoritarian capacities to subtly dominate elections? Finally, I analyze the role of coercive capacity as well as informal aspects of economic control further in the cases of Zimbabwe in 2008 and 2013. What strategies finally won Mugabe and his ZANU(PF) the chaotic 2008 elections, and did they have the expected effects on regime stability? And what changed prior to the calmer 2013 elections? The case studies thus test the theoretical apparatus and lend nuance to the quantitative findings of this and the preceding chapter.

Notes

1 As one of the subcomponents of the index, regulation of credit markets, is available earlier than the full index for many regimes, I rely solely on this subcomponent for years when the full index is missing so as not to exclude that country-year from the analysis. Whenever the full index is available, I use this rather than the subcomponent.
2 Setting the standardized variable $z = (\ln(1 + x) - \text{mean}(\ln(1 + x))) / (\text{standard deviation}(\ln(1 + x)))$.
3 Curiously, with this reduced sample, coercive capacity – unlike in the previous chapter – is found to significantly reduce the risk of regime breakdown independent of the holding of elections. This is in correspondence with expectations in the literature (Bellin 2004; Albertus and Menaldo 2012).

References

Albertus, Michael, and Victor Menaldo. 2012. "Coercive Capacity and the Prospects for Democratization." *Comparative Politics* 44 (2): 151–69.
Bellin, Eva. 2004. "The Robustness of Authoritarianism in the Middle East: Exceptionalism in Comparative Perspective." *Comparative Politics* 36 (2): 139–57.
Camp, Roderic A. 1990. "Camarillas in Mexican Politics: The Case of the Salinas Cabinet." *Mexican Studies/Estudios Mexicanos* 6 (1): 85–107.
Collier, Ruth. 1992. *The Contradictory Alliance: State-Labor Relations and Regime Change in Mexico*. Berkeley: University of California at Berkeley.
Cornelius, Wayne, and Ann Craig. 1991. *The Mexican Political System in Transition*. San Diego: Center for US-Mexican Studies.
Fox, Jonathan. 1994. "The Difficult Transition from Clientelism to Citizenship: Lessons from Mexico." *World Politics* 46 (2): 151–84.
Geddes, Barbara, Joseph Wright, and Erica Frantz. 2014. "Autocratic Breakdown and Regime Transitions: A New Data Set." *Perspectives on Politics* 12 (2): 313–31.
Greene, Kenneth. 2007. *Why Dominant Parties Lose: Mexico's Democratization in Comparative Perspective*. Cambridge: Cambridge University Press.
Gwartney, James, Robert Lawson, and Walter Block. 1996. *Economic Freedom of the World, 1975–1995*. Vancouver: Fraser Institute.
Gwartney, James, Robert Lawson, and Joshua Hall. 2013. "2013 Economic Freedom Dataset." Economic Freedom of the World: 2013 Annual Report. Fraser Institute. www.freetheworld.com/datasets_efw.html.
Haber, Stephen, and Victor Menaldo. 2011. "Do Natural Resources Fuel Authoritarianism? A Reappraisal of the Resource Curse." *American Political Science Review* 105 (1): 1–26.
Hanmer, Michael J., and Kerem Ozan Kalkan. 2013. "Behind the Curve: Clarifying the Best Approach to Calculating Predicted Probabilities and Marginal Effects from Limited Dependent Variable Models." *American Journal of Political Science* 57 (1): 263–77.

Langston, Joy, and Scott Morgenstern. 2009. "Campaigning in an Electoral Authoritarian Regime: The Case of Mexico." *Comparative Politics* 41 (2): 165–81.

Levitsky, Steven, and Lucan Way. 2010. *Competitive Authoritarianism: Hybrid Regimes after the Cold War*. Cambridge: Cambridge University Press.

Magaloni, Beatriz. 2006. *Voting for Autocracy*. New York: Cambridge University Press.

McMann, Kelly. 2006. *Economic Autonomy and Democracy: Hybrid Regimes in Russia and Kyrgyzstan*. Cambridge and New York: Cambridge University Press.

Messiant, Christine. 2001. "The Eduardo Dos Santos Foundation: Or, How Angola's Regime Is Taking over Civil Society." *African Affairs* 100 (399): 287–309.

Morrison, Kevin M. 2009. "Oil, Nontax Revenue, and the Redistributional Foundations of Regime Stability." *International Organization* 63 (1): 107–38.

Penn World Table. 2013. "Penn World Table." https://pwt.sas.upenn.edu/php_site/pwt_index.php.

Ross, Michael. 2003. "The Natural Resource Curse: How Wealth Can Make You Poor." In *Natural Resources and Violent Conflict*, edited by Ian Bannon and Paul Collier, 17–42. Washington, DC: The World Bank.

———. 2013. *The Oil Curse: How Petroleum Wealth Shapes the Development of Nations*. Reprint edition. Princeton, NJ: Princeton University Press.

5 State capacity, economic control, and two divergent elections in Malaysia and the Philippines

In the 1980s, electoral authoritarianism persisted in the Southeast Asian regimes of Malaysia and the Philippines. Malaysia had held regular multi-party elections since independence in 1957 (and still does so), but these contests had been heavily biased in favor of the main Malay party, United Malays National Organization (UMNO), and its ruling coalition Barisan Nasional (BN), a multi-ethnic alliance. Muhammad Mahatir became prime minister in 1981 and continued the tradition of regular yet biased elections. In the Philippines, Fernando Marcos gained the presidency in democratic elections in 1965. He turned the regime increasingly autocratic, culminating in the declaration of martial law in 1972, but he later reinstated elections and continued to hold them until his departure from power in 1986. However, whereas Mahatir presided over an effective administration and an imposing coercive force and extended his grip on the economy through distributive policies and public enterprises, authoritarian capacities were limited in the Philippines. Marcos's army slowly disintegrated in the face of corruption and political patronage, and the administrative force was underpaid.

This chapter examines the dynamics of elections that occurred under autocrats endowed with such different capacities. The quantitative analyses showed that both administrative capacity and economic control condition the effect of authoritarian elections but that coercive capacity has no such general effects. Where all capacities are lacking, the analyses indicated that authoritarian elections are more likely to be followed by breakdown.

The aim of this chapter is twofold. First and foremost, it examines whether there is evidence that it was indeed the capacities available to the ruling groups that shaped electoral outcomes and regime developments in Malaysia and the Philippines. This chapter does not claim to reveal causation but rather seeks to assess whether the general argument finds support in the cases. Did Mahatir employ his administrative apparatus to subtly manipulate elections? And did elections contribute to regime stability? Did Marcos fail to carry out discreet manipulation of elections because he lacked the capacity to do so? And did that cost him his power? Second, the case studies also seek to nuance the quantitative findings, as they allow for better assessments of the conditioning factors: the authoritarian capacities.

Method and case selection: Malaysia and the Philippines in the late 1980s

The aim of this and the following chapter is to assess whether the correlations found in the quantitative analyses conform more closely to the theoretical mechanisms that are expected to drive them. It is an attempt to identify the mechanisms through which elections affect regime stability. The method employed approximates what Campbell (1975) and Mahoney (2003) term pattern-matching. The goal is not to carry out a thorough process-tracing study that attempts to trace the causal chain (see Beach and Pedersen 2013, 14–16). Instead, I examine in each case whether there is evidence of the observable implications of the theoretical apparatus, which were summarized in Table 2.4. In addition to a more detailed assessment of the phenomena of interest – regime stability, elections, and capacities – the qualitative analyses investigate the strategies employed by the rulers and responses by the main actor groups (citizens, opposition, and regime elites).

If the case material supports theoretical expectations, this does not in itself constitute a full test of the theory, nor does it rule out alternative explanations for regime stability or breakdown. But in combination with the cross-national findings, such evidence can enhance our confidence in the theoretical claims. Vice versa, if the case material does not provide evidence of the expected mechanisms, the credibility of the theory has suffered in spite of the cross-national correlations.

As the main goal is to examine whether there is evidence of the expected theoretical mechanisms when the explanatory factors take on certain values, the cases are chosen based on their values on the main explanatory factors. I choose cases in which elections were held but authoritarian capacities varied according to the scenarios sketched in Chapter 2: stabilization by elections, breakdown by elections, and electoral survival. Thus, the cases are not picked at random among the cases that fall closest to the regression lines of Chapters 3–4, but are chosen to shed light on particular scenarios of authoritarian electoral dynamics. They are, however, still an approximation of typical cases. As the expected correlation between explanatory and dependent variables is present, they lend themselves neatly to assessing whether the theoretical mechanisms derived in Chapter 2 indeed lie behind the correlations of Chapters 3–4 (see Gerring 2007, 92–3).

In this chapter, I investigate whether the Malaysian election of 1990 and the Philippine election of 1986 conform to the suggested theoretical mechanisms. As shall be discussed later, Malaysia, with high levels of state capacity and the ruling party's control over the economy, should approximate the scenario of *stabilization by elections*, whereas the Philippines, where the capacities available to the leader were limited, appears to be a case of *breakdown by elections*. The expectations regarding these two scenarios are summarized in the following section.

Looking at the main control factors employed in the quantitative analyses – namely wealth, growth, societal unrest or protests, and time period – these two Southeast Asian regimes are arguably alike on some of the parameters. Societal unrest or protest occurred in both cases, taking the form of Muslim uprisings and communist insurgencies in the Philippines and clashes between ethnic Malay and

Chinese in Malaysia, to which both countries' leaderships referred in order to defend their authoritarian practices (Thompson 1995, 75; Crouch 1996, 22–4). But there are also important differences between the two cases, particularly in terms of economic growth and the international environment. The 1986 election in the Philippines was preceded by two years of economic crisis, and the former colonial power, the United States, interfered in support of both the regime and the opposition (Bonner 1987, 420, 432; Adesnik and McFaul 2006, 13–15). Malaysia, on the other hand, experienced modest growth and little intervention from the outside, although its 1990 election occurred in the immediate aftermath of the collapse of the Berlin Wall. These differences between the cases do not pose a problem to the analyses, as the attempt is not to approximate a most similar system design in which alternative explanations of regime change are controlled for. This exercise was undertaken in the quantitative analyses. Rather, the goal here is to assess whether the observable implications of the theory are visible in what ought to be two typical cases of opposing effects of authoritarian elections. That is, the study examines whether the cases render probable the claim that authoritarian state capacities conditioned the effect of elections, but it does not rule out alternative explanations in these particular cases.

State capacity and economic control in Malaysia and the Philippines

Judged by the data employed in Chapter 3, Malaysia and the Philippines exemplify respectively a high- and a low-capacity state. By the Philippine election of 1986, the country's tax extraction rate placed it in the 28th percentile of all authoritarian regimes, whereas Malaysia was in the 78th percentile. Similarly, Malaysia's military expenditures were in the 64th percentile for authoritarian regimes whereas the Philippines's was in the 25th. Malaysia and the Philippines also differed in terms of economic control, but not as much. On the index of economic control used in Chapter 4, the Philippines was among the quarter of authoritarian regimes that had the lowest degree of economic control in 1986, the year of its final authoritarian election and following breakdown. In 1986, Malaysia was slightly higher (the 29th percentile), but was as low as the Philippines during its 1990 election. Going beyond these simple measures to more fully account for levels of administrative and coercive capacity and economic control in these two regimes largely supports this overall pattern.

When Mahatir became prime minister in 1981, he inherited a strong state. Malaysia's administrative capacity is reflected in the reach of its civil service as well as in the economic policies implemented since independence. The managerial and professional division of the Malaysian civil services grew from 9,545 members in 1975 to 58,000 in 1990, and the expansion was especially pronounced in the prime minister's department, leaving him in control of a large part of the bureaucratic workforce (Puthucheary 1987, 102–4; Crouch 1996, 132–3). Whereas these bureaucrats were not necessarily directly involved in elections, public employees still played a significant role in Malaysian elections, as discussed later.

Furthermore, programs such as the New Economic Policy (NEP), a large-scale policy initiative intended to shift ownership of the corporate sector from ethnic Chinese to Malay hands (and which largely succeeded in doing so), reflected the capacity of the Malaysian leadership to implement its desired policies and contributed to increasing government control over state resources, as discussed later (Jesudason 1989, 78–9). Furthermore, Malaysia's extractive capacity demonstrates the existence of a machinery capable of monitoring and extracting resources – skills that also make the control of elections seem achievable (Hamilton-Hart 2002, 148). This is exemplified by the Employees Provident Fund (EPF), a government agency that extracts and administrates pension savings for private and some public enterprises from employees and employers. It had some of the highest contribution rates in the world, and in 1993 "the Malaysian state was collecting 22 percent of the salaries of 89 percent of the Malaysian workforce through the EPF, in addition to the country's already high rates of direct taxation" (Slater 2010, 153). In addition to reflecting an effective and wide-reaching bureaucracy, the taxes collected helped enforce the administrative and coercive powers of the state.

Malaysia's effective administrative machinery stands in contrast to that of the Marcos leadership, which was increasingly dependent on patronage networks, family, and friends rather than strong institutions (Thompson 1995, 4–5). From 1972–1981, Marcos upheld a period of martial law, citing a threat from communist insurgents. During this period, the president opted to divide power positions and patronage among his narrow circle of supporters rather than strengthen state institutions (Hutchcroft 2000, 300; Slater 2010, 175–6). Technocrats were left "constantly undercut by the presidential favors bestowed on cronies" (Thompson 1995, 4). Although Wurfel reports that the early Philippine bureaucracy was fairly well educated, the salaries of top-level civil servants were less than half of those in Malaysia, and corruption became so widespread that it "undermined the normal functioning of government" (Wurfel 1988, 79–80; see also Noble 1986, 101–2; Overholt 1986, 1144). The low administrative capacity of the Philippines was also illustrated – and further exacerbated – by its lack of a strong revenue collection authority: the Philippine tax extraction-to-GDP ratio in the early Marcos era was estimated to be 36% below the expected ratio (Cheetham and Hawkins 1976, 396–7, 391–3).

Although military expenditures, personnel, and salaries were increased both prior to and during the martial law period, and the Philippine Armed Forces benefited from significant financial support from the United States (Wurfel 1988, 140–1; Thompson 1995, 65), the military budget of the Philippines was lower than Malaysia's. From 1980 to 1985, Philippine military spending averaged slightly below 13 USD per capita per year compared to 120 USD in Malaysia (Singer et al. 1972). The military was, in some instances, deployed against citizens. Under the Preventive Detentions Act, citizens accused of constituting a threat to national security were frequently arrested and could be incarcerated by military units while awaiting government charges (US Department of State 1985, 853). However, the Philippine Armed Forces struggled with the de-professionalizing and demoralizing effects of political patronage. Marcos-favored officers from his home region, Ilocos, instated his relative, Fabian Ver, as army chief of staff, and distributed patronage (Overholt 1986, 1148; Wurfel 1977, 24–5). While ensuring the loyalty of parts of the military, the strategy also caused grievances among those who did not benefit and left the military de-professionalized and split (Noble 1986, 101; see also Slater 2010, 178–9; Thompson 1995, 54–5).

Malaysia's military expenditures were the second highest per capita in the region, surpassed only by those of Singapore (Singer et al. 1972). In addition to the well-organized army built up under British rule, Malaysia was home to an effective special branch force, a Federal Reserve Unit and Light Strike Force, a paramilitary wing, and a police force that covered all Malaysian territory (Barraclough 1985, 800; Ahmad 1987, 116–17). Its army, paramilitary, and police force were supplemented by legal measures allowing for widespread government responses to opposition, including the Internal Security Act (ISA), allowing ample room for detention of anyone considered a threat to the security, functioning, or economic development of Malaysia (Barraclough 1985, 807; Crouch 1996, 79–82; Munro-Kua 1996, 31–6); the Sedition Act, prohibiting public debate of "sensitive" issues (Crouch 1996, 82–4); and the Universities and University Colleges Acts, which prohibited political activities and party affiliations for students and university faculty (Crouch 1996, 92–3).

Although the differences in terms of economic control are less striking, they are still present. Traditionally, the Philippine economy "was controlled and dominated by the private sector" (Cheetham and Hawkins 1976, 387), and public enterprises played a modest role (Cheetham and Hawkins 1976, 411–12). Although this gradually changed throughout the 1970s, government expenditure as a share of GDP decreased again from the mid-1970s, and at the time of the 1986 elections, government spending accounted for 12% of GDP, leaving the Philippines among the 25% of authoritarian regimes with the lowest public spending that year (data from Penn World Table 2013).

The public sector budget in Malaysia was not markedly higher. With 16% of GDP accounted for by public spending in 1986, Malaysia was ranked higher than the Philippines (the 49th percentile), but it was not among the authoritarian regimes that had large public sectors. The strong Malaysian state was used by the government to intervene in the economy in many respects, particularly to eliminate wealth disparities between ethnic Malays and Chinese dating back to the colonial period (Pepinsky 2009, 62–3). Exemplified by the NEP, with its target of indigenous (primarily Malay) ownership of 30% of the corporate sector, the government in the early 1970s shifted toward active involvement in the economy (Jesudason 1989, 76–80; Gomez and Jomo 1997, 24). The Economic Planning Unit, which was responsible for steering the NEP, was situated under the prime minister, giving that office a greater say in choosing the projects that benefitted from the NEP. Thus, government control over the economy expanded and the opportunities for political patronage, which could potentially be employed to strengthen the stabilizing effect of elections, increased (Gomez and Jomo 1997, 25–6). The NEP was also followed by the creation of large state-owned enterprises such as the national oil company,

PETRONAS, and investment trust funds (e.g., Pernas), through which benefits and jobs were biased toward ethnic Malays, again allowing the rulers control over large parts of the economy (Pepinsky 2009, 65, 69–74; Jesudason 1989, 84–100; Gomez and Jomo 1997, 29–39).

In terms of natural resource income, there were also discrepancies between Malaysia and the Philippines. Whereas Malaysia's oil resources placed it in the top 20% of authoritarian regimes in terms of resource income as a share of GDP in the period, the Philippines was more modestly placed at the 50th percentile in 1986 (data from Haber and Menaldo 2011). Malaysia's oil production took off in the late 1970s and increased markedly throughout the 1980s, leaving extra resources in government hands (Jesudason 1989, 82–4).

Thus, when Marcos and Mahatir both conducted authoritarian elections in the 1980s, they did so with no intention of giving up power but also with varying levels of administrative and coercive capacity at their disposal and with varying degrees of control over the economy. But did these capacities affect the rulers' strategies, electoral outcomes, and regime stability?

Theoretical expectations

In terms of the capacities available to rulers, Malaysia and the Philippines approximate two of the three different scenarios sketched in Chapter 2. Malaysia, with its substantial levels of state capacity and non-negligible control over the economy, is expected to be a case of *stabilization by elections*. Recall from Chapter 2 that if the theoretical mechanisms indeed drive the relationship between elections, capacities, and authoritarian regime stability, the following implications follow (see also Table 2.4): a high-capacity case (where rulers preside over a strong administrative apparatus and/or control the economy) such as Malaysia should show the employment of subtle manipulation strategies, namely systemic manipulation, manipulation of voters' preference formation, restricted access to the vote, and legal and economic harassment of the opposition. These strategies should be directed from above, carried out by agents representing the ruling group, and lead to an incumbent victory. Finally, according to the existing literature on authoritarian elections, the election should have a number of stabilizing effects such as the prevention of elite defections, co-optation of the opposition, and generation of legitimacy (see Table 2.1, first column).

The Philippines, with the ruler's limited capacities both in terms of the administrative and coercive apparatuses and control over the economy, is a case of expected *breakdown by elections*. In this scenario (a regime where the autocrat is low on all capacities), some of the more overt strategies of electoral dominance, manipulation of voters' preference expression, manipulation of vote counting, and physical harassment of opponents could come into play, although they should largely fail to achieve the overall goal of regime stability. The use of subtle strategies should be limited. Rather than stabilizing the regime, a number of the destabilizing effects of elections, including elite defections, opposition mobilization, loss of legitimacy, and protests (which the rulers should not be able to effectively suppress), should play out, resulting in the breakdown of the authoritarian regime. In the following, I assess whether these observable implications of the theory were visible in the cases of Malaysia and the Philippines.

Electoral dynamics

Managed elections and authoritarian stability in Malaysia

Approaching the 1990 elections, the Malaysian party regime was (and still is) run by UMNO through the BN. Earlier elections under Mahatir were won with roughly 60% of votes and had been used to legitimate the new prime minister and co-opt important parts of the opposition. However, the 1990 general election followed a tumultuous period of elite defections. In 1987, two prominent ministers, Razaleigh and Musa, split with Mahatir's forces and ran for UMNO's presidency and vice presidency. Following an extremely close vote, Razaleigh and Musa lost the internal UMNO elections to Mahatir's team. A court dispute in 1987–1988 left Mahatir in control of the majority of the old UMNO, now "UMNO Baru," while Razaleigh and other prominent former UMNO members formed the opposition party Semangat '46.

When Mahatir called elections for October 11, 1990, BN faced its greatest opposition challenge so far. Semangat had negotiated alliances with both major opposition parties, the Democratic Action Party (DAP) and the Party Islam SeMalaysia (PAS), and offered voters an alternative to BN that also spanned ethnic divides. Although deprived of UMNO's resources and control over the state apparatus, Semangat had an extensive network of members (Nathan 1990, 213). In the face of this new competition, it is perhaps not surprising that for the first time in its history, the BN did not succeed in winning a true supermajority victory. It won 53.4%, yet, thanks to gerrymandered districts, still attained 127 seats, amounting to more than two-thirds of the 180 total seats in Parliament (Tan 2002).

Even lacking a supermajority of votes, the victory was substantial enough to have important stabilizing effects. First, it clearly signaled continued BN dominance and thus deterred further elite defections while co-opting the newly founded opposition back into UMNO. Brownlee reports how "Razaleigh's partisans [. . .] reaffiliated when they saw that their success depended on renewed loyalty to the ruling party rather than autonomous, ineffectual action among the opposition" (Brownlee 2007, 144). The BN had effectively demonstrated its monopoly on power and celebrated the 1995 general election with an impressive supermajority victory, gaining 65.2% of the votes. After the 1995 defeat, Razaleigh returned to UMNO. Second, the election legitimated continued BN rule by giving it yet another electoral mandate in the face of real opposition (Case 1993, 187–8). Thus, the election did indeed seem to have the stabilizing effects expected by the literature on electoral authoritarianism. But was this victory dependent on the subtle strategies of electoral dominance? And was the effectuation of these strategies dependent on BN's administrative capacity and/or economic control?

Systemic manipulation contributed significantly to BN's large victories under Mahatir. Malaysia's system of plurality victories in single-member constituencies was highly skewed in favor of UMNO, in part because of the side-lining and co-optation of the electoral commission in the 1950s and 1960s (Hing and Ong 1987, 118–23; Rachagan 1987, 217–18). By using the ability to construct districts with unequal numbers of voters, the rulers ensured that predominantly Malay districts were much smaller than non-Malay districts. This allowed UMNO to secure a dominant role in government as long as it was the most popular party among ethnic Malays, who comprised over 50% of the population (Hing and Ong 1987, 122).

Other types of systemic manipulation also worked in favor of the rulers. The nine-day campaign period, set by the incumbent, was the shortest yet. While this did not pose a problem to the BN candidates, who had already been campaigning for months, it was a huge disadvantage to the new opposition. The 1974 ban on open-air rallies left the opposition seriously disadvantaged. It had to hold more meetings to reach the same number of people and faced additional costs as indoor facilities needed to be hired and transport organized (Hing and Ong 1987, 124–5; Khong 1991, 21). BN candidates, on the other hand, could still spread their message through the largely government-owned press, and BN ministers were allowed to address large crowds (Crouch 1996, 84–8; Khong 1991, 21; Milne and Mauzy 1999, 116; Jomo 1996, 94–5).

The campaign also provides numerous examples of manipulation of voters' preference formation, founded in both administrative capacity and economic control. Some tactics were underpinned by control over state personnel. Workers at the Community Development Program (Kemas), a unit under the Ministry of Rural and National Development providing adult education, conducted pro-BN propaganda, and the Minister for Education ordered local officials to defend the government (Crouch 1996, 62–3). The BN's appointees at the municipal level would not let the opposition book community halls for indoor rallies, and the BN-controlled Village Security and Development Committees (JKKK) projected the BN as the provider of the community services (Hilley 2001, 86; Khong 1991, 21) and surveyed the population to identify opposition. If members of the JKKKs did not support the BN, they were threatened with removal (Crouch 1996, 62). Another invention for the 1990 election was the "adopted daughters" strategy, in which young, unemployed women who had participated in a state-sponsored training program were placed as "adopted daughters" with local families who were potential swing voters. The families received 200 USD and were expected to vote for UMNO – and if still in doubt as to whom to vote for on election day, the families were followed to the polling station by their adoptee (Crouch 1996, 63).

The large public sector also allowed BN excessive control over voters. The BN directly targeted constituencies with development projects and state support to win over voters (Khong 1991, 21–2; Crouch 1996, 61–2). Prior to the 1990 election, Pillai reported how "The government is freer with its finances now, giving extra income to civil servants and upgrading long-forgotten or long-promised services in areas where major blocks of votes are at stake" (Pillai 1990, 1387). And the Information Ministry admitted spending 172,000 USD "to encourage the voters to go to the polls" (Crouch 1996, 63; Khong 1991, 22). The change to the voting act prior to the 1990 election allowed for more effective targeting. Reducing the number of voters at each station to a maximum of 700, moving the vote-counting process to the polling stations, and giving each ballot a separate number allowed the incumbents to better monitor constituencies, identify opposition strongholds, and distribute state spoils accordingly (Crouch 1996, 60–1; Milne and Mauzy 1999, 116).

The more overt tactic of manipulating voters' preference expression was not as widespread but did occur. The incentives used were largely economic and drew on the state's access to public resources. In some places, voters were threatened with the removal of state support were they to support the opposition, and decisive vote buying was also reported in the most competitive districts (Khong 1991, 42).

In the 1990 election, flaws in the electoral roll – either registered voters whose names were missing from the roll or "phantom" voters included on the roll – affected around 300,000 voters. But rather than being a systematic attempt at manipulating access to the vote, the flaws were largely accepted as stemming from human error (Lim 2002, 115–16). Furthermore, in correspondence with theoretical expectations, manipulation of vote counting was not widely reported (Case 1991, 473; US Department of State 1990, 959–60). It thus seems the BN was more focused upon subtle manipulation of preference formation and electoral institutions than restricting access to the vote or conducting fraud on election day. Given the effective abuse of the state's administrative apparatus and economic control, fraud was not necessary (Khong 1991, 47).

But BN's electoral strategies were not solely targeted at voters. Particularly legal and economic harassment of the opposition was widely used. DAP faced an administrative hassle when it initially attempted to register as a party, and both DAP and PAS have been threatened with de-registration (Barraclough 1985, 809–10). DAP in particular was targeted and was refused permits to hold meetings and prosecuted for illegal assemblies and for raising "sensitive issues" (Barraclough 1985, 809–11). In 1990, opposition forces cancelled large meetings in three cases because of a lack of police permits (US Department of State 1990, 957). Throughout the 1980s, legal sanctions were implemented, and the police force was deployed against opposition parties and members. Although prosecution against opposition members was largely unsuccessful, its financial, emotional, and reputational costs still hampered opposition politicians (Barraclough 1985, 809).

However, in the context of the 1990 election, such repression remained largely legal and economic. Observers stress the preventive effect of the massive coercive apparatus, which was "always ready to intervene" (Crouch 1996, 95; see also Case 1993, 186–7; Tan 2002, 145), but instances of police violence were rare in the period (Ahmad 1987, 114). The coercive apparatus was not widely used to physically harass opposition members.

Following BN's victory, Semangat slowly dissolved. No major post-electoral protests arose, and the full employment of the coercive apparatus following the election never occurred. Prior and later events – the declaration of emergency law in 1969 and the violent crackdown on Anwar Ibrahim and his *Reformasi* movement in the late 1990s – suggest that both the ability and willingness to intervene by force were present, but given UMNO's electoral dominance fed by more subtle forms of manipulation, it simply was not necessary.

Thus, in many ways, the Malaysian elections of 1990 exhibit signs of the expected theoretical mechanisms. The case is summarized in Table 5.1. The ruling coalition employed its administrative capacity and control over the economy to dominate elections. All the more subtle strategies of manipulation apart from deliberate tampering with access to the vote were widely used. In particular, the ruling front relied on systemic manipulation, manipulation of voters' preference formation, and legal harassment of the opposition. The strategies were carried out by agents of the government, including a biased electoral commission, the police force, and a range of public servants at the national and local levels who worked to sustain BN rule. The strategies were thus dependent upon the rulers' control over an effective administrative apparatus as well as extant public resources. However, one more overt strategy was also used, as manipulation of voters' preference formation – primarily in the form of vote buying – was carried out in certain districts.

These strategies were sufficient to buy the BN a supermajority victory, and the remaining overt strategies of electoral dominance, election day fraud and violence against opposition and protesters, were not employed. The subtle manipulation strategies effectively limited the opposition, and the electoral victory served to both cement and legitimate UMNO rule and drive defected elites back into the fold. Could this incumbent victory be accounted for simply by UMNO's popularity? UMNO did indeed enjoy the support of a large part of the population, particularly the ethnic Malays. But this support was in part secured exactly through the coalition's control over the administration and the economy, which served to bind voters to the BN through preference manipulation. Furthermore, in spite of its public appeal, the coalition still unfolded the panoply of electoral manipulation – including the more overt strategy of vote buying – indicating that authoritarian capacities played an important part in securing electoral victory.

The case study of Malaysia in 1990 supports the findings in Chapter 3 that established a correlation between high levels of administrative capacity and regime stability following elections. In the case of Malaysia in 1990, most of the observable implications derived from the theoretical apparatus are present. This indicates that the statistical correlation between administrative capacity, elections, and regime breakdown could indeed stem from the electoral strategies that rulers endowed with high administrative capacity can carry out. However, there is evidence that the rulers in Malaysia used not only their administrative capacity but also their domination of the economy to control elections. These findings also support the results of the cross-national analyses. Although economic control was not found to correlate with regime stability following elections in the cross-national tests (Chapter 4), it was found to reduce the risk of breakdown following elections. The following section explores whether a different pattern is visible in the low-capacity case of the Philippines under Marcos.

Post-electoral collapse in the Philippines

The Philippines has a long history of elections, but in contrast to Malaysia, the Philippines had electoral turnovers until Marcos took power in a democratic election in 1965. He declared martial law in 1972, and in the following years elections took the form of plebiscites engineered to support Marcos's rule. After multi-party elections were reintroduced, the opposition boycotted the 1981 elections. The February 7, 1986 election was thus the first presidential election since 1969 in which Marcos and his newly invented New Society Movement (KBL) faced true opposition. The opposition was personified by Corazon Aquino, the widow of Marcos's long-time political enemy, Benigno Aquino, who had been assassinated, and by a former Marcos ally-cum-opponent, Salvador Laurel, who ran for vice president. On paper, Marcos won the violent and fraudulent elections. But rather than consolidate his rule, the election had the opposite effect. Before assessing signs of the effect of the flawed election on the final regime developments, I discuss the extent to which the Marcos leadership not only failed to employ the more subtle manipulation strategies that were heavily used in Malaysia, but was also restricted in carrying out even the more overt tactics due to lack of capacities.

In correspondence with theoretical expectations, the ruling group did not rely much on systemic manipulation. Marcos initially called elections for mid-January, but in order to achieve opposition acceptance, he was forced to postpone election day by three weeks, allowing the opposition more time to prepare (Timberman 1987, 240). Although the media was heavily biased against the opposition, there were no legal restrictions on opposition campaigning (Bonner 1987, 402; Thompson 1995, 146; US Department of State 1985, 849). The opposition campaigned vigorously across the archipelago, and two days before the election, they staged what was then the biggest rally in Philippine history, gathering between half a million and one million supporters in Manila.

However, other more subtle – and more capacity-demanding – strategies were carried out. Even though the Philippine government at the time could not be said to preside over a strong administrative apparatus nor efficiently control the economy, manipulation of voters' preference formation was still attempted. Government resources were employed as development projects were targeted at Marcos strongholds, and local governments were handed extra money to distribute (Bonner 1987, 242; Wurfel 1988, 298; Aquino 1986, 156).

Overt manipulation of voters' preference expression also took place as an estimated 500 million USD was set aside for vote buying (Thompson 1995, 142). But "the machinery didn't work quite as it had in the past" (Overholt 1986, 1161). Less fearful of army reprisals, government employees increasingly turned against the ruling front, carrying out their tasks less efficiently. Overholt describes how, after the assassination of Benigno Aquino, the rulers' attempt to arrange a pro-government demonstration among public employees backlashed when participants showed up with anti-Marcos posters (1986, 1157). Thus, the manipulation of voters' preference formation and expression was hampered by the decreasing threat from the coercive apparatus and the declining control over the bureaucracy. In desperation, the Marcos leadership resorted to violence, not only against opposition activists as discussed later, but also on election day in an attempt to hamper voters' preference expressions: on election day, four volunteers for the independent public poll watcher NAMFREL and close to a hundred other civilians died (Bonner 1987, 369–70; US Department of State 1985, 851, 1986, 795; Villegas 1987, 195).

Instead of subtle manipulation of voters' preference formation, two other strategies became central. The more subtle strategy of restricting access to the vote was widespread. Various observers estimate that between two and four million voters were disenfranchised (Timberman 1987, 245; Villegas 1987, 195; Thompson 1995, 143–4; US Department of State 1986, 801; Bonner 1987, 414–15). The procedure was not random but deliberately carried out by Marcos's agents, who collected information from previous elections to determine opposition strongholds and eliminate names from the voters' roll (Thompson 1995, 142–4; Aquino 1986, 156–7).

But in spite of the use of some of the more subtle forms of manipulation, including of voters' preference formation and their access to the vote, it was primarily outright fraud that secured Marcos his nominal victory. Whereas little fraud was reported in Malaysia, Marcos "won" the 1986 election in the counting process. The vote counting and tabulation process saw massive irregularities: ballot boxes were stuffed and stolen, tabulation sheets were bought for manipulation, teachers serving as electoral inspectors were paid off to ignore obvious fraud, and 30 computer operators quit the tallying, claiming that the results they had arrived at did not match the ones publicized in favor of Marcos (Bonner 1987, 424; Thompson 1995, 142; Timberman 1987, 245; Villegas 1987, 195). In the end, the official result gave Marcos 53.6% of the votes, whereas NAMFREL claimed that Aquino had won with 52% of the vote (Hartmann, Hassall, and Santos Jr 2002, 228) and the CIA put the share of votes won by the opposition even higher (Bonner 1987, 425). The importance of election day fraud for Marcos's victory is also highlighted by the discrepancies between observed and unobserved districts. In both the 1984 and 1986 elections, the ruling front fared markedly better in unobserved districts where no independent forces were present to report on election day manipulation (Thompson 1995, 129, 150).

Marcos still controlled an administrative apparatus capable of mustering the money and manpower to steal the elections through overt as well as subtle manipulation strategies. But the lack of capacity to fully pressure citizens into compliance before election day contributed to his vulnerability both internally and internationally (Thompson 1995, 150). He was forced to rely on blatant fraud under the eyes of national and international observers (Wurfel 1988, 299). Rather than subtly securing a victory, the ruler's desperate measures heightened the citizens' grievances. The results were heavily and openly contested by the opposition, the Church, and NAMFREL.

Working against the discreet generation of a supermajority victory was also the successful mobilization of an otherwise weak opposition. Rather than divide and rule, the elections "gave new purpose and focus to the widespread but fragmented opposition" (Timberman 1987, 241; see also Villegas 1987, 195). Pressured by the election, the opposition candidates, Aquino and Laurel, were forced to work together and agreed to run on the same slate despite disagreements (Bonner 1987, 391–2). Whereas the Islamic authorities in Malaysia were tightly controlled by the bureaucracy and prevented from supporting the opposition, the Catholic Church in the Philippines played a prominent oppositional role in the mid-1980s and, led by Manila's Archbishop Cardinal Sin, consistently spoke out against Marcos's rule without retaliation (Wurfel 1988, 279–80, 199; Thompson 1995, 117–18, 151–2). In the famous 1986 walkout from the official Philippine vote-tallying process, the protesting computer operators sought refuge in a nearby convent, whereas "the Malaysian state's longstanding tight control over Islamic practice and organization meant that mosques could not become 'free spaces' for oppositionists" (Slater 2010, 215).

Thus, incapable of effectively preventing opposition from emerging through legal and economic harassment, the Marcos leadership was forced to crack down violently. A wide variety of high-intensity coercion tactics were reported, ranging from the killings of groups of protesters and violence against opposition supporters in the years preceding the elections to the assassination of opposition politician Javier in the aftermath of the 1986 election (Bonner 1987, 369–70; US Department of State 1985, 851, 1986, 795; Villegas 1987, 195). These developments are especially striking in comparison to the limited reports of army and police brutality in Malaysia. But as with the instances of obvious fraud, these demonstrations of violence caused grievances that helped set in motion post-electoral protests. While such grievances are not unheard of in stable authoritarian regimes, the Philippine leadership no longer had the coercive power to effectively deal with them.

Although the heavy reliance on high-intensity coercion documents that Marcos possessed coercive capacity, the coercive apparatus was slowly disintegrating. A significant part of the political violence against both voters and opposition activists was committed by warlords who were affiliated with Marcos but not fully under his control (Thompson 1995, 142; US Department of State 1985, 850–1). Military officers were embarrassed by their low public standing and demoralized by the corruption of the military and its complete subservience to Marcos and his cronies (Overholt 1986, 1160).

On February 22, 1986, military leaders Enrile and Ramos defected, and the people, infuriated by blatant electoral fraud and violence, moved in to protect them. Within 24 hours, at least 20,000 people were on the streets in front of the camps in which the defectors had taken refuge. On several occasions throughout this so-called "People Power Revolution," the Marcos leadership could have retaliated but proved incapable of cracking down. Immediately after the defections and before the people took to the streets, the remaining part of the military could still have overwhelmed the rebels, but General Ver, appointed as army chief because of his loyalty rather than his professionalism, was unable to deliver a successful strategy (Thompson 1995, 156; Timberman 1987, 247; Overholt 1986, 1163). Similarly, when the crowds dispersed during the night several days after the defections, the military still proved incapable of attacking (Timberman 1987, 247; Wurfel 1988, 303). When Marcos finally deployed his army against the people, by now

128 *Elections in Malaysia and the Philippines*

numbering hundreds of thousands, officers refused to shoot and deserted (Overholt 1986, 1162–3; Villegas 1987, 196; Wurfel 1988, 303). Thus, the "People Power Revolution" is not only a story of massive post-electoral popular protests but also of a "hollow regime's inability to deploy force against an adversary" (Overholt 1986, 1162). A crackdown on protesters was never accomplished. Marcos and his allies departed the presidential palace in a helicopter and sought refuge in Hawaii while Aquino assumed the presidency.

In many respects, the 1986 Philippine election is the antithesis of the 1990 contests in Malaysia. The dynamics are summarized in Table 5.1. The leadership's

Table 5.1 Capacities, election strategies, and effects – Malaysia and the Philippines

		Malaysia		Philippines	
Conditioning variables	**DV IV** Multi-party election	+		+	
	Regime breakdown	–		+	
	Administrative capacity	High		Low	
	Coercive capacity	High		Low	
	Economic control	Medium/high		Low	
	Electoral victory	+		+	
	Stabilizing effects	Legitimacy Signaling Opposition co-optation Rent distribution			
	Destabilizing effects			Information on incumbent weakness Opposition mobilization Post-electoral protests	
	Strategies		*Carried out by government agents?*		*Carried out by government agents?*
Observable implications	**Subtle** Systemic manipulation	+	+	–	
	Manipulation of voters' preference formation	+	+	+	+
	Restricting access to the vote	–		+	+
	Legal and economic harassment of opposition	+	+	–	
	Manipulation of voters' preference expression	+	+	+	+/–
	Overt Manipulation of vote counting	–		+	+
	Physical harassment of opposition	–		+	+/–
	Violent crackdown on protesters	N/A		–	

capacities were limited, and that seemed to affect its electoral strategies. But rulers were not incapable of manipulating elections. In fact, through manipulation of voters' preference expression, access to the vote, and vote counting, and by physically harassing opposition politicians, they secured electoral victory. In this process, the ruling group did to some extent rely on its own agents, but it also experienced mass defections from both its coercive and administrative apparatus and had to draw in more loosely affiliated warlords to generate chaos on election day. Thus, contrary to expectations, Marcos's leadership succeeded in some attempts at both subtle and overt manipulation. But, conforming to expectations, the overt strategies resulted in widespread protests and loss of legitimacy. Marcos did not muster the capacities to either prevent or quell expressions of opposition activity and mass dissatisfaction, and the electoral victory ended in regime breakdown.

In contrast to theoretical expectations, it thus seems that even in the low-capacity case of the Philippines, Marcos and his ruling front could carry out more subtle forms of manipulation. But in line with the theoretical expectations, since these strategies were not sufficient and had to be combined with more overt measures, the result was a backlash that the rulers did not have the capacity to handle. There is also evidence that this relationship stems from a low-capacity autocrat's inability to successfully dominate elections. Thus, the case material from the Philippines in 1986 supports the cross-national findings of Chapter 4. The Philippine president lacked the capacities to effectively manipulate elections and, eventually, multi-party elections led to regime breakdown. But the ruler is not necessarily as incapacitated as expected: at least in the Philippines, a range of electoral manipulation – even more subtle forms – still unfolded.

Conclusion

These two typical cases representing the differing effects of authoritarian elections support the claim that the capacities available to the authoritarian ruling group shape the effect of elections because they enable or limit manipulative and repressive strategies. The ruling front in Malaysia during the 1990 election relied heavily on its administrative apparatus and control over the economy to carry out subtle forms of manipulation that secured a supermajority victory. Its impressive coercive apparatus was never put to use, as the rulers could dominate elections without it. The elections underpinned regime stability in numerous ways. In the Philippines, limited capacities restricted the room for maneuver. The leadership did attempt a number of strategies, both overt and subtle, but ultimately they largely backfired. Although they resulted in an election victory, this victory had all the adverse effects on stability that have been listed by the literature on authoritarian elections. The rulers lacked the capacity to prevent subversion by elections, including the coercive apparatus needed to quell protests, and the regime succumbed in the aftermath of elections.

The cases not only reveal an overall pattern; they also show that the correlation between elections, capacities, and stability established in Chapters 3–4 can potentially be explained by the theoretical framework on electoral strategies spelled out in Chapter 2, although alternative explanations for regime stability cannot be ruled out in the individual cases. The large-N analyses supported the overall claim that capacities condition the effect of elections. There was also support for H4 (elections are stabilizing at high levels of administrative capacity) as well as H6 (elections at low levels of authoritarian capacities are regime destabilizing). The quantitative evidence did not lend support to H5 (elections are stabilizing at high levels of economic control). The case study of Malaysia, however, shows that the ruling group used not only its administrative capacity but also its extensive control over economic activity – and a large public sector – to control elections. It seems that in Malaysia, high levels of administrative capacity and economic control not only helped the rulers avoid breakdown following election. It helped them stabilize their rule through the holding of elections.

However, the cases also reveal a number of nuances. Despite its low level of capacities, Marcos's ruling group was able to "win" an election, and it did carry out some of the more subtle strategies. But its heavy reliance on the more overt strategies and ultimately its failure to fully accomplish these strategies, namely the full-scale crackdown on opposition and protesters, led to its demise. In Malaysia, the ruling coalition primarily relied on more subtle manipulation strategies, but more overt measures were also taken, such as intensive vote buying. Overall, elections were so subtly manipulated and widely controlled that no major protests erupted. It thus seems that although the deployment of successful strategies of manipulation may secure a regime stabilization by election, this effect can be undermined if the leadership is forced to combine these strategies with more overt measures that can cause backlash. In the following chapter, I examine whether the destabilizing effects of such a backlash may be avoided if the autocrat masters the coercive capacity necessary to clamp down on opposition and protesters, as exemplified by President Robert Mugabe in Zimbabwe.

References

Adesnik, David, and Michael McFaul. 2006. "Engaging Autocratic Allies to Promote Democracy." *The Washington Quarterly* 29 (2): 5–26. doi:10.1162/wash.2006.29.2.7.

Ahmad, Zakaria Haji. 1987. "The Police and Political Development in Malaysia." In *Government and Politics of Malaysia*, edited by Zakaria Haji Ahmad. Singapore: Oxford University Press.

Aquino, Belinda. 1986. "The Philippines: End of an Era." *Current History* 85 (510): 155–85.

Barraclough, Simon. 1985. "The Dynamics of Coercion in the Malaysian Political Process." *Modern Asian Studies* 19 (4): 797–822.

Beach, Derek, and Rasmus Brun Pedersen. 2013. *Process-Tracing Methods: Foundations and Guidelines*. Ann Arbor: University of Michigan Press.

Bonner, Raymond. 1987. *Waltzing with a Dictator*. London: Macmillan.

Brownlee, Jason. 2007. *Authoritarianism in an Age of Democratization*. New York: Cambridge University Press.

Campbell, Donald T. 1975. "III. 'Degrees of Freedom' and the Case Study." *Comparative Political Studies* 8 (2): 178–93.

Case, William. 1991. "Comparative Malaysian Leadership: Tunku Abdul Rahman and Mahathir Mohamad." *Asian Survey* 31 (5): 456–73.

———. 1993. "Semi-Democracy in Malaysia: Withstanding the Pressures for Regime Change." *Pacific Affairs* 66 (2): 183–205.

Cheetham, Russel, and Edward Hawkins. 1976. *The Philippines: Priorities and Prospects for Development*. Washington: The World Bank.

Crouch, Harold. 1996. *Government and Society in Malaysia*. Ithaca: Cornell University Press.

Gerring, John. 2007. *Case Study Research: Principles and Practices*. Cambridge: Cambridge University Press. www.lavoisier.fr/livre/notice.asp?id=OA3WRSAA63SOWO.

Gomez, Edmund, and K. S. Jomo. 1997. *Malaysia's Political Economy: Politics, Patronage and Profits*. Cambridge: Cambridge University Press.

Haber, Stephen, and Victor Menaldo. 2011. "Do Natural Resources Fuel Authoritarianism? A Reappraisal of the Resource Curse." *American Political Science Review* 105 (1): 1–26.

Hamilton-Hart, Natasha. 2002. *Asian States, Asian Bankers: Central Banking in South-East Asia*. Ithaca: Cornell University Press.

Hartmann, Christof, Graham Hassall, and Soliman Santos Jr. 2002. "Philippines." In *Elections in Asia and the Pacific: A Data Handbook*. Vol. 2, edited by Dieter Nohlen, Florian Grotz, and Christof Hartmann. Oxford: Oxford University Press.

Hilley, John. 2001. *Malaysia: Mahatirism, Hegemony and the New Opposition*. London: Zed Books.

Hing, Lee Kam, and Michael Ong. 1987. "Malaysia." In *Competitive Elections in Developing Countries*, edited by Myron Weiner and Erun Özbudun, 112–46. Durham, NC: Duke University Press.

Hutchcroft, Paul. 2000. "Colonial Masters, National Politicos, and Provincial Lords: Central Authority and Local Autonomy in the American Philippines, 1900–1913." *The Journal of Asian Studies* 59 (2): 277–306.

Jesudason, James. 1989. *Ethnicity and the Economy: The State, Chinese Business, and Multinationals in Malaysia*. Singapore: Oxford University Press.

Jomo, K. S. 1996. "Elections' Janus Face: Limitations and Potential in Malaysia." In *The Politics of Elections in Southeast Asia*, edited by R. H. Taylor, 90–113. Cambridge: Cambridge University Press.

Khong, Kim Hoong. 1991. "Malaysia's General Election 1990: Continuity, Change, and Ethnic Politics." 74. Research Notes and Discussions Paper. Singapore.

Lim, Hong Hai. 2002. "Electoral Politics in Malaysia: 'Managing' Elections in a Plural Society." In *Electoral Politics in Southeast and East Asia*, edited by Aurel Croissant, Gabriele Bruns, and Marei John, 101–48. Singapore: Friedrich Ebert Stiftung. https://aceproject.org/ero-en/regions/asia/MY/01361005.pdf/view.

Mahoney, James. 2003. "Strategies of Causal Assessment in Comparative Historical Analysis." In *Comparative Historical Analysis in the Social Sciences*, edited by James Mahoney and Dietrich Rueschemeyer, 337–72. New York: Cambridge University Press.

Milne, Robert Stephen, and Diane K. Mauzy. 1999. *Malaysian Politics under Mahatir*. London: Routledge.

Munro-Kua, Anne. 1996. *Authoritarian Populism in Malaysia*. New York: St. Martin's Press, Inc.

Nathan, K. S. 1990. "Malaysia in 1989: Communists End Armed Struggle." *Asian Survey* 30 (2): 210–20.

Noble, Lela Garner. 1986. "Politics in the Marcos Era." In *Crisis in the Philippines: The Marcos Era and Beyond*, edited by John Bresnan, 70–113. New Jersey: Princeton University Press.

Overholt, William. 1986. "The Rise and Fall of Ferdinand Marcos." *Asian Survey* 26 (11): 1137–63.

Penn World Table. 2013. "Penn World Table." https://pwt.sas.upenn.edu/php_site/pwt_index.php.

Pepinsky, Thomas. 2009. *Economic Crises and the Breakdown of Authoritarian Regimes: Indonesia and Malaysia in Comparative Perspective*. New York: Cambridge University Press.

Pillai, M. G. 1990. "Election Prospects in Malaysia." *Economic and Political Weekly* 25 (26): 1387–8.

Puthucheary, Mavis. 1987. "The Administrative Elite." In *Government and Politics of Malaysia*, edited by Zakaria Haji Ahmad. Singapore: Oxford University Press.

Rachagan, Sothi. 1987. "The 1986 Parliamentary Elections in Peninsular Malaysia." *Southeast Asian Affairs* 14 (1): 217–35.

Singer, David, Stuart Bremer, John Stuckey, and Bruce Russett. 1972. "Capability Distribution, Uncertainty, and Major Power War, 1820–1965." In *Peace, War, and Numbers*, 19–48. Beverly Hills: Sage.

Slater, Dan. 2010. *Ordering Power: Contentious Politics and Authoritarian Leviathans in Southeast Asia*. New York: Cambridge University Press.

Tan, Kevin. 2002. "Malaysia." In *Elections in Asia and the Pacific: A Data Handbook*. Vol. 2, edited by Dieter Nohlen, Florian Grotz, and Christof Hartmann. Oxford: Oxford University Press.

Thompson, Mark. 1995. *The Anti-Marcos Struggle*. New Haven: Yale University Press.

Timberman, David. 1987. "Unfinished Revolution: The Philippines in 1986." *Southeast Asian Affairs* 14: 239–63.

US Department of State. 1985. *1985 Human Rights Report: Philippines*. Washington, DC: Bureau of Democracy, Human Rights, and Labor.

———. 1986. *1986 Human Rights Report: Philippines*. Washington, DC: Bureau of Democracy, Human Rights, and Labor.

———. 1990. *1990 Human Rights Report: Malaysia*. Washington, DC: Bureau of Democracy, Human Rights, and Labor.

Villegas, Bernardo. 1987. "The Philippines in 1986: Reconstruction in the Post-Marcos Era." *Asian Survey* 27 (2): 194–205.

Wurfel, David. 1977. "Martial Law in the Philippines: The Methods of Regime Survival." *Pacific Affairs* 50 (1): 5–30.

———. 1988. *Filipino Politics: Development and Decay*. Ithaca: Cornell University Press.

6 Electoral ups and downs, state capacity, and economic control in Zimbabwe

The pressure was on for the 2008 parliamentary and presidential elections in Zimbabwe. President Robert Mugabe and his Zimbabwe African National Union-Patriotic Front (ZANU[PF]) had ruled the country and regularly won non-democratic elections since independence in 1980. But opposition to Mugabe's authoritarian rule had built up through civil society since the mid-1990s. The Southern African Development Community (SADC) headed mediation efforts aimed at free, fair, and peaceful 2008 elections. Indeed, the first election round was deemed relatively peaceful, and when the election results were finally released, they revealed an opposition victory for the two separate fronts of the Movement for Democratic Change (MDC) in combination. The presidential election results put opposition candidate Morgan Tsvangirai ahead of incumbent President Mugabe, but the official results did not give Tsvangirai the required majority, and a second round was needed. Widespread violence orchestrated by the ruling party followed. In the end, Tsvangirai withdrew from the second round, and Mugabe proceeded to win the presidency. Prolonged negotiations headed by SADC resulted in a Global Political Agreement (GPA) that stipulated the rules for a coalition government with Tsvangirai as prime minister and Mugabe as president, with continued control over the security apparatus.

Under the framework of the GPA, Zimbabwe headed toward the 2013 elections under the so-called Inclusive Government (IG). The road was bumpy and plagued by power struggles both within and between the MDC and ZANU(PF) as well as a severe economic crisis. When the 2013 elections approached, although ZANU(PF) continuously sought to dominate the process and prominent SADC figures declared that sufficient electoral reforms had not been implemented (Research & Advocacy Unit 2013b), the MDC factions agreed to proceed with the election, believing that they would win (Raftopoulos 2013a, 977). The elections were, in comparison with the post-electoral violence in 2008, peaceful (Raftopoulos 2008; ZESN 2013). The results revealed a sound incumbent victory. Mugabe had attained 61% of votes, and ZANU(PF) had secured a great majority of parliamentary seats. The MDC parties declared the elections fraudulent and exited the IG, leaving Zimbabwe once again to authoritarian one-party rule by ZANU(PF).

This chapter investigates electoral dynamics in Zimbabwe in 2008 and 2013. The claim is not that authoritarian capacities were the sole cause of the electoral outcomes in the particular cases. Rather, the chapter employs pattern-matching and assesses the degree to which the strategies used by the incumbent, and the results thereof, conform to the theoretical expectations of Chapter 2. As was the case for Malaysia, Zimbabwe can in many respects be classified as a high-capacity regime. In this chapter, I first analyze the extent to which the strategies leading to the 2008 victory were similar to those proposed in Chapter 2 – and thus to those practiced in Malaysia in 1990. Second, I ask whether and how the victory and the employed strategies affected regime stability. For this purpose, the analyses are extended to include the 2013 elections. Noting that the 2008 elections involved heavy reliance on the security apparatus, I ask how Mugabe – following widespread violence and a resulting loss of legitimacy in 2008 – moved on to secure victory in largely peaceful elections in 2013 and whether the changed tactics proved to have a different effect on long-term regime stability.

Method and case selection: Zimbabwe in the 2000s

In Chapters 3 and 4, the quantitative analyses supported the claim that the relationship between elections and regime stability is conditioned by administrative capacity and economic control. But unlike administrative capacity and economic control, coercive capacity was not found to condition the effect of authoritarian elections. However, these findings could be dependent on the proxies available to capture coercive capacity on a cross-national scale. Whereas coercive capacity was defined as encompassing all arms of the coercive apparatus, including the police and private militias, only data on military capacity are available across countries and over time. Chapter 5 showed that in the high-capacity case of Malaysia, coercive capacity was not put to use, and the ruling party – in correspondence with theoretical expectations – relied primarily on administrative capacity and economic control. In the Philippines, these capacities were too low for the ruling group to dominate elections through subtle measures, and when protests erupted, the coercive apparatus failed. However, the counterfactual – that an efficient and loyal coercive force could have secured an incumbent victory (the scenario of *electoral survival*) – cannot be confirmed from this scenario of *breakdown by election*. Furthermore, although economic control significantly conditions the effect of elections, the effect primarily runs through a large public sector and thus supports accounts of the PRI's abuse of public money in 20th century Mexico. However, some autocrats control the economy in more informal ways.

The case of Zimbabwe is chosen to allow for a more thorough assessment of the role of the coercive apparatus as well as the more informal methods of economic control. At least on paper, Zimbabwe in 2008 was a typical case of *stabilization by election*. The capacities available to the ruling coalition were high, the election was won, and the regime did not break down. But as the analysis will demonstrate, the use of the coercive apparatus was markedly more abundant than expected from a high-capacity case. Employing the strategy of pattern-matching, the first part of this chapter analyzes the degree to which the dynamics surrounding the 2008 election correspond to the observable implications of the scenario of *stabilization by election* derived in Chapter 2. The expectations are summarized later. In the second part of the chapter, I turn to the 2013 elections and ask what changed over time as the costs of relying on repression became evident. Although the economy was in disarray, the case of Zimbabwe during the 2013 elections demonstrates more informal ways of controlling the economy including the appropriation of natural resources administered directly by party members rather than the Ministry of Finance. Throughout, the analyses rely on a combination of academic literature, reports from human rights activists, newspaper material, and interviews conducted in Harare and Bulawayo in May–June 2014.[1]

The 2008 elections in Zimbabwe: winning office, losing legitimacy

Zimbabwe has been ruled by Mugabe and ZANU(PF) since independence from white rule in 1980 and until Mugabe was unseated by the military and elements in his own party in November 2017. Multi-party elections haven been held throughout the period. In the 1980s, parliamentary multi-party elections were primarily between ZANU(PF) and its rival guerilla movement from the independence struggle, PF-ZAPU. But after a period of hardboiled ZANU(PF) repression of PF-ZAPU, the party was merged into ZANU(PF) in 1987, and Mugabe was sworn in to the new post of president. In the following elections, now for both Parliament and the presidential office, only smaller parties competed against Mugabe and ZANU(PF) (Darnolf 2000; Baumhögger 1999).

In 1999, a new party, the MDC, sprang out of the union movement, and with Morgan Tsvangirai as leader it formed an opposition to ZANU(PF). The two parties contested non-democratic elections in 2000, 2002, and 2005, which ZANU(PF) won with 49–60% of the vote. In 2005, the MDC split into two factions, the smaller MDC and the larger MDC-T led by Tsvangirai. Although the MDC parties led separate campaigns, they both remained in staunch opposition to ZANU(PF), and in the 2008 elections, Mugabe thus faced an established opposition. Before examining electoral dynamics in the 2008 elections, I assess the level of capacities prior to the elections.

Authoritarian capacities in Zimbabwe prior to the 2008 elections

Administrative capacity

Judged by the available government statistics, the Zimbabwean administrative force was strong compared to many of its African neighbors. The tax-to-GDP ratio averaged 0.34 between 1984 and 1999, far higher than neighboring countries (0.23 in South Africa and 0.18 in Mozambique) and the East African states of Tanzania (0.16), Kenya (0.21), and Uganda (0.03) (data from Hendrix 2010). Although preferences for taxation are partly determined by ideology and not merely capacity, this level of extraction also demonstrates a capacity on the part of the administration to extract resources. Furthermore, Zimbabwe had registered 168,000 central government employees in 1990 and 174,000 in 1996 (Therkildsen 2001, app. 3), translating into a little less than 2% of the population. In comparison, the roughly equally sized neighboring countries of Zambia and Mozambique employed between 0.6% and 1.4% of the population and South Africa between 3% and 3.5% (Therkildsen 2001, app. 3). However, it is generally noted that national accounts data are often unreliable in developing countries in particular, and a qualitative assessment of the strength of the administrative force is therefore also necessary (Jerven 2013).

Zimbabwe's administrative apparatus has traditionally been described as strong and well-developed. Upon independence, Zimbabwe inherited a strong, centralized, technocratic state from the previous Rhodesian regime (Alexander and McGregor 2013, 751; Bratton and Masunungure 2011, 8). The state was expansive in comparison to many African regimes of the 20th and 21st centuries. But the increasingly tumultuous post-independence period also saw an erosion of the state apparatus, and the severe economic crisis in particular resulted in "the loss of the state's capacity to supply basic services for its citizens" after 2000 (Raftopoulos 2008, 226; Bratton and Masunungure 2011, 16–17; Meredith 2002, 159–61). The economy collapsed, and governance was widely criticized. The traditionally high public sector wages were undercut by hyperinflation, and the crisis – both economically and politically – also led to a massive brain drain, pushing well-educated Zimbabweans to migrate (Naing 2012, 215–17). Thus, in spite of Zimbabwe's tax extraction rate-to-GDP ratio of 0.26 in 2006, placing it in the 85th percentile of all authoritarian regimes that year, its administrative capacity had been dealt a blow over the past decade. Although its administrative capacity may have remained higher than that of many other African regimes, it was clearly at its lowest in the post-independence period.

ZANU(PF) remained in tight control over the administrative resources still available. Since independence, ZANU(PF) had sought to establish its control over the state, compromising local government structures and allowing the party's central Politburo to control government ministries (Muzondidya 2008, 178). In parallel to the crumbling of parts of the state apparatus, the 2000s saw an increasing politicization of the civil services and the courts (Alexander and McGregor 2013, 752; Bratton and Masunungure 2011, 45–6; Naing 2012, 217–18). Mugabe retained control over appointments to all important positions in the civil service (Meredith 2002, 79). Veterans of the liberation struggle, along with military officers and other known ZANU(PF) supporters, were placed across the administrative force and judges were appointed on a partisan basis (Raftopoulos 2008, 213). Thus, ZANU(PF) slowly merged itself with the state (interview with anonymous political science professor). As one civil society activist repeatedly explained, "ZANU is the state and the state is ZANU" (interview with anonymous civil society activist, Harare).

In sum, while Zimbabwe's ruling party has traditionally presided over a strong state and still controls networks of public employees that span the territory, its administrative capacity had eroded during the decade leading up to the 2008 elections, both due to the economic crisis and the politicization of the state apparatus. Nevertheless, the state structures and employees that remained were tightly controlled by and interwoven into the ruling party.

Coercive capacity

The coercive apparatus of Zimbabwe has its origins both in its predecessor, the colonial state of Rhodesia, and in the guerilla movements of the liberation war. Many mercenaries and soldiers of the colonial regime left after independence, and there are large discrepancies in reports on the size of the army following independence (Jackson 2014, 53–4). But British advisers stayed on, and the creation of a national army was successful (Jackson 2014, 57).

Military spending per capita had steadily decreased since independence and in 2007 was significantly lower than that of most neighboring countries, reflecting the economic crisis (Raftopoulos 2008, 211). Nonetheless, Zimbabwe's military spending placed the country just above the 50th percentile for authoritarian regimes in 2007 (data from Singer et al. 1972), and the only country in the region with greater military capability is South Africa (Jackson 2014, 62).

Today, the army boasts manpower, a strong organizational structure, and an array of repressive laws inherited from the colonial era. The Joint Operations Command (JOC), originally set up by the Rhodesian rulers, retains its position as the central organ coordinating the Zimbabwe National Army (ZNA), the air force, prison service, the Central Intelligence Organization (CIO), and the Zimbabwe Republic Police (ZRP). There is also a special military wing, the Fifth Brigade, which was active in the 1980s and was behind the killings of 20,000 civilians during Operation *Gukurahundi*, aimed at oppressing ZAPU, the other liberation-era guerilla group and ZANU(PF)'s only competitor for power in the early post-independence period (Jackson 2014, 58–9). The brigade was trained in North Korea, had the specific purpose of dealing with internal trouble, and answered directly to President Mugabe (Ndlovu-Gatsheni 2006, 66).

The army and police can refer to a great selection of repressive laws covering everything from public order to privacy, such as the Law and Order Maintenance Act retained from colonial times, the Public Order and Safety Act (POSA), instated in 2002 and aimed at regulating public meetings and gatherings, and the Access to Information and Protection of Privacy Act, also introduced in 2002 to regulate the media environment. One activist in Bulawayo, when I asked which law he was typically detained under, referred to an array of different laws that the police would usually invoke (interview with anonymous journalist and civil society activist, Bulawayo).

A large part of the coercive apparatus is of a more informal character and is not captured by measures of military spending. The veterans of the liberation struggle, some 40,000 of whom were not integrated into the army upon independence (Human Rights Watch 2002, 8), are organized in the Zimbabwe Liberation War Veterans' Association (ZLWVA), tied to ZANU(PF) through pensions and land, and supplied with military arms (Ndlovu-Gatsheni 2006, 72; Kriger 2003). They were the main force behind the land evictions of the "Fast Track" land reforms discussed later. Furthermore, ZANU(PF) controls the youth militias such as Chipangano, which is known to control the Mbare Township in Southern Harare. The coercive capacity of Zimbabwe's current government is thus not solely dependent on the army – the security services have several important branches complemented by private militias.

The control that ZANU(PF) exerts over the administration is even more pronounced in the security sector, leading one expert to state that "the factor that best explains the regime is the symbiosis between the party and the security sector" (Masunungure 2011, 47; see also Ndlovu-Gatsheni 2006). After independence, the army was dominated by ZANU(PF)'s military wing, ZANLA, and ZANU(PF) remains in control of the army, air force, intelligence, police, and prison services (Bratton and Masunungure 2008, 48). The loyalty of every branch of the security apparatus is secured in part by the history of the liberation struggle, ensuring that most top ZANU(PF) politicians throughout the 2000s had fought side by side with serving high-ranking military personnel (Ndlovu-Gatsheni 2006, 74). The then-head of the Zimbabwe Defense Force (ZDF), the army and air force in combination, General Vitalis Zvinavashe, famously stepped forward in 2001 to announce that the armed forces supported ZANU(PF) and would not tolerate leadership by anyone who had not fought in the war for independence (Tendi 2013; Ndlovu-Gatsheni 2006, 52–3). The history of the liberation struggle is also used as propaganda during training of youth militias (interview with anonymous political science professor; Ndlovu-Gatsheni 2006, 72–3).

Patronage also plays an important part (Bratton and Masunungure 2008, 47; Jackson 2014). Military officers are offered lucrative contracts and leading positions in, for instance, the Reserve Bank, the Zimbabwe Electoral Commission (ZEC), the National Oil Company, and ZANU(PF)'s central organs (Bratton and Masunungure 2008, 49; Ndlovu-Gatsheni 2006, 75–6; Dawson and Kelsall 2011, 20). Additionally, war veterans benefit from government subsidies as well as the land reforms discussed in the following section (Raftopoulos 2008, 211–12; Bratton and Masunungure 2011, 22).

Thus, while Zimbabwe's coercive force contributed to its control over the economy, as discussed later, economic resources also helped ensure the loyalty of the coercive apparatus, which is among the strongest in the region.

Economic control

According to two observers, "The major prize that ZANU-PF won at independence was the apparatus of the state, including its military machinery and economic resources" (Bratton and Masunungure 2008, 44). Based on the index of economic control employed in Chapter 7, combining data on government share of GDP, business regulations, and natural resources, Zimbabwe was in 2007 placed at the 77th percentile of all authoritarian regimes. Although the Zimbabwean economy has dipped several times since independence, this section argues that the government to a large extent controls economic activity within its territory, including farm land, exports, mineral revenues, trade, and employment opportunities.

The state inherited by Mugabe and his ruling group was one "that deeply penetrated the economy" (Bratton and Masunungure 2011, 8), but sources suggest that two-thirds of the economy was still in foreign hands at independence (Dawson and

Elections, capacity, and control in Zimbabwe 139

Kelsall 2011, 8). From 1980 onward, ZANU(PF) moved to gain control over the economy (Magure 2012, 69), and during the 1990s, the policy of "indigenization" of the economy was used to distribute patronage through a system not unlike that of Malaysia's pro-Malay economic policies (Raftopoulos and Compagnon 2003, 24–6). The government set in place state-owned enterprises or companies held by the party itself, such as the M & S Syndicate, which held party properties, and Zidco Holdings, focused on the import and export business. The latter was said to employ 10,000 people by 1992 and had favorable access to government contracts (Dawson and Kelsall 2011, 18–19; Meredith 2002, 82). The government gained control over the prices of agricultural outputs, controlled salaries, and attempted to regulate the mining sector through the Minerals Marketing Corporation (Markowitz 2013, 140–1; Raftopoulos and Compagnon 2003, 19). In 1992, then-Minister of Justice Emmerson Mnangagwa estimated ZANU(PF)'s assets and businesses at around 75 million USD (Meredith 2002, 82).

These economic activities contributed to the party's funds and allowed ample room for patronage (Bratton and Masunungure 2011, 28–9; Muzondidya 2008, 171–2; Dawson and Kelsall 2011, 9, 19). Mugabe's closest companions became some of the richest people in the country through lucrative business contracts and opportunities to trade foreign currency (Bratton and Masunungure 2011, 28; Meredith 2002, 82; Dawson and Kelsall 2011, 13). The network of patronage extended across the country, as ZANU(PF) supporters on the ground received farming supplies, government funding, and housing (Markowitz 2013, 141; Zamchiya 2013; Raftopoulos and Compagnon 2003, 19–20).

But the Structural Adjustment Packages and economic crisis of the 1990s limited this original state control over the economy (Dawson and Kelsall 2011, 13) and the trend of economic decline continued more or less uninterrupted. Going into the 2008 elections, the Zimbabwean economy was in a state of crisis. The early 2000s saw recession, hyperinflation, a shortage of foreign currency, a collapse of the agricultural sector, food shortages, shortages of basic commodities and farming inputs, enormous poverty, an unemployment rate above 80%, and a corresponding upsurge in the informal sector (Tarisayi 2009, 12–14). Such economic decline can potentially unsettle a government, but it can also render more citizens dependent on the resources controlled by the rulers (Alexander and McGregor 2013, 758). Zimbabwe's recent history provides several examples of this latter dynamic. According to Le Bas, ZANU(PF)'s power from 2000 onward was increasingly based on "the extralegal appropriation and redistribution of resources along partisan lines" (LeBas 2014, 57).

Most prominent among the resources controlled by the ruling group in Zimbabwe is perhaps land. A great part of arable land was in the hands of white commercial farmers throughout colonial times and, by 2000, white farmers still occupied nearly 30% of land while more than a million black Zimbabweans were restricted to arid "communal areas," resulting in "a significant land hunger" (Human Rights Watch 2002, 2). Land redistribution schemes had been in place since independence but did not succeed in significantly redistributing land (Muzondidya 2008, 172; Human Rights Watch 2002, 6–7; Meredith 2002, chap. 7).

Some observers speculate that one reason why the land question was not settled in the 1990s was the government's desire to use it for political gains (Hellum and Derman 2004).

In 2000, the Mugabe government took advantage of the sensitive process of land redistribution through the so-called "Fast Track" land reforms. First, property rights were weakened through legal measures, and the right to compensation following land acquisitions was limited (Hellum and Derman 2004). Government control over the Supreme Court helped speed up this process. Second, farms were designated for acquisition, and war veterans and youth militias, sometimes with the help of the CIO, army, or police and guided by ZANU(PF), invaded commercial farms and evicted both owners and farm workers, with stories of violence and other human rights violations reaching the international press (Human Rights Watch 2002; Sachikonye 2003, 30–2; Meredith 2002, 169). Thus, the ruling front's coercive capacity contributed to strengthening its economic control. By 2002, 90% of white farmers had had their land acquired by the government, totaling 11 million hectares (Sachikonye 2003, 15).

On top of the multiple and much-debated consequences for the Zimbabwean economy in the long term, these land acquisitions had political effects that also matter to electoral dynamics. First, they were a form of harassment of the opposition and sought to discourage opposition activity, as white farm owners and black farm workers were predominantly opposition supporters (Human Rights Watch 2002, 20–3; Meredith 2002, 169). Second, the land acquisitions provided ZANU(PF) with enormous resources for patronage. Numerous studies document how the land was distributed on a partisan basis and how particularly ZANU(PF) and military elites along with the war veterans, but also lower-level ZANU(PF) supporters, have benefitted from it (Marongwe 2011; Human Rights Watch 2002, 27–31; Dawson and Kelsall 2011, 14–15; Matyszak and Reeler 2013, 12–13). Third, of at least 320,000 people employed on white-owned commercial farms before 2000 (and up to two million people who depended on these for their livelihood, equaling 20% of the population), 200,000 were evicted by 2003 (Sachikonye 2003, 15). The farm invasions thus diminished the economic independence of a great part of the population (Sachikonye 2003, 39–41). Land thus forms an important source of government control over the economy that can be exploited at election time but is not captured in the typical, cross-national measures of economic control used in Chapter 4.

In addition to its firm control over land, the government controls the economy in a number of other formal and informal ways. The granting of business licenses and access to foreign currency has been discussed previously, and privileged access to trading in foreign currency became an especially attractive perk during hyperinflation (Bratton and Masunungure 2011, 28). The scarcity of essential goods during the economic crisis also made other strategies even more valuable. Price regulations were used to supply ZANU(PF) supporters with cheap goods (Dawson and Kelsall 2011, 16), and privileged access to import licenses became even more attractive (Bratton and Masunungure 2011, 28).

On top of its control over business licenses, trade agreements, foreign currency, and various forms of formal government benefits such as agricultural support and housing, the government also sought to control the informal sector, especially through its coercive apparatus. ZANU(PF)-controlled youth militias continued to dominate the informal economy even in MDC-run areas. In Mbare in central Harare, stalls at the market – on which thousands of people depend for their living – were distributed (for a significant fee) by the Chipangano militia to known ZANU(PF) supporters, and the militia also financed its activities by demanding fees from intercity buses for accessing the local bus terminal (McGregor 2013; LeBas 2014, 62; Dawson and Kelsall 2011, 10–11; interview with anonymous political science professor; interview with Eddie Cross, MDC-T parliamentarian, Bulawayo). Again, such informal ways of controlling the economy are not captured by measures of economic control, including government spending and regulation of business, used for the cross-national analyses of Chapter 4.

In sum, in spite of economic catastrophe, Mugabe and his ruling group retained control over rents from land, trade, and natural resources (Dawson and Kelsall 2011, 22). And while the continuing economic crisis pushed more people into the informal sector and left fewer dependent on the government for salaries (Tarisayi 2009), people still depended on the government for patronage in the form of everything from land and farming equipment to subsidies, housing, or access to stalls at the local Harare markets.

Theoretical expectations for the 2008 elections

In sum, judging by the statistics employed in Chapters 3–4, Zimbabwe was a high-capacity regime. Approaching the case qualitatively with a broader range of evidence may detract slightly from this assessment. The state apparatus had undoubtedly eroded prior to the 2008 elections and the economy was in shambles. But Zimbabwe was not a low-capacity regime. It scored at least moderate to high on all three types of capacities. Thus, in the following sections, I hold the evidence of first the 2008 and then the 2013 elections against the observable implications of the *stabilization by elections* scenario presented in Chapter 4. Recall that the following implications of the theory were derived: a high-capacity case (where rulers control a strong bureaucracy and/or dominate the economy – coercive capacity could be either high or low) should rely on subtle manipulation strategies, namely systemic manipulation, manipulation of voters' preference formation, restricted access to the vote, and legal and economic harassment of the opposition. The strategies should be directed from above, carried out by agents of the ruling group, and lead to an incumbent victory. The overt manipulation strategies should not prove necessary. Finally, according to the existing literature on authoritarian elections, the election should have a number of stabilizing effects, including the prevention of elite defections, co-optation of the opposition, and generation of legitimacy (see Table 2.4).

Electoral dynamics in 2008

The 2008 elections proceeded in two rounds. The first round was for the presidency, Parliament, Senate, and local councils and was held on March 29. The main contestants were the ruling ZANU(PF), led by President Mugabe, and the two opposition parties, MDC-T, headed by presidential candidate and original opposition leader Tsvangirai, and MDC, led by Mutumbara. Makoni, a former ZANU(PF) finance minister, ran as an independent with support from Mutambara.

The first electoral round was described as the most peaceful in Zimbabwe's recent history (Masunungure 2009b, 61; Matyszak 2009, 137–8). The government did employ its capacities to manipulate elections, and reported issues include propaganda and hate speech, a biased media, the banning of opposition rallies, abuse of government funds for vote buying, and a biased voter registration (Matyszak 2009; Masunungure 2009b; ZESN 2008). But on polling day, the domestic observer organization ZESN noted major problems at only 3% of polling stations (ZESN 2008, 42), and the results were generally recognized as representing the will of the people (Masunungure 2009a, 79). The result was astonishing: MDC-T had won 99 seats, MDC had won ten, and ZANU(PF) 97. ZANU(PF) had thus lost its parliamentary majority. However, the results of the presidential election were not immediately announced, and things changed dramatically in the second round and the aftermath of the first round, on which this analysis focuses.

Government strategies and resources in the second round of the 2008 elections

The most notable issue of the first round of the presidential election was the delayed announcement of results, and this shaped the second electoral round. ZEC, with its six members as well as its head appointed by the president, is not recognized as an unpartisan institution (Linington 2009, 98–9). After the announcement of parliamentary results, the release of presidential results was postponed, and they did not reach the public until 32 days later – a process that observers judged should have taken no more than 36 hours (Matyszak 2009, 141). In comparison, the announcement of the results of the second round, which Mugabe won, took only 24 hours (ZESN 2008, 65).

When the first-round results of the presidential elections were finally revealed, Tsvangirai had attained 47.9% of votes, Mugabe 43.2%. But seeing that no presidential candidate had achieved 50% plus one additional vote, a run-off presidential election was announced to take place on June 27.

Whether the period in which results were withheld was used to tamper with tabulation procedures in order to ensure that the opposition did not come out with 50% plus one victory is debated (Matyszak 2009, 141–2; Makumbe 2009, 128–9). But the prolonged period between the two rounds of the presidential election – the constitution allows for only 21 days between the two rounds (ZESN 2008, 21–2) – with the government allegedly having had access to the results from the outset (Masunungure 2009a, 81; ZESN 2008, 51; International Crisis Group 2008, 3), allowed the government to prepare its strategies in the second round (Matyszak 2009, 141–2). Overt manipulation of the administration of elections thus initiated the second electoral round of 2008 and the accompanying tactics that were enabled by the ruler's dominance over the administrative apparatus, including the electoral commission. The following section discusses which strategies were used and whether administrative, coercive, and economic resources were essential in ensuring incumbent President Mugabe his eventual victory in the second round in June 2008.

Whereas systemic manipulation has not been raised as an issue in the second round of the 2008 elections, manipulation of voters' preference formation and expression are emphasized throughout reports. A range of more subtle ways of manipulating voters' preference formation was observed and reported. Some relied on the abuse of government funds. Government food relief, and in particular the resources of the Grain Marketing Board, was distributed on a partisan basis and at ruling party rallies in an attempt to manipulate vote choice. The availability of government funds for the ruling party's campaign was made even more important when in early June the government banned NGOs from carrying out humanitarian tasks (Matyszak 2009, 146–7). This move left an even greater part of the population economically dependent on the rulers and susceptible to manipulation of vote choice.

Government facilities were also widely available for the ruling party's – and only the ruling party's – campaign, and the opposition was denied permits to hold rallies (Zimbabwe Human Rights NGO Forum 2008, 3; ZESN 2008, 57). But it was not only the administrative apparatus that was put to use. ZANU(PF) abused its economic dominance as well as its coercive force as its youth militias had strict control over Harare markets. For instance, it was reported how street vendors were forced to wear ZANU(PF) t-shirts in order to maintain their stalls (ZESN 2008, 54). Furthermore, the ruling party's control over the media also allowed its propaganda to reach the population (ZESN 2008, 60–1). Thus, both the administrative and coercive apparatuses and the rulers' control over the economy served the strategy of manipulating voters' preference formation.

But the dominant strategy in this electoral round was overt manipulation of voters' preference expression and the tool was state-sponsored violence. With the run-off described as "a one-race contest in an environment drenched in blood" (Masunungure 2009a, 94), and ZESN reporting that 171 deaths, 16 rapes, and 9,148 assaults – all related to the elections – had been verified and many more recorded (ZESN 2008, 54), it is clear that coercive capacity played the most central role in this election.

Electoral violence was visibly carried out by ZANU(PF) agents and directed from above (Zimbabwe Human Rights NGO Forum 2008, 4). According to observers, the JOC took over the planning of the run-off campaign as soon as the government realized that the first round of elections was lost (Bratton and Masunungure 2008, 51; Eppel 2009, 969; Alexander and Tendi 2008, 10; International Crisis Group 2008, 5). Two hundred army officers were spread across the country to oversee the electoral violence, primarily carried out by war veterans and youth militias while the police either looked the other way or even actively participated in the harassment (International Crisis Group 2008, 6; Zimbabwe Human Rights NGO Forum 2008, 4–5; Alexander and Tendi 2008, 11; Solidarity Peace Trust 2008, 27–30; Bratton and Masunungure 2008, 51).

The manipulation of voters' preference expression occurred both by threats and outright violence. Ruling party politicians, including the president, and army officers made references to the liberation war in public speeches and assured the public that they would not be defeated by an electoral loss but would rather take up arms (Masunungure 2009a, 83). The police erected road blocks in certain areas and confiscated mobile phones and looked through their contents (ZESN 2008, 55). But the ruling front did not rely on threats alone. Operation *Makavhoterapapi* (meaning "Where did you put your cross?"), a voter intimidation campaign to punish first-round MDC voters and make sure that the ruling party would win the second round, was initiated (International Crisis Group 2008, 6). Base camps were set up across the country, to which suspected MDC supporters would be taken for torture and reeducation by youth militias and war veterans (Zimbabwe Human Rights NGO Forum 2008, 2).

In urban areas, especially in Harare, voters were forced to attend political meetings, whereas rural areas were "sealed off" for both opposition candidates and observers (Tarisayi 2009, 22). Curfews were put in place and there were serious restrictions on freedom of assembly, movement, and expression (Tarisayi 2009, 22). Opposition supporters were barred from participating in MDC-T rallies by youth militias and police (ZESN 2008, 62). When polling day finally arrived, and even though Tsvangirai at that point had withdrawn his candidacy, there were still reports of voter intimidation in polling stations. These included the presence of weapons in voting stations, local chiefs interfering with the vote, opposition voters being "assisted" in the voting booth, and voters being forced to hand over the serial number of their ballots along with their personal information, and being threatened with violence if they had not supported the incumbent (Masunungure 2009a, 94; ZESN 2008, 64–5).

Restriction of the access to the vote – not on election day but through disenfranchisement prior to elections – was not carried out in the second round, as the primary registration of voters occurred prior to the first round. In the first round, however, allegations of manipulation of the voter roll conducted by ZEC and the Registrar-General were widespread. The 5,934,768 people who had officially registered to vote comprised 45% of the population in a country where 50% of the population are below voting age and millions have emigrated. Along with the final – alleged – voter turnout of the second round of around 2.5 million people, this is taken as evidence that the ZEC inflated the voter list (Makumbe 2009, 122).

Manipulation of the administration of elections, which was crucial in the first round of elections with ZEC's maneuver to postpone the announcement of results, was not widely reported in the second round. As described later, Tsvangirai withdrew before election day because of widespread violence, and Mugabe therefore ran uncontested even though Tsvangirai appeared on the ballot. However, election results are still questioned, as observers argue that the reported turnout rate was surprisingly high, given that many observed polling stations were virtually empty on election day (Makumbe 2009, 126)

Economic and legal harassment of opposition members was widespread (interview with Eddie Cross, Bulawayo; interview with David Coltart, former MDC minister and current member of Senate). Party officials were targeted and arrested, the MDC headquarters in Harare was raided by police, and campaign vehicles were confiscated (International Crisis Group 2008, 6; ZESN 2008, 57). Both Tsvangirai and the Secretary-General of MDC-T, Tendai Biti, as well as numerous other opposition politicians, were arrested several times during the run-off campaign, charged with treason and other offenses (Tarisayi 2009, 22; ZESN 2008, 55).

In this election, subtle manipulation of opposition figures was overshadowed by the heavy use of overt, physical harassment of opposition candidates. The campaign of violence, in particular in the ruling party's original strongholds but reaching across the country, brought "the opposition party's network of activists to the verge of oblivion" (Masunungure 2009a, 85). Houses of alleged MDC supporters were burned, and political activists were intimidated, arrested, abducted, and in some instances killed (Solidarity Peace Trust 2008, 32–6; Zimbabwe Human Rights NGO Forum 2008). Public employees, especially teachers and ZEC officials, suspected of supporting the opposition were harassed, attacked, and beaten by youth militias (Tarisayi 2009, 19; Solidarity Peace Trust 2008, 24, 43). An opposition politician described how houses were burned in his home village, where he had initiated opposition politics, and his elderly father was forced to hide in the mountains for weeks (interview with anonymous parliamentarian). By election day, "more than 80 opposition supporters were dead, hundreds were missing, thousands were injured and hundreds of thousands were homeless" (Masunungure 2009a, 85).

By mid-June, Tsvangirai withdrew from the race, citing the violence and the bleak prospects of a fair vote, and took refuge at the Dutch embassy. Mugabe proceeded to win the election. After the coercive capacity of the ruling group had been on full display for several months, post-electoral protests did not occur, and violent crackdowns on protesters were rendered obsolete.

The government's strategies in the 2008 elections are summarized in the first column of Table 6.1. It is clear that the ruling group, contrary to expectations, did not restrict itself to the use of subtle manipulation strategies. In fact, if one includes the first electoral round, in which the registration of voters occurred, there is evidence of all types of manipulation apart from the more subtle, systemic kind. And all types were carried out by government agents, whether the police, the army, youth militias, ZEC, or public servants. The rulers were relying on both administrative and coercive capacity as well as control over the economy. But in contrast to theoretical expectations for a high-capacity autocracy, the subtle types of manipulation, such as limiting access to the vote prior to election day and altering voters' preference formations, were not the dominant strategies. Rather, the elections were dominated by more overt manipulation of voters' preference expression on election day and physical intervention in the opposition's campaign by members of the coercive apparatus.

Table 6.1 Capacities, election strategies, and effects – Zimbabwe

		2008		2013	
DV IV	Multi-party election	+		+	
	Regime breakdown	–		–	
Conditioning variables	Administrative capacity	Medium		Medium	
	Coercive capacity	High		High	
	Economic control	High		High	
Observable implications	Electoral victory	+		+	
	Stabilizing effects	Opposition demobilization Voter protests prevented		Legitimacy Signaling Opposition split	
	Destabilizing effects	Lost legitimacy		Rent distribution	
	Strategies		Carried out by government agents?		Carried out by government agents?
Subtle	Systemic manipulation	–		+	+
	Manipulation of voters' preference formation	+	+	+	+
	Restricting access to the vote	+ (1st round)	+	+	+
	Legal and economic harassment of opposition	+	+	+	+
	Manipulation of voters' preference expression	+	+	+	+
Overt	Manipulation of vote counting	+	+	(+)	+
	Physical harassment of opposition	+	+	(+)	
	Violent crackdown on protesters	N/A		N/A	

Note: (+) indicates that the strategy was employed to a very low degree or that it was uncertain whether the strategy was used or not.

Thus, although the Mugabe government should have had the capacities to subtly manipulate elections, the strategies employed in the second round were more overt and correspond more closely to the scenario of *electoral survival*. Recall from Chapter 2 that in the scenario of electoral survival, the rulers do not have the administrative capacity or control over the economy to subtly manipulate elections, but instead rely primarily on the coercive apparatus to carry out overt manipulation and avoid electoral loss (see Table 2.4). Given the common assumption that autocrats wish to hold on to power and act rationally according to that wish, the possession of capacities will make the domination of elections through subtle manipulation more likely. Yet the case of Zimbabwe in 2008 illustrates that possessing the capacities to subtly dominate elections does not always imply using them.

It is beyond the scope of this analysis to explain why the Mugabe government, in spite of its significant capacities, did not subtly manipulate elections to secure a victory in the first round. Authoritarian leaders may choose not to employ their capacities (an unlikely scenario in Zimbabwe in 2008, given the ruler's willingness to manipulate the second electoral round a few months later); be restrained in doing so, for instance, by international actors (also unlikely in the case of Zimbabwe in 2008, where the capacities were put to use a few months later in spite of the heavy presence of, for instance, SADC); or may simply miscalculate their popularity and refrain from manipulating elections to the degree required to win. Evidence indicates that this is what happened in Zimbabwe in 2008. Believing that he was sure to win (International Crisis Group 2008), Mugabe did not apply his full force in the first round of elections. According to two observers, "ZANU(PF) had not lost its capacity to mobilise [...] However, the relative lack of violence, and the opening of political space it allowed, was sufficient for ZANU(PF) to lose its advantage" (Alexander and Tendi 2008, 9). The ruling group failed to see the seriousness of the situation and lost the relatively peaceful yet flawed first round.

But Mugabe learned a lesson. The second round was just around the corner, and there was no time to change to long-term, subtle strategies of well-covered-up manipulation (interview with anonymous political science professor; interview with anonymous civil society leader, Harare). Unlike Marcos in the Philippines, Mugabe controlled his coercive apparatus, and he used it to secure electoral survival. ZANU(PF)'s electoral victory was thus attributed to the "sheer force of the state" (Raftopoulos 2013a, 984). The strategies used were thus heavily reliant on authoritarian capacities as was expected, but the employed strategies did not comply with the expected mechanisms, likely because the government miscalculated its popularity. But did the presidential victory have the expected effects?

The effect of the 2008 electoral turmoil

The electoral victory did not have all of the stabilizing effects that could likely occur in the case of stabilization by elections. Mugabe won the presidential elections, but the loss of ZANU(PF)'s parliamentary majority robbed the ruling front of its ability to legislate uninterrupted (Masunungure 2009b, 77). Furthermore, it dealt a severe blow to their image of invincibility (Bratton and Masunungure 2008, 42). Yet the opposition victory in parliamentary elections did not constitute a regime breakdown. In the aftermath of elections, mediators from SADC negotiated a power-sharing deal, with Mugabe as president and Tsvangirai as prime minister. But as shall be discussed later, the resulting Inclusive Government (IG) was heavily criticized for leaving Mugabe and ZANU(PF) in control.

Furthermore, Mugabe's victory in the presidential race brought some stabilizing effects. The opposition was clearly demobilized by the massive violence that had succeeded in undermining their structures and raising the costs of opposition activism (Masunungure 2009a, 85, 92–3; interview with David Coltart; interview with Eddie Cross, Bulawayo). Large-scale violence left the population in a state of shock, ensuring that no protests occurred (Matyszak 2009, 135).

As expected in the scenario of *electoral survival* to which the government's strategies in 2008 correspond more closely, the use of violence rather than subtle manipulation, although perhaps from the rulers' perspective less expensive than losing the elections, was nonetheless costly. They won the presidential contest but lost their legitimacy both internally and externally (Raftopoulos 2013a, 972; Masunungure 2011, 57; Bratton and Masunungure 2008, 51–2; Alexander and McGregor 2013, 757).

Thus, despite the presence of authoritarian capacities, the Mugabe government relied on overt manipulation. The conducted strategies correspond to those expected in the scenario of *electoral survival* rather than that of *stabilization by elections*, and the effects also approximate those expected where rulers secure electoral victory through violence rather than subtle manipulation: the ruling front survived but it was wounded. The analysis now turns to the 2013 elections. Had Mugabe's and ZANU(PF)'s capacities changed? And did the strategies and effects conform more closely to theoretical expectations?

The 2013 elections in Zimbabwe: reinstating power through a supermajority victory

Analyzing the July 2013 elections in light of what happened in 2008 serves to further test the theoretical arguments of Chapter 2. After the 2008 parliamentary defeat and the widespread violence that followed, and with a continued economic crisis and a power-sharing agreement, many observers, including the opposition itself, expected an opposition victory that could only be quelled by another round of intense, government-directed violence (Raftopoulos 2013a, 978; interview with anonymous parliamentarian; interview with Eddie Cross, Harare). Neither occurred. Mugabe and ZANU(PF) secured a supermajority victory in a much more peaceful one-round election. Mugabe attained 60.6% of votes compared to Tsvangirai's 33.7%, and ZANU(PF) secured 160 seats against 49 for MDC-T and none for MDC. What strategies did Mugabe and ZANU(PF) rely on? What resources contributed to this superior strategy in the 2013 elections? And have the electoral dynamics had the expected effects? These are the questions pursued in the following sections.

The GPA and the Inclusive Government

Before assessing the 2013 electoral dynamics, I briefly turn to the so-called power-sharing period that occurred in the intermezzo of the 2008 and 2013 elections. Following the second round of the violent 2008 elections, SADC intervened and negotiated the tripartite Global Political Agreement (GPA), inspired by the recent settlement in Kenya following its violent 2007 elections. The power-sharing agreement was signed by ZANU(PF) and the two MDCs in September 2008 and implemented in February 2009. It formed an Inclusive Government (IG) by preserving Mugabe as president, instating Tsvangirai as prime minister, and splitting the ministries among the three parties. But the agreement was criticized for being biased from the outset as executive power remained in the hands of Mugabe, who also held on to "hard power" through important ministries such as Defense, Mining, and Land, and the staff of many government agencies remained loyal to ZANU(PF) (Muzondidya 2013, 49). Furthermore, throughout the GPA, Mugabe's ruling front succeeded in upholding a parallel structure of government, redirecting important decisions from the cabinet to a tight group centered around the JOC and the president, and Mugabe retained and expanded his informal patronage networks (Muzondidya 2013, 50; Kriger 2012). These issues will be discussed further in the following section on Mugabe's and ZANU(PF)'s capacities in the 2013 elections.

The GPA was designed to steer Zimbabwe toward free and fair elections, originally scheduled for 2012, and to "normalize" the political environment. But throughout, Mugabe and ZANU(PF) used a number of strategies to dominate the political landscape, stall the reform process, and prepare for victory in the upcoming elections. While the ruling group upheld its tactics of legal harassment of the opposition, now its coalition partner, through arrests, detentions, and court cases (Mazarire 2013, 90–3), they also turned to various other forms of manipulation. The reforms of the security sector, the civil service, and the media environment were halted (Mazarire 2013, 110; Kriger 2012), and the constitutional reform process was hijacked. One of the important aspects of the GPA was the drawing and signing of a new constitution prior to the next election round. Following both fights between the parties of the IG and numerous ZANU(PF)-designed obstacles, including a re-draft of the original constitutional draft in the summer of 2012, a compromise constitution was finally put to the vote in a referendum in March 2013 (Raftopoulos 2013a, 973; Mazarire 2013, 83–3). The constitution was accepted by an overwhelming majority, but also with allegations of an inflated voter roll (Matyszak 2013). The debacle around the constitutional reform had postponed the elections, and a full "normalization" of the political environment was still to be attained. Following the referendum, SADC warned that in spite of the new constitution, the necessary reforms to ensure free and fair elections had not been "adequately implemented" (Raftopoulos 2013a, 976; ZESN 2013, 19). Nonetheless, Mugabe moved to rush through elections – a process that is analyzed later.

This was the environment in which the presidential and parliamentary elections of 2013 occurred. There were numerous indications that although ZANU(PF) had not given up on its more overt and repressive tactics, it had not wasted the time since the 2008 elections but instead subtly worked the system to its advantage. In the following sections, I analyze the changes to Mugabe's and ZANU(PF)'s capacities during the course of the IG before turning to the dynamics and effects of the July 2013 elections.

A changed environment? ZANU(PF)'s coercive and administrative capacity and economic control during the IG

The four-year IG to some extent affected the capacities Mugabe and ZANU(PF) had at their disposal in the 2013 election campaign. The administrative apparatus was, as discussed previously, affected by the economic crisis that peaked in 2008.

But the quality of the administration does not appear to have changed markedly during the IG. What could potentially have changed is Mugabe's and ZANU(PF)'s control over the apparatus. From 2009 to 2013, ZANU(PF) governed along with the opposition, which ran a number of ministries, but ZANU(PF) retained its control over the administration. Top civil servants remained loyal to ZANU(PF) as the permanent secretaries even in MDC-led ministries were not replaced during the IG, and MDC ministers and mayors experienced obstructions from ZANU(PF)-loyal staff throughout their governing period (McGregor 2013; Mazarire 2013, 89–90; Bratton and Masunungure 2011, 38; interview with David Coltart; interview with Eddie Cross, Bulawayo; interview with anonymous parliamentarian). In 2012, Kriger reported that nearly 40% of civil servants were youth militia members taken in by ZANU(PF) in 2008 (2012, 15). While MDC ministers were present at cabinet meetings, the ZANU(PF)-appointed Registrar-General was in charge of voter registration, Mugabe and ZANU(PF) still had the option of moving administrative issues surrounding the elections into the offices of the military and the CIO, and ZEC remained dominated by ZANU(PF)-loyal staff (LeBas 2014, 59; interview with anonymous parliamentarian; interview with anonymous political science professor; Muzondidya 2013, 49–50).

The coercive apparatus remained under Mugabe's leadership (LeBas 2014, 56; Raftopoulos 2013b). As one local confided in me: "The old man held on to all ministries with guns – even the national parks services" (interview with anonymous businessman, Bulawayo). ZANU(PF) thus controlled the Ministry of Defense and the Ministry of Justice, and the army reported directly to Mugabe, who retained the presidency (Bratton and Masunungure 2011, 34; Mazarire 2013, 88–9). Both Tsvangirai as prime minister and the MDC co-minister of home affairs had limited influence on the running of the police, as they were bypassed by police reporting to the ZANU(PF) co-minister or directly to the president (interview with anonymous political science professor; LeBas 2014, 58). The remaining branches of the coercive apparatus, the youths and war veterans, remained active and loyal to ZANU(PF) (Mazarire 2013, 81–5).

As discussed previously, the economic crisis throughout the 2000s did not rob the ruling group of all its patronage resources, but instead served to make the rents under ZANU(PF)'s control even more attractive. Approaching the 2013 elections, observers stated that in spite of the IG, ZANU(PF) still held a strong resource advantage and had retained and expanded its patronage networks (International Crisis Group 2013, 1; Raftopoulos 2013b, xvi). The dollarization of the economy that followed from the GPA from 2009 onward stabilized the economy, but this stabilization also benefitted ZANU(PF) as it worked to undergird its patronage system and support ZANU(PF) loyalists' business ventures (Muzondidya 2013, 43–4). State-owned enterprises fell under the MDC-T portfolio, but their boards were still loyal to ZANU(PF) (Mazarire 2013, 89–90).

When asked what had changed the economic situation from 2008 to 2013, a great number of interviewees agreed on one factor: diamonds (interview with anonymous political science professor; interview with anonymous parliamentarian; interview with anonymous civil society leader, Harare; interview with anonymous civil society activist, Harare). Diamond production increased dramatically from late 2008 onward, and at the same time, the decrease in agriculture meant an increase in the mining sector's share of exports, leaving it to account for nearly half of external revenues by 2010 (Bratton and Masunungure 2011, 39).

According to some sources, ZANU(PF), desperately wanting to perform better in the next election but inhibited by the power-sharing agreement that had put Tendai Biti of the MDC-T at the head of the Finance Ministry, strategically moved to secure control of the mining sector (Nyamunda and Mukwambo 2012, 164; interview with anonymous political science professor; interview with anonymous civil society activist, Harare). In the Marange diamond fields, discovered in 2006 and estimated to be the largest diamond discovery in history, small-scale miners had been allowed to operate freely until the 2008 elections (Nyamunda and Mukwambo 2012, 148; Bond and Sharife 2012, 356). But in late 2008 and early 2009, the army was deployed to evict small-scale miners from the area, and the diamond industry was taken over by companies that had shared ownership between the Zimbabwean government and foreign companies (Bond and Sharife 2012, 357–8). Although the potential yield of the Marange diamond fields was estimated at minimum one billion USD a year, MDC-T Minister of Finance Biti complained of few diamond rents reaching the treasury (Bond and Sharife 2012, 355; International Crisis Group 2013, 24–5; interview with David Coltart; interview with anonymous parliamentarian). Instead, diamond money was said to find its way to high-profile army officers, ZANU(PF) politicians, and on to the ruling party, where it could be spent on patronage, political campaigns, and election rigging (Bratton and Masunungure 2011, 39; International Crisis Group 2013, 24–5; interview with anonymous political science professor; interview with Eddie Cross, Bulawayo; interview with anonymous parliamentarian; interview with anonymous civil society activist, Harare). However, it must be underscored that whereas the abuse of the diamond industry appears to be common knowledge in Zimbabwe, there is very little documentation on the actual output and its use.

Nonetheless, a pattern emerges in which ZANU(PF) by 2013 had retained control over great parts of the state, in particular the coercive apparatus, and in spite of the economy being in a state of permanent crisis had found new resources over which it had secured control.

Theoretical expectations to the 2013 elections

The IG did not change the capacities of Mugabe's ruling front significantly. ZANU(PF) still largely controlled the administration and had full control over the coercive apparatus. The party's domination of the economy had not been rolled back either – rather, evidence points to a ZANU(PF) takeover of the diamond trade that can potentially have provided the ruling group with a great inflow of extra resources. Thus, if Zimbabwe was a high-capacity regime in 2008, this was still – if not even more so – the case in 2013, despite the contested 2008 elections. Thus, the theoretical expectations remain the same. The Zimbabwean elections should largely conform to the scenario of *stabilization by elections*: the rulers should rely on subtle manipulation strategies, namely systemic manipulation, manipulation of voters' preference formation, restricted access to the vote, and legal and economic harassment of the opposition. The strategies should be directed from above, carried out by government agents, and lead to an incumbent victory. The overt manipulation strategies should not prove necessary. The elections should have a number of stabilizing effects, including the prevention of elite defections, co-optation of the opposition, and generation of legitimacy.

Electoral dynamics in 2013

The following sections investigate the use of state capacity and economic resources in the 2013 election campaign. However, it is important to state that these manipulative strategies were not the sole cause of the 2013 incumbent victory. There were signs of increasing popularity ratings for ZANU(PF). A 2012 public opinion poll by Freedom House showed that 31% of respondents would vote for ZANU(PF) (an increase of 14 percentage points since 2010), and 20% would support MDC-T (a drop of 18 percentage points from 2010) (Booysen 2012). However, only 53% of respondents wished to express whom they would vote for, so it is hard to estimate the scale of ZANU(PF)'s increased popularity. Furthermore, former opposition supporters expressed disappointment with the perceived corruption and lack of delivery on policy promises by ministers from the two MDCs during the IG (interview with David Coltart; interview with anonymous journalist and civil society activist, Bulawayo). It thus seems that the ruling party's campaign on indigenization and land reform appealed to parts of the population (interview with anonymous political science professor (2)), that their status as liberators should not be underestimated (interview with anonymous political science professor (2); interview with anonymous political science professor), and that the opposition was being punished for internal skirmishes and being held accountable for four years in coalition government (LeBas 2014, 60; Raftopoulos 2013a, 985).

In spite of this, manipulation did occur and was estimated to have significantly affected the results (ZESN 2013; Matyszak and Reeler 2013; interview with anonymous civil society leader, Harare). But it is debated whether this manipulation secured ZANU(PF) a victory or simply made the difference between a majority victory and a supermajority victory (Matyszak and Reeler 2013, 10).

Undoubtedly, the electoral defeat and descent into violence in 2008 had taught Mugabe and ZANU(PF) a lesson (interview with anonymous political science professor; interview with anonymous civil society leader, Harare), and they dealt with it effectively. Even though the IG allowed the opposition to take substantial part in government, Mugabe's ruling group went to work on its 2013 electoral strategy immediately after the electoral shock of 2008 (interview with anonymous political science professor). Their tactics were visibly different than in previous campaigns. Whereas ZANU(PF) seemed surprised by their first-round loss in 2008 and could only revert to violence in order not to lose, they were well aware that they could not afford to secure another electoral victory through violence (interview with anonymous civil society leader, Harare). In the following, I investigate whether the employed manipulation strategies correspond to those expected in the theoretical framework.

Systemic manipulation

The setting of the date for the 2013 elections for local councils, the Senate, Parliament, and the presidency constitutes an example of the ruling group relying on systemic manipulation. Whereas Mugabe and ZANU(PF) wanted elections held before the original date set for the expiry of the IG, the opposition upheld that this was not possible, as the reforms agreed upon in the GPA were not yet implemented and the government did not have the funds to hold elections. But the ruling front was aided by its control of the state apparatus. On May 31, the Constitutional Court, controlled by ZANU(PF) (Raftopoulos 2013a, 976–7; International Crisis Group 2013, 3–6), ruled that elections should be held by July 31, and this date was confirmed by the president on June 13 in spite of protests from SADC (Matyszak and Reeler 2013, 2; Raftopoulos 2013a, 976; ZESN 2013, 19). Regardless of whether the setting of the election date broke with the constitution, it was a form of systemic manipulation: the swift elections were an advantage to Mugabe and ZANU(PF), as they inhibited the final moves toward a free and fair electoral environment. There simply was not enough time to revise media laws or allow for voter registration and campaigning as demanded in the constitution, and the rushed election caused chaos in ZEC (LeBas 2014, 59; ZESN 2013, 19; Matyszak and Reeler 2013, 2).

Other examples of systemic manipulation include gerrymandering of election districts and the disenfranchisement of the diaspora. Gerrymandering was not noted as an issue by the Zimbabwe Election Support Network (ZESN), the independent election observation organization that reports on Zimbabwean elections, and there was no formal delimitation process prior to the 2013 election (Research & Advocacy Unit 2013c, 5). But opposition politicians accuse ZANU(PF) of having pushed the boundaries of urban districts, typical opposition strongholds, to include rural areas or communal land, inhabited by ZANU(PF) supporters, so as to tip the balance in those particular districts (interview with Eddie Cross, Bulawayo). Furthermore, international election experts who visited Zimbabwe prior to election day expressed concerns that the electoral system had been designed to give ZANU(PF) an advantage in the distribution of reserved seats in Parliament and the Senate (interview with Jørgen Elklit, election expert). Finally, the Constitutional Court supported Mugabe and ZANU(PF) and denied voting rights to Zimbabweans in the diaspora (ZESN 2013, 31) – a great part of whom are opposition supporters.

Observers agree that the strategies that contributed to distorting electoral results were neither systemic manipulation nor the more brute forms of harassment. Rather, it was the manipulation of voters' preference formation and expression and of their access to the vote that mattered.

Manipulation of voters' preference formation

Manipulation of voters' preference formation took many forms. With the elections being called before the revisions of the media laws, state media was still dominant. A clear bias toward ZANU(PF) was documented (ZESN 2013, 37; Matyszak and Reeler 2013, 11), and the opposition reported that their advertisements were rejected by news outlets, which were dominated by ZANU(PF) or worried about their future if they allowed room for the opposition (interview with anonymous parliamentarian). Mugabe and ZANU(PF) used the biased media as a channel for propaganda, continuously depicting the MDC as "puppets of the West" (Matyszak and Reeler 2013, 11).

ZANU(PF)'s control over the economy, including the rents acquired from the diamond trade, were also used to finance the election campaign. Sources reported that ZANU(PF) had 100 million USD to spend on the campaign (interview with anonymous civil society activist, Harare; interview with Eddie Cross, Bulawayo). ZANU(PF) candidates were equipped with vehicles, posters, and t-shirts to distribute to potential supporters at a level where opposition parties could not compete (interview with anonymous political science professor; interview with anonymous civil society activist, Harare). In his Bulawayo constituency, MDC candidate David Coltart described a "t-shirt battle": "Here, there are no TV debates. Our main way of communicating with people is through visibility on the streets," he said, and continued, "I was able to purchase 400 t-shirts. ZANU was driving around with trucks literally full of t-shirts, handing them out" (interview with David Coltart).

There were also stories of ZANU(PF) handing out gifts, such as kitchen utensils (interview with David Coltart; interview with Eddie Cross, Bulawayo), and the First Lady donating food (although this was also attempted by the opposition) (ZESN 2013, 38). Public resources were abused as ZANU(PF) distributed food relief on a partisan basis and took credit for the canceling of utility bills just one week before the elections (LeBas 2014, 62; Raftopoulos 2013a, 983; ZESN 2013, 37). These various forms of clientelism were perceived as having great effects on voter preferences (interview with anonymous parliamentarian). As a civil society activist explained to me:

> Zimbabwean citizens no longer believe in the democratic role of casting a ballot. They see elections as places where you trade something for something else. We are all clients of the state now. The state brings us something. We buy it with our vote or by beating up someone. Because ultimately, we do not have the power to change anything.
> (interview with anonymous civil society activist, Harare)

The administrative and coercive apparatus was also put to use: civil servants, the police, and uniformed soldiers were used to campaign for the ruling party, and chiefs were encouraged to gather votes for ZANU(PF) in their districts (ZESN 2013, 37–8; interview with anonymous parliamentarian; interview with anonymous civil society activist, Harare).

Manipulation of voters' preference expression

Even more important in affecting vote choice was perhaps the manipulation of voters' preference expression. However, this typically overt form of manipulation occurred in a more subtle fashion. Most observers agree that there was little violence on or before election day (LeBas 2014, 52; ZESN 2013; Research & Advocacy Unit 2013b, 3; interview with anonymous political science professor (2)). Zimbabwe's history of political violence, not just from the 2008 election, where whole districts that supported the MDC were targeted after the elections, but dating back to the *Gukurahundi*, should not be underestimated (ZESN 2013, 19). ZANU(PF) drew on what has been dubbed the "harvest of fear" (Alexander and McGregor 2013, 761; International Crisis Group 2013, 5; interview with anonymous political science professor; interview with Eddie Cross, Bulawayo; interview with David Coltart, Bulawayo; interview with anonymous civil society activist, Harare). The subtle threat of violence being unleashed, for instance, by army officers advising the population to vote for ZANU(PF) (Zimbabwe Peace Project 2013, 2) or the presence of police at some polling stations (ZESN 2013, 44), could have pushed many voters to support ZANU(PF). When asked what went wrong in the 2013 elections, Eddie Cross, MP for MDC-T, told me that:

> Insecurity could do more than we had expected. We are talking about a population who is dependent on the state and who feels that there is no alternative to ZANU(PF). [. . .] We underestimated the issue of money, we underestimated the power of financial resources.
> (interview with Eddie Cross, Harare)

Another sign of manipulation of voters' preference expression was the high number of assisted voters and issues with special voting. At 38% of polling stations, more than 25 people were reported to require assistance to vote, resulting in around 300,000 assisted voters. ZESN estimates that, given Zimbabwe's literacy rate of 95%, there should have been only 30,000 (ZESN 2013). Assisted voting is a common type of vote manipulation, especially in rural areas where local chiefs can easily identify MDC supporters and coerce them into requesting voting assistance by someone identified by the chief, who will then make sure that ZANU(PF) receives the vote (ZESN 2013, 42–3, 51) (interview with anonymous parliamentarian).

Thus, in carrying out manipulation of voters' preference formation and expression, Mugabe's ruling group drew on its dominance of the administrative apparatus, on the threat supplied by the huge coercive apparatus that it commands, and on its control over the economy, including the newfound diamond resources. But in this election, even the more overt manipulation of preference expression on election day was conducted in a more implicit and subtle way. Violence was not dominant, and the prevalent manipulation strategy turned out to be restriction of access to the vote prior to election day.

Restricting access to the vote

Issues with the voter roll, the document listing those eligible to vote, and the voter registration process are discussed in every report and were mentioned by all interviewees I spoke with in Zimbabwe in May–June 2014. The bias in the registration of voters is understood to have affected the election results significantly (Matyszak and Reeler 2013, 5–6). The voter roll was controlled by the Registrar-General, which also ran the voter registration process jointly with ZEC (Research & Advocacy Unit 2013d, 3). On top of not making the voter roll publicly available in electronic form for everyone to inspect as demanded by the constitution (it was released in hard copy on the night of the election), the roll had many flaws. The Zimbabwean think tank the Research and Advocacy Unit estimated that new voters, those under 30, were systematically underrepresented, and that for all age groups above 30, there were more people on the voter roll than in the population, including 116,000 people over 100, in a country with life expectancy rates just above 50 (Research & Advocacy Unit 2013a, 5–6).

Furthermore, the voter registration process was biased, with the bulk of disenfranchisement being borne by opposition strongholds. According to an MP for MDC-T, there were 19 registration centers in the country's largest province, Harare, compared to 100 centers in each of the traditionally ZANU(PF)-dominated provinces of Mashonaland East, West, and Centre (interview with anonymous parliamentarian). ZESN found that registration rates ran at 99.97% in rural areas, ZANU(PF)'s traditional strongholds, and 67.94% in urban areas, where the opposition dominates, leaving an estimated 750,000 people disenfranchised in the opposition's urban strongholds (ZESN 2013, 22).

The debacle of the registration process also manifested itself on election day, when a large number of voters were turned away from polling stations in spite of having registered. This was more prominent in opposition areas, where ZESN observers reported more than 25 people turned away on election day in 82% of all wards (ZESN 2013, 42). A local businessman in Bulawayo told me that he had driven one of his employees from the polling station where she had always voted to one at the other end of the city, at which she was suddenly registered on election day. Had he not had a car to offer her, her vote would have been lost. According to my source, this was a common phenomenon in opposition strongholds (interview with anonymous businessman, Bulawayo).

This strategy of more subtle manipulation of access to the vote through the voter registration process was based on the ruling group's control of the administration, in particular the Registrar-General and elements of ZEC. However, sources state that the coercive apparatus and the economic resources available to Mugabe and ZANU(PF), in particular the diamond windfall, were essential in carrying out this strategy. Thus, manipulation of the voter roll is seen as a calculated strategy chosen by the ruling group in the realization that ballot-stuffing or other more obvious types of fraud would be picked up by election observers and denounced by the international community (interview with anonymous civil society activist, Harare).

Instead, the JOC is said to have worked closely with the Israeli security company, Nikuv, at the army headquarters (KGVI) in Harare, to design a more subtle strategy for electoral manipulation, including the "massaging" of the voter roll ("Election Rigging Scandal Deepens" 2014; interview with anonymous political science professor; interview with MDC-T parliamentarian Eddie Cross, Bulawayo). It is, as with the diamond windfalls, hard to find evidence of these allegations, but Nikuv was in charge of issues such as the voter roll, and the Home Affairs Department confirmed hiring Nikuv in 2000 to handle the computerization of the central registry (Zimbabwe Independent 2014a). The national newspaper, *Zimbabwe Independent*, has revealed details of money transfers from the Registrar-General's office to Nikuv, and parts of the press have referred to Mugabe's victory as a "made-in-Israel landslide" Zimbabwe Independent 2014b). Thus, the subtle manipulation of voter registration seems to have depended on Mugabe and ZANU(PF)'s full range of authoritarian capacities.

Manipulation of tabulating and counting

Manipulation of tabulating and counting was not widely reported. The only sign of ballot-stuffing is discrepancies in the number of special voters. Special voting taking place in advance of election day is allowed for those parts of the police force who are on duty on election day. ZEC registered 69,322 voters as eligible for special voting, while the MDC-T co-minister of home affairs reported that the police force totaled only 38,000 (ZESN 2013, 27). This led to speculations of attempts at ballot-stuffing, but it was the debacle surrounding voter registration that was estimated to have affected results, and ballot-stuffing was not reported as a problem by national observers.

Economic and legal harassment of the opposition

Economic and legal harassment of opposition candidates was less pronounced than in 2008. ZESN reported a relatively free campaigning environment "with no extra-judicial impediments against those wishing to submit their papers to the nomination courts" (ZESN 2013, 35). However, being an opposition member in Zimbabwe still involves much hassle. Former MDC minister David Coltart recounted how a leader of his youth campaign in Bulawayo had been arrested under accusations of ripping up a ZANU(PF) poster, but when ZANU(PF) party activists tore down every MDC poster on the main road leading to Bulawayo Airport, the police did not intervene, even though the MDC reported the incident (interview with David Coltart). Similar reports of brief arrests of numerous civil society and opposition activists abound (Zimbabwe Peace Project 2013, 5–9; US Department of State 2013, 14). There was also an abundance of stories of opposition supporters being refused business licenses and foreign exchange licenses and of companies losing customers and public contracts (interview with Eddie Cross, Harare).

Physical harassment of the opposition

In sharp contrast to previous elections, physical harassment of the opposition was limited. Intimidation tactics were "tempered" (International Crisis Group 2013, 2) and the opposition candidates with whom I met reported being much less fearful than in previous years and that assassination attempts had dwindled (interview with Eddie Cross, Bulawayo; interview with David Coltart). Human rights organizations still reported politically motivated abductions and torture, primarily against MDC candidates, and often carried out by plain-clothes police officers (US Department of State 2013, 2–5). Thus, although markedly reduced, physical harassment was still employed.

In the end, subtle manipulation of voters' preference formation, manipulation of voters' preference expression, and, in particular, manipulation of access to the vote, supported by the strong security sector and heavy control over the economy, served to boost the votes for Mugabe and ZANU(PF). A supermajority victory resulted without a descent into violence, and the results, although initially contested by the opposition, were not taken to the courts nor protested by the public. Violent crackdown on protesters was not necessary given the complete lack of post-election protests – the reason for which shall be discussed in the following section.

Mugabe's and ZANU(PF)'s use of strategies is summed up in Table 6.1. They do not fully conform to theoretical expectations: whereas the employed strategies were carried out by agents of Mugabe's ruling group, it was not only the subtle strategies expected from a high-capacity regime that were used. ZANU(PF) also relied on more overt measures such as manipulation of voters' preference expressions, partly through threats of violence, and physical harassment of opposition figures. However, there were marked changes from the previous election. Relying on an extensive coercive apparatus and allegedly drawing on newfound resources thanks to control over diamond fields, the ruling group's dominant strategy was subtle manipulation of access to the vote through the voter roll. Furthermore, as had also been witnessed throughout the GPA and the constitutional referendum, subtle systemic manipulation also played an important part in the 2013 election, in contrast to the previous contest.

Thus, at first sight, the case does not conform to expectations because all types of strategies, subtle and overt (with the exception of clamp-down on protesters), were used. On the other hand, apart from the manipulation of voters' preference expression, the overt strategies were much more limited than in previous elections. Observers stress that the two most influential strategies were the more subtle strategy of restricting access to the vote and the more overt attempt at affecting voters' preference expression on election day. But even this more overt strategy was in fact carried out in a much more subtle way. Rather than relying on outright violence, ZANU(PF) employed the "harvest of fear" and needed only to hint at violent previous elections. The mere sight of a military officer in the presence of a ZANU(PF) candidate was, in some districts, enough to affect voters' choice on election day. Unlike the more overt type of manipulation of preference expression that involves outright threats and acts of violence, this new strategy left very little direct evidence for the opposition and international actors to point to. Mugabe and ZANU(PF) still used overt strategies, in contrast to theoretical expectations. But along the lines of the theoretical apparatus, the more subtle strategies – or more subtle versions of typically overt strategies – were the most widely used and proved most important for altering outcomes. The question remains whether the tactics had the expected effects on actor choices and thus on regime stability.

The effect of the 2013 electoral dominance

First of all, the strategies seemed to have affected vote choice as ZANU(PF) and Mugabe, in contrast to previous elections, gained a majority of votes. One obvious effect of the electoral victory was ZANU(PF)'s regained ability to legislate uninterrupted and change the constitution at will due to its two-thirds majority in Parliament. But the clear victory in what many judged to be relatively free – and indeed much more peaceful – elections also served to boost Mugabe's and ZANU(PF)'s legitimacy, both internally and externally (interview with anonymous civil society activist, Harare; interview with anonymous political science professor). SADC and the African Union (AU) endorsed the elections (Raftopoulos 2013a, 978). Although the freedom and fairness of the elections were not complimented by the EU and the United States, the EU proceeded to ease its sanctions against the country (Croft 2014).

Electoral dynamics also affected both rulers and opposition in various other ways expected in the scenario of stabilization by election. Thus, the victory boosted the ruling party's attractiveness in the eyes of internal elites. One civil society leader explained to me how, outside of ZANU(PF), politicians are "fish out of water" (interview with anonymous civil society activist, Harare). Votes matter, and as has clearly been demonstrated, voters follow Mugabe. Therefore, ZANU(PF) elites hedge their bets on promotions inside the party rather than challenging it from the outside, and defections remain limited (interview with anonymous civil society activist, Harare; interview with anonymous political science professor).

Furthermore, continued electoral losses have seriously inhibited opposition progress. In 2005, the MDC split during debates over whether to compete in flawed senatorial elections. In early 2014, eight months after the 2013 electoral defeat, MDC-T split again when Secretary-General Tendai Biti challenged Tsvangirai. Both high-ranking opposition politicians and outside observers named the electoral defeat as one of the main catalysts of skirmishes and criticisms of MDC-T leader Tsvangirai (interview with Eddie Cross, Bulawayo; interview with David Coltart, Bulawayo; interview with anonymous diplomat at the Danish Embassy to Zimbabwe). While opposition politicians and civil society leaders still hope for change through elections and not in spite of elections, and note improvements in, for instance, civil liberties throughout recent decades (interview with anonymous journalist and civil society activist, Bulawayo; interview with anonymous civil society activist, Harare), many observers agree that it will be a while before the

Zimbabwean opposition has recovered from its latest electoral defeat (interview with anonymous diplomat at the Danish Embassy to Zimbabwe).

Finally, citizens never challenged Mugabe and ZANU(PF) through post-electoral protests. The lack of protests could be attributed to the fact that opposition support was dwindling and electoral manipulation was more subtle and less overt, and the population thus to a large extent saw elections as reasonably free (interview with anonymous journalist and civil society activist, Bulawayo; interview with anonymous parliamentarian; interview with anonymous political science professor (2)). But it could also be caused by the "dividend of fear" from previous campaigns of violence directed against opposition activists and ordinary voters alike (interview with anonymous civil society activist, Harare). When I asked a local Harare taxi driver who had expressed doubts in the electoral results why there were no anti-ZANU(PF) protests, he looked at me in disbelief: "Protests? Do you think we want the kind of trouble that follows?"

Thus, the effects of the ruling group's strategies widely correspond to the scenario of *stabilization by election*. Although the Mugabe and ZANU(PF) mixed subtle with more overt measures, the elections seemed to have a stabilizing effect, binding in elites and splitting the opposition. When Mugabe was finally removed from power through military interference in November 2017, the developments were unrelated to elections and ZANU(PF) remained in power headed by former vice president Emmerson Mnangagwa.

Conclusion

The case of Mugabe's Zimbabwe is not a clear-cut fit with theoretical expectations, but the diverging dynamics of the 2008 and 2013 elections demonstrate a number of points. First, the cases illustrate that – at least in some autocracies – coercive capacity does matter. Although the importance of coercive capacity could not be documented in statistical analyses relying on measures of military capacity, the coercive apparatus clearly played a large role – albeit in different ways – in the last two elections in Zimbabwe. In 2008, a strong and loyal coercive force bought Mugabe his second-round victory. In 2013, the presence of the coercive apparatus was less clear, and violence was limited. But the military had an important role to play, both in securing the so called "harvest of fear" and in coordinating the more subtle manipulation of elections, for instance, manipulation of the voter roll.

Second, the cases underscore that the finding in Chapter 3 that coercive capacity does not significantly condition the effect of elections could be biased by the limited measure of coercive capacity. Measuring coercive capacity solely through the military apparatus would neglect, for instance, the role played in Zimbabwe by a staunchly pro-Mugabe police force, a great number of loyal war veterans, and active youth militias. Thus, Zimbabwe's coercive capacity was just around the 50th percentile among authoritarian regimes prior to the 2008 election if we rely solely on a measure of military spending. However, a qualitative approach reveals that the coercive force of the Mugabe government was likely greater than what was revealed by statistics of military expenditure. Thus, based on case evidence from

Zimbabwe, it is worth developing a more full-fledged measure of coercive capacity in future studies of the relationship between state capacity and regime stability.

Third, the case of Zimbabwe points to the numerous informal ways in which an autocrat may control the economy. These tactics are hard to pick up on in government or NGO statistics available on a cross-national basis. Cross-national analyses may underestimate the economic power of rulers who – like Mugabe – appropriate natural resources without publicly registering the wealth generated or who control a huge informal economy, for instance, by relying on their coercive forces. This is a challenge that future research on autocrats' economic power should address.

Fourth, the 2008 elections in particular serve to nuance the theory of authoritarian strategies. Although Mugabe and ZANU(PF) enjoyed high levels of capacity – both state and economic – they did not focus on subtle manipulation strategies. Thus, a high-capacity regime will not necessarily conform to the scenario of *stabilization by elections*. It is more likely to do so, as the more subtle manipulation strategies will often be the rational choice. In some instances, such as Zimbabwe in 2008, the incumbent may overestimate his own popularity or underestimate his opponent, and face an immediate electoral threat that demands more overt measures if it is to be eradicated. When the Mugabe government realized the seriousness of the situation, it drew on all its authoritarian capacities, particularly its coercive force, to ensure electoral survival through more overt strategies. The case illustrates how high-capacity autocrats may sometimes misjudge the situation and find themselves in the scenario of *electoral survival* rather than *stabilization by elections*. But the effects of the elections and the strategies employed – the demobilization of the opposition on the one hand, and the loss of legitimacy and the blow to the ruler's image of invincibility on the other – conformed quite well to the expected scenarios of *electoral survival* where the ruling group employs more overt measures to win elections.

Fifth, in line with expectations, the ruling group learned a lesson in 2008, and the 2013 elections conform more closely to the expectations for high-capacity rulers and their ability to stabilize their rule through elections. However, they still differed from the more clear-cut, subtle strategies applied by a high-capacity ruling group such as the UMNO leadership in Malaysia. Although the Mugabe government primarily used its capacities to generate a victory through subtle strategies such as restricting access to the vote, the case also reveals a number of nuances to the theoretical expectations. One of the more overt strategies, manipulating voters' preference formation, was used, but in a more subtle version. Thus, the distinction between subtle and overt measures of manipulation is not always clear-cut. And although subtle strategies dominated, Mugabe and ZANU(PF) did not fully refrain from employing overt strategies, such as physical harassment of the opposition. In the short run, this did not seem to alter the stabilizing effects of elections, but the long-term effects are not yet known.

Finally, in carrying out subtle types of manipulation, the ruling front relied not only on administrative capacity and economic control. The infrastructure of the armed forces seems to have played a significant role in some of the more subtle manipulation strategies, including the tampering with the voter roll that disenfranchised a significant part of the opposition's voters. Thus, just like the distinction between manipulation strategies is not clear-cut, the coercive force may also be employed for some of the more subtle strategies. Again, this finding hints at the potential importance of coercive capacity and thus supports the call for further studies on the effect of coercive capacity on authoritarian electoral dynamics across the globe.

Overall, the case underlines the quantitative findings. Although not always through the measures expected, in the high-capacity regime of Zimbabwe, the ruling front under Mugabe succeeded in stabilizing authoritarian rule through elections, and its strategies depended in part on its state capacity and control over the economy. In the short run, the 2013 elections bought Mugabe and ZANU(PF) more time in power and took the air out of the opposition. As this book is going into press, Zimbabwe is once again headed towards an election (scheduled for 2018). This time, however, even though the ruling party remains in power, the military has removed an aging Mugabe from the presidency, and former vice president, Emmerson Mnangagwa, has been instated in his place.

Note

1 Interviewees were chosen based on their knowledge of and experience with the elections of 2008 and 2013. Interviews capturing as broad a representation of the political spectrum as possible were attempted, but interviewees over-represent the opposition and civil society, as these groups are easiest to gain access to. Therefore, the analyses present relatively little evidence on how the internal regime elites responded to regime strategies and electoral outcomes, and more information on the choices and actions of voters and opposition. The true identities of interviewees are revealed when the interviewees agreed to this. Whenever possible, arguments presented by interviewees were confirmed by other sources. Where further evidence was difficult to find, this is reported in the analysis.

References

Alexander, Jocelyn, and JoAnn McGregor. 2013. "Introduction: Politics, Patronage and Violence in Zimbabwe." *Journal of Southern African Studies* 39 (4): 749–63.

Alexander, Jocelyn, and Blessing-Miles Tendi. 2008. "A Tale of Two Elections: Zimbabwe at the Polls in 2008." *Concerned Africa Scholars Bulletin* (80): 5–17.

Baumhögger, Goswin. 1999. "Zimbabwe." In *Elections in Africa: A Data Handbook*, edited by Dieter Nohlen, Bernard Thibaut, and Michael Krennerich, 963–80. Oxford: Oxford University Press.

Bond, Patrick, and Khadija Sharife. 2012. "Zimbabwe's Clogged Political Drain and Open Diamond Pipe." *Review of African Political Economy* 39 (132): 351–65.

Booysen, Susan. 2012. "Change and 'New' Politics in Zimbabwe: Interim Report of a Nationwide Survey of Public Opinion in Zimbabwe: June–July 2012." Freedom House. www.freedomhouse.org/sites/default/files/Change%20and%20New%20Politics%20 in%20Zimbabwe.pdf.

Bratton, Michael, and Eldred Masunungure. 2008. "Zimbabwe's Long Agony." *Journal of Democracy* 19 (4): 41–55.

———. 2011. "The Anatomy of Political Predation: Leaders, Elites and Coalitions in Zimbabwe, 1980–2010." 9. Developmental Leadership Program. www.dlprog.org.

Croft, Adrian. 2014. "EU Eases Zimbabwe Sanctions, Keeps Them on Mugabe." *Reuters*, February 17. www.reuters.com/article/2014/02/17/us-zimbabwe-eu-idUSBREA1G11R20140217.

Darnolf, Staffan. 2000. *Democratic Electioneering in Southern Africa: The Contrasting Cases of Botswana and Zimbabwe*. Denver: International Academic Publishers.

Dawson, Martin, and Tim Kelsall. 2011. *Anti-developmental Patrimonialism in Zimbabwe*. Working Paper 19: Africa Power and Politics Programme. http://www.institutions-africa.org/filestream/20111110-appp-working-paper-19-anti-developmental-patrimonialism-in-zimbabwe-dawson-and-kelsall-nov-11.

Eppel, Shari. 2009. "A Tale of Three Dinner Plates: Truth and the Challenges of Human Rights Research in Zimbabwe." *Journal of Southern African Studies* 35 (4): 967–76.

Hellum, Anne, and Bill Derman. 2004. "Land Reform and Human Rights in Contemporary Zimbabwe: Balancing Individual and Social Justice through an Integrated Human Rights Framework." *World Development* 32 (10): 1785–805.

Hendrix, Cullen S. 2010. "Measuring State Capacity: Theoretical and Empirical Implications for the Study of Civil Conflict." *Journal of Peace Research* 47 (3): 273–85.

Human Rights Watch. 2002. "Fast Track Land Reform in Zimbabwe." 1. New York. www.hrw.org/reports/2002/zimbabwe/ZimLand0302.pdf.

International Crisis Group. 2008. "Zimbabwe: Prospects from a Flawed Election." 138. Africa Reports. Brussels. www.crisisgroup.org/en/regions/africa/southern-africa/zimbabwe/138-zimbabwe-prospects-from-a-flawed-election.aspx.

———. 2013. "Zimbabwe's Elections: Mugabe's Last Stand." 95. Africa Briefing. Johannesburg/Brussels. www.crisisgroup.org/en/regions/africa/southern-africa/zimbabwe/b095-zimbabwes-elections-mugabes-last-stand.aspx.

Jackson, Paul. 2014. "Military Integration from Rhodesia to Zimbabwe." In *New Armies from Old: Merging Competing Military Forces after Civil Wars*, edited by Roy Licklider, 49–67. Washington, DC: Georgetown University Press.

Jerven, Morten. 2013. *Poor Numbers: How We Are Misled by African Development Statistics and What to Do about It*. 1st edition. Ithaca: Cornell University Press.

Kriger, Norma. 2003. "Zimbabwe's War Veterans and the Ruling Party: Continuities in Political Dynamics." In *Twenty Years of Independence in Zimbabwe: From Liberation to Authoritarianism*, edited by Staffan Darnolf and Liisa Laakso, 104–21. New York: Palgrave Macmillan.

———. 2012. "ZANU(PF) Politics under Zimbabwe's 'Power-Sharing' Government." *Journal of Contemporary African Studies* 30 (1): 11–26.

LeBas, Adrienne. 2014. "The Perils of Power Sharing." *Journal of Democracy* 25 (2): 52–66.

Linington, Greg. 2009. "Illegality & Zimbabwe's 2008 Presidential Elections." In *Defying the Winds of Change: The 2008 Elections in Zimbabwe*, edited by Eldred Masunungure, 98–118. Harare: Weaver Press.

Magure, Booker. 2012. "Foreign Investment, Black Economic Empowerment and Militarised Patronage Politics in Zimbabwe." *Journal of Contemporary African Studies* 30 (1): 67–82.

Makumbe, John. 2009. "Theft by Numbers: ZEC's Role in the 2008 Elections." In *Defying the Winds of Change: The 2008 Elections in Zimbabwe*, edited by Eldred Masunungure, 119–32. Harare: Weaver Press.

Markowitz, Lawrence P. 2013. *State Erosion: Unlootable Resources and Unruly Elites in Central Asia*. Ithaca: Cornell University Press.

Marongwe, Nelson. 2011. "Who Was Allocated Fast Track Land, and What Did They Do with It? Selection of A2 Farmers in Goromonzi District, Zimbabwe and Its Impacts on Agricultural Production." *Journal of Peasant Studies* 38 (5): 1069–92.

Masunungure, Eldred. 2009a. "A Militarized Election: The 27 June Presidential Run-Off." In *Defying the Winds of Change: The 2008 Elections in Zimbabwe*, edited by Eldred Masunungure, 79–97. Harare: Weaver Press.

———. 2009b. "Voting for Change: The 29 March Harmonized Elections." In *Defying the Winds of Change: The 2008 Elections in Zimbabwe*, edited by Eldred Masunungure, 61–78. Harare: Weaver Press.

———. 2011. "Zimbabwe's Militarized Electoral Authoritarianism." *Journal of International Affairs* 65 (1): 47–64.

Matyszak, Derek. 2009. "Civil Society & the Long Election." In *Defying the Winds of Change: The 2008 Elections in Zimbabwe*, edited by Eldred Masunungure, 133–48. Harare: Weaver Press.

———. 2013. "Odd Numbers?" Harare: Research and Advocacy Unit. www.researchandadvocacyunit.org/publications.

Matyszak, Derek, and Tony Reeler. 2013. "Report on the Conditions for the 2013 Harmonised Elections." Harare: Research and Advocacy Unit. www.researchandadvocacyunit.org/.

Mazarire, Gerald. 2013. "ZANU(PF) and the Government of National Unity 2009–12." In *The Hard Road to Reform: The Politics of Zimbabwe's Global Political Agreement*, edited by Brian Raftopoulos, 71–116. Harare: Weaver Press.

McGregor, JoAnn. 2013. "Surveillance and the City: Patronage, Power-Sharing and the Politics of Urban Control in Zimbabwe." *Journal of Southern African Studies* 39 (4): 783–805.

Meredith, Martin. 2002. *Our Votes, Our Guns: Robert Mugabe and the Tragedy of Zimbabwe*. 1st edition. New York: PublicAffairs.

Muzondidya, James. 2008. "From Bouancy to Crisis, 1980–1997." In *Becoming Zimbabwe: A History from the Pre-Colonial Period to 2008*. Harare: Weaver Press.

———. 2013. "The Opposition Dilemma in Zimbabwe." In *The Hard Road to Reform: The Politics of Zimbabwe's Global Political Agreement*, edited by Brian Raftopolos, 39–70. Harare: Weaver Press.

Naing, Myo. 2012. "Upgrading Zimbabwe's Bureaucratic Quality." In *Zimbabwe Mired in Transition*, edited by Eldred Masunungure and Jabusile Shumba, 205–29. Harare: Weaver Press.

Ndlovu-Gatsheni, Sabelo. 2006. "Nationalist-Military Alliance and the Fate of Democracy in Zimbabwe." *African Journal on Conflict Resolution* 6 (1): 49–80.

Nyamunda, Tinashe, and Patience Mukwambo. 2012. "The State and the Bloody Diamond Rush in Chiadzwa: Unpacking the Contesting Interests in the Development of Illicit Mining and Trading, c.2006–2009." *Journal of Southern African Studies* 38 (1): 145–66.

Raftopoulos, Brian. 2008. "The Crisis in Zimbabwe, 1998–2008." In *Becoming Zimbabwe: A History from the Pre-Colonial Period to 2008*, edited by Brian Raftopoulos and Alois Mlambo, 201–32. Harare: Weaver Press.

———. 2013a. "The 2013 Elections in Zimbabwe: The End of an Era." *Journal of Southern African Studies* 39 (4): 971–88.

———, ed. 2013b. *The Hard Road to Reform: The Politics of Zimbabwe's Global Political Agreement*. Harare: Weaver Press.

Raftopoulos, Brian, and Daniel Compagnon. 2003. "Indigenization, State Bourgoise and Neo-Authoritarian Politics." In *Twenty Years of Independence in Zimbabwe: From*

Liberation to Authoritarianism, edited by Staffan Darnolf and Liisa Laakso, 15–33. New York: Palgrave Macmillan.
Research & Advocacy Unit. 2013a. "An Audit of Zimbabwe's 2013 Voters' Roll." Harare. www.researchandadvocacyunit.org/.
———. 2013b. "Brief Report on the 2013 Harmonised Elections." SAPES Policy Dialogue Forum Meeting. Harare. www.researchandadvocacyunit.org/.
———. 2013c. "Key Statistics from the June 2013 Voters' Roll." Harare. www.researchandadvocacyunit.org/.
———. 2013d. "Numbers Out of Tune? An Examination of the Vote in Harmonised July 2013 Election: A Brief Report." Harare. www.researchandadvocacyunit.org/.
Sachikonye, Lloyd. 2003. *The Situation of Commercial Farm Workers after Land Reform in Zimbabwe*. London: Farm Community Trust of Zimbabwe.
Singer, David, Stuart Bremer, John Stuckey, and Bruce Russett. 1972. "Capability Distribution, Uncertainty, and Major Power War, 1820–1965." In *Peace, War, and Numbers*, 19–48. Beverly Hills: Sage.
Solidarity Peace Trust. 2008. "Punishing Dissent, Silencing Citizens: The Zimbabwe Elections 2008." Johannesburg. www.solidaritypeacetrust.org/133/punishing-dissent-silencing-citizens/.
Tarisayi, Eustinah. 2009. "Voting in Despair: The Economic & Social Context." In *Defying the Winds of Change: The 2008 Elections in Zimbabwe*, edited by Eldred Masunungure, 11–24. Harare: Weaver Press.
Tendi, Blessing-Miles. 2013. "Ideology, Civilian Authority and the Zimbabwean Military." *Journal of Southern African Studies* 39 (4): 829–43.
Therkildsen, Ole. 2001. "Efficiency, Accountability and Implementation Public Sector Reform in East and Southern Africa." Democracy, Governance and Human Rights Programme Paper Number 3, United Nations Research Institute for Social Development. http://www.ucl.ac.uk/dpu-projects/drivers_urb_change/urb_governance/pdf_trans_corrupt/UNRISD.pdf
US Department of State. 2013. "2013 Human Rights Report: Zimbabwe." Washington, DC. www.state.gov/documents/organization/220388.pdf.
Zamchiya, Phillan. 2013. "The Role of Politics and State Practices in Shaping Rural Differentiation: A Study of Resettled Small-Scale Farmers in South-Eastern Zimbabwe." *Journal of Southern African Studies* 39 (4): 937–53.
ZESN, Zimbabwe Election Support Network. 2008. "Report on the Zimbabwe 29 March 2008 Harmonized Elections and 27 June Presidential Run-Off." Harare.
———. 2013. "Report on the Zimbabwe 31 July 2013 Harmonised Elections." Harare.
Zimbabwe Human Rights NGO Forum. 2008. "Political Violence Report." Harare. www.hrforumzim.org/category/reports-on-political-violence/.
Zimbabwe Independent. 2014a. "Election Rigging Scandal Deepens." Accessed June 13. www.theindependent.co.zw/2013/08/09/election-rigging-scandal-deepens/.
———. 2014b. "Nikuv Polls Rigging Saga Takes New Twist." Accessed June 13. www.theindependent.co.zw/2013/08/16/nikuv-polls-rigging-saga-takes-new-twist/.
Zimbabwe Peace Project. 2013. "July 2013. ZPP Monthly Monitor." Harare. www.zimpeaceproject.com/.

Interviews

Interview with anonymous businessman, Bulawayo, May 25 2014.
Interview with anonymous civil society activist, Harare, May 27 2014.

Interview with anonymous diplomat at the Danish Embassy to Zimbabwe, Harare, May 23 2014.
Interview with anonymous journalist and civil society activist, Bulawayo, May 24 2014.
Interview with anonymous parliamentarian, Harare, May 30 2014.
Interview with anonymous political science professor, Harare, May 21 2014.
Interview with anonymous political science professor (2), Harare, May 28 2014.
Interview with David Coltart, former MDC minister during the IG and current member of Senate, Bulawayo, May 24 2014.
Interview with Eddie Cross, MDC-T parliamentarian, Bulawayo, May 24 2014.
Interview with Eddie Cross, MDC-T parliamentarian, Harare, May 30 2014.
Interview with Jørgen Elklit, election expert visiting Zimbabwe for IFES, Aarhus, Denmark, December 16 2014.

7 Conclusion

Authoritarian elections, capacities, and regime stability

The literature on authoritarian elections has encountered an apparent paradox. While some researchers have found a destabilizing and in some instances even a democratizing effect of authoritarian multi-party elections, others argue that elections contribute to authoritarian regime stability. Why do multi-party elections sometimes stabilize authoritarian regimes while at other times they lead to their demise?

This book has argued that the effect of authoritarian multi-party elections on regime stability is conditional upon the capacities available to rulers. Administrative capacity, coercive capacity, and control over the economy increase the probability that elections will contribute to authoritarian regime stability. Autocrats who preside over strong states and/or exhibit extensive control over the economy are more likely to see their regimes stabilize when holding authoritarian elections. Authoritarian rulers who have limited capacities will be more likely to experience breakdown following a multi-party election.

Authoritarian capacities enable and constrain electoral strategies aimed at affecting choices made by internal regime elites, opposition candidates, and ordinary citizens. In carrying out these strategies, autocrats attempt to ensure that the elites remain loyal, the opposition is demobilized or co-opted into the ruling front, voters support the ruling party, and protesters stay quiet after elections, thus using elections as tools to secure authoritarian regime survival. When we take account of the capacities that autocrats possess, the paradox of authoritarian elections is not so paradoxical after all.

This concluding chapter reflects upon this claim, the tests of the claim performed throughout the book, and the implications of the results for both theory and practice. First, I summarize the findings. Second, I discuss their implications for the literature on electoral authoritarianism and the literature on electoral integrity. Third, I ask what happens once an authoritarian regime has broken down following elections, and what other ramifications multi-party elections under autocracy might have. Finally, I briefly reflect upon the implications for democracy promotion efforts. Throughout, I suggest a number of avenues for future research.

The findings and the need for further research

Authoritarian elections are neither a new nor a rare phenomenon. Chapter 1 showed that in 2008, 84% of all autocracies held some form of elections. 62% held multi-party elections. Authoritarian multi-party elections were rarer during the Cold War. Only since 1991 have we witnessed a dramatic increase in multi-party authoritarian elections – what the literature terms hegemonic (and in some instances competitive) regimes. Today, authoritarian multi-party elections occur across regions and across authoritarian regime types. But what happens when autocrats open up for multi-party competition?

This book has argued that the effect of authoritarian elections on regime stability depends on the context in which elections are embedded. Autocrats with high levels of state capacity – administrative and coercive – or extensive control over the economic sphere are more likely to use elections to stabilize their rule. Rulers who lack such capacities face a higher risk of regime breakdown following multi-party elections. Administrative state capacity or extensive economic control allows the ruler to subtly manipulate elections, for instance, through propaganda, abuse of state spending, or harassment of opposition forces.

Where the ruler is unable to carry out such electoral strategies – or the strategies simply fail – high coercive state capacity may secure stability nonetheless. However, an electoral victory enforced by the coercive apparatus is unlikely to legitimate prolonged rule. It often serves as a short-term solution to electoral pressure as in Zimbabwe in 2008. Here, the ruling front was surprised by what could have been an opposition victory in elections and turned to the coercive apparatus to secure control over the second round of presidential elections. In the longer term, however, the rulers scaled down repression, and violence was much less pronounced as an electoral strategy in 2013 when the ruling front had time to prepare more subtle electoral manipulation. In cases where administrative capacity and economic control are lacking, coercive capacity may still secure stability through elections in the short term. But where rulers also lack the repressive capacity necessary to steal elections and quell the protests that follow, elections are much more likely to lead to regime breakdown.

The argument on administrative capacity and economic control found support in cross-national analyses and case studies of authoritarian multi-party elections, whereas the evidence for an effect of coercive capacity was mixed. However, the statistical analyses also revealed that although multi-party elections may stabilize authoritarian rule where the autocrat's capacity to control such elections is very high, most authoritarian regimes are destabilized by elections.

In Chapter 3, I found that administrative capacity, proxied by tax extraction ratios, negatively conditions the effect of multi-party elections on the risk of regime breakdown. For the 50% of autocracies that have lower levels of administrative capacity, holding multi-party elections increases the risk of authoritarian regime breakdown. In regimes where tax extraction rates are above 0.26, corresponding to the top 10% of the sample, holding elections decreases the likelihood of breakdown and more so the more tax extraction rates increase. The results lend cross-national support to the original claims put forth by Slater and collaborators that state capacity supports authoritarian rule (Slater 2010; Slater and Fenner 2011).

Proxying the incumbent's degree of control over the economy by an index comprising information on regulation of business, labor, and credit, income from natural resources, and the size of the public sector, the analyses in Chapter 4 showed a significant, negative conditional effect of economic control on the relationship between elections and regime breakdown. Although the effect was not statistically significant when for elections held within the past three years, economic control did condition the effects of elections after one, five, and seven years. However, there was no evidence that elections are regime stabilizing at high levels of economic control: elections correlate with regime breakdown where economic control is at low or medium values, but even at extremely high values of economic control, elections are not stabilizing. Thus, economic control may explain how dictators avoid losing power following elections but cannot on its own explain how elections become regime stabilizing.

Overall, the analyses reveal that for low and medium levels of economic control and administrative capacity, elections are more likely to destabilize the regime. Only where administrative capacity is at its highest do elections correlate with regime stability. The statistical results thus indicate that the argument that multi-party elections support authoritarian rule (i.e., Magaloni 2006; Lust-Okar 2006; and the long-term effects unveiled by Knutsen, Nygård, and Wig 2017) may in fact refer to a limited group of regimes with very high capacity to control elections. In the majority of autocracies, elections are destabilizing. The paradox of authoritarian elections may describe a situation where multi-party elections promote stability in very specific instances but are likely to destabilize regimes most of the time. Most autocracies simply do not control a state that is strong enough to subtly manipulate elections without provoking widespread public dissatisfaction.

Chapter 4 also revealed that the effect of economic control runs through the indicator of government spending. Thus, the findings primarily support the theoretical argument that a dictator controlling the economy through a large public sector may subtly manipulate elites, opposition, and citizens, for instance, by doling out public money or threatening public employees. This finding resonates with studies of the tactics of the PRI in Mexico that delivered patronage through the formal state apparatus (Greene 2007; Magaloni 2006). There was no statistical support for an effect of regulation of business or of natural resource wealth. This finding is discussed further later.

The quantitative analyses demonstrated an overall correlation between elections, regime breakdown, and administrative capacity and economic control. But they left open the question of whether it was indeed the expected mechanisms, namely the presence or absence of subtle electoral manipulation, that explained this correlation. Chapters 5–6 explored the mechanisms of electoral stabilization and breakdown in selected cases. They attempted to assess whether the suggested micro-level mechanisms are indeed what underlie the macro-level correlations.

The dynamics surrounding the elections in Malaysia in 1990 and the Philippines in 1986 largely support the argument. The evidence suggests that the ruling UMNO in Malaysia relied on its large and effective public workforce, control over the electoral commission, and control over public resources to subtly manipulate elections. The strategies of systemic manipulation, manipulation of voters' preference formation, and legal harassment of the opposition were predominant in securing a supermajority victory, in turn co-opting defected elites back into the ruling party and sustaining legitimacy. There is thus evidence that it may indeed be administrative capacity and economic control that allow autocrats to stabilize their rule through elections.

In the Philippines, contrary to expectations, more subtle manipulation strategies such as restricting access to the vote by disenfranchising suspected opposition supporters were carried out despite a lack of administrative capacity and control over the economy. But as expected, the Marcos leadership's primary measures were overt fraud on election day and physical harassment of the opposition, and the result was a backlash of public protests. Lacking the control over the coercive forces necessary to quell this "People Power Revolution," the regime collapsed. Thus, although the case studies do not rule out alternative explanations for electoral outcomes and regime survival in Malaysia and collapse in the Philippines, the dynamics in the cases are in line with theoretical expectations. There is evidence that high levels of administrative capacity and economic control allow rulers to stabilize their regime through subtle electoral manipulation and that rulers who lack such capacities are forced to turn to blatant electoral manipulation and eventually hand over power.

The cases also served to nuance the cross-national findings on the effect of economic control and point to the need for further research. In Zimbabwe, the rulers used economic control in several ways, especially during the 2013 electoral campaign. However, these dynamics related to the informal rather than the formal economy. Diamond wealth bypassed state coffers but was still used to the advantage of the ruling party. Simultaneously, the coercive force was used to appropriate and distribute land to the advantage of the ruling group's supporters and to control the informal sector such as the large street markets. These tactics are hard to pick up on in government or NGO statistics available on a cross-national basis. Thus, in cross-national analyses, we may underestimate the economic power of rulers who – like Mugabe – appropriate natural resources without publicly registering the wealth generated or who control a huge informal economy, for instance, by relying on their coercive forces. A blossoming literature on the importance of land rights as a source of political patronage promises to advance this field further and can contribute to our knowledge of the various tools autocrats use to hold on to power via elections (Albertus and Menaldo 2012a; Boone 2014). This study underscores the importance of finding ways to document such informal tools of authoritarian control in cross-national analyses.

Whereas conditioning effects of administrative capacity and economic control were detected in Chapters 3–4, no such effect of coercive capacity was found. Based on data on military capacity, Chapter 3 rejected the hypothesis that coercive capacity conditions the effect of authoritarian multi-party elections on regime stability. This finding, however, is nuanced in the case studies, particularly by the evidence of the authoritarian leadership's strategies in Zimbabwe during the 2008 and 2013 elections. With medium levels of administrative capacity and high levels of coercive capacity and control over the economy, Zimbabwe was a high-capacity case. In this light, it is surprising that Mugabe's ruling front relied primarily on overt strategies of election day fraud and physical harassment of the opposition to survive the 2008 elections. The case thus demonstrates that merely possessing capacities does not necessarily mean that the rulers will use these capacities. In the case of Zimbabwe in 2008, it seems the government underestimated the threat from elections, and that once it realized its precarious position, its only option was to turn to emergency measures of overt repression.

The analysis of the elections in Zimbabwe thus nuances the findings on the role of coercive capacity. At least in Mugabe's Zimbabwe, the coercive force of the ruler proved decisive for electoral dynamics. Had it not been for its colossal coercive apparatus, including the military, the police force, the war veterans, and the youth militias, Mugabe and ZANU(PF) most likely would have been unable to turn what looked like an electoral loss in the first round of the 2008 elections into a victory and a power-sharing agreement that ultimately turned out to their advantage. Similarly, although the dynamics that unfolded in the 2013 elections correspond more closely to the theoretical apparatus – ZANU(PF) drew on its dominance of the administration as well as its economic resources from the diamond fields to restrict access to the polls in opposition strongholds and to obstruct the opposition campaign – the coercive apparatus still played an important role. Thus, whereas the coercive apparatus played only a minor role in Malaysia, where UMNO instead relied on its administrative capacity and control over the economy, the Mugabe government in Zimbabwe kept turning to its coercive apparatus even though it had other capacities on which to rely.

The contrasting findings of the quantitative and qualitative studies on the role of coercive capacity could easily be explained if Zimbabwe is simply considered a unique case in which the coercive apparatus played an exceptionally large part. However, it is also likely that the quantitative analyses simply cannot fully take into account the effect of coercive capacity, as only cross-national data on military spending and personnel are available. In Zimbabwe, the loyal police force that carried out the day-to-day harassment of the opposition, the large group of war veterans who were the main actors behind the farm invasions, and the youth militias in charge of parts of Harare all played an important role in both the 2008 and 2013 elections. However, such groups are not captured in the cross-national analyses that rely solely on data on military capacity.

Developing more complete measures of coercive capacity could thus provide a fruitful avenue for future studies. Relying on measures of military personnel, researchers have investigated the effect of coercive capacity on the prospects for democratization in authoritarian regimes (Albertus and Menaldo 2012b), the effect of military spending on the likelihood of authoritarian breakdown (Andersen et al. 2014), and civil-military relations in democratizing regimes (Croissant and

Kuehn 2017). But there is still a need to further explore the effect of coercive apparatuses beyond military capacities on regime stability – in both electoral and non-electoral regimes. Such endeavors would line up neatly with the blossoming research agenda on state repression (e.g., Davenport 2007; Wood 2008; Bhasin and Gandhi 2013; Regan and Henderson 2002; Escribà-Folch 2013).

Implications for the literature on authoritarian elections

Supporting the claims made by researchers such as Geddes (1999) and Svolik (2012), this book has demonstrated that it can be rewarding to take seriously the many traits that vary across dictatorships. Both administrative capacity and control over the economy have been shown to affect the relationship between multi-party elections and authoritarian regime stability. Thus, taking the capacities available to rulers into account, the paradox of authoritarian elections is not so paradoxical after all. The effect of authoritarian elections on regime stability is conditioned by the administrative capacity at the disposal of the autocrat as well as her control over the economy.

The findings have several implications for the future study of authoritarian regimes. First, researchers have realized that the great variation among authoritarian regimes matters to both durability and a wide range of policy decisions. But the focus has primarily been on the effect of authoritarian regime type (e.g., Geddes 2003; Magaloni 2008; Wright 2008; Fjelde 2010; Knutsen and Fjelde 2013; Weeks 2012, 2). Researchers have argued that the group from which leaders are drawn and the structure for accessing power and making policy decisions matter, i.e., party regimes behave differently from personalist or military regimes. This book has demonstrated that other traits, in the form of capacities and their interactions with elections, also matter to regime dynamics. Thus, it would be fruitful to look at other variations across authoritarian regimes in addition to the various regime types.

A potential avenue for further research would be to apply the distinction between various levels of capacities to existing findings in the literature on authoritarian elections. For instance, the literature on electoral authoritarianism has commonly separated regimes that hold multi-party elections into competitive regimes, those with unfair elections but some level of uncertainty over electoral outcomes, and hegemonic autocracies, in which the incumbent always wins, and argued that hegemonic regimes are more stable than competitive regimes (e.g., Schedler 2013, 167–8). This finding is hardly surprising (regimes in which rulers do not lose elections are more stable than those in which they occasionally do), and it is also unclear what is driving the relationship. The proposition almost begs the question why some authoritarian regimes remain hegemonic while others turn competitive. Some of the regimes that the literature classifies as competitive are excluded from the analyses of this book because they feature uncertainty over electoral outcomes and are thus classified as democratic, but the distinction between different levels of capacities may still help shed light on the relationship. Could the observed differences between the so-called competitive and hegemonic autocracies be explained by differing levels of capacities? Perhaps the rulers of hegemonic regimes (i.e., Singapore) are successful in generating supermajority victories and thus having their regime classified as hegemonic, precisely because they have, on average, higher levels of capacities than competitive regimes (i.e., Kenya during the 1990s).

Second, the book challenges the voluntarist perspective that the effect of authoritarian elections primarily depends on actor choices (Schedler 2013). Whereas the choices of central actors may indeed be decisive in the two-level game of authoritarian elections, this does not mean that we should not attempt to unfold the factors that shape such actor choices and search for more general patterns. The claims made by Howard and Roessler (2006); Bunce and Wolchik (2011); and Donno (2013) that opposition party mobilization and unity matter to the effect of authoritarian elections or the notion that the people's choice of protesting electoral fraud brings down authoritarian regimes (Kuntz and Thompson 2009) may indeed be true. But this book has demonstrated that the capacities at the disposal of the autocrat can affect the choices made by the opposition, the citizens, and the internal regime elites. In doing so, these capacities also condition the effect of elections.

Thus, the possibility of a transfer of power following elections in Zimbabwe was diminished by the opposition's splits in 2005 and 2014. However, these internal opposition skirmishes did not occur in a vacuum. They reflect the choices of opposition leaders, but they were also affected by the strategies of opposition harassment and manipulation carried out by ZANU(PF). Relying on its strong coercive apparatus and a loyal bureaucracy, even during the coalition government from 2009–2013, Mugabe's leadership was able to continuously inhibit opposition activity and attempted to portray the opposition as incompetent. These strategies have undoubtedly contributed to the opposition's current state of crisis and thus also to the diminished prospects for regime change. Moving forward, this link between the micro and the macro levels, between actors and structures, should receive even more attention.

One way of doing so would be to test the interaction between actors, capacities, and strategies further by performing quantitative, cross-national tests of the theoretical mechanisms linking the micro to the macro level. In this book, I have assessed such claims against the evidence provided by selected cases, but a number of these questions could – and should – be tested across countries. For instance, judged on data across countries and over time, are elite defections rarer where state capacity and control over the economy abound? Are opposition splits or co-optation of opposition figures more common in regimes where the state apparatus and control over the economy are used to harass the opposition? Do autocrats with high levels of administrative capacity tend to use more subtle forms of electoral manipulation? Although attaining such data across authoritarian regimes is tricky, it can indeed be done, as has been proven by Reuter and Gandhi (2011), who analyze the effect of economic crises on the likelihood of elite defections in electoral autocracies, as well as Bhasin and Gandhi (2013), who examine the timing and targeting of authoritarian repression during election campaigns. Such analyses would further test the claims of this book and generate new knowledge on authoritarian regime dynamics on the micro level.

Third, the findings also beg the question what other factors may shape the effect of authoritarian elections. Knutsen, Nygård, and Wig (2017) have recently shown that multi-party elections destabilize autocrats in the short term but may bring regime stability once this immediate period of uncertainty has passed. This book has demonstrated that regimes with very high levels of state capacity are more likely to survive the potentially destabilizing electoral event and move on to reap the long-term benefits that elections offer to autocrats. Regimes with low and medium levels of administrative capacity and economic control are more likely to break down immediately after elections. What other factors shape this relationship? Donno (2013) and Levitsky and Way (2010) emphasize the importance of the international community in determining when elections promote democratization. Can international actors also support autocracies through potentially destabilizing electoral events and thus help explain why some dictatorships stabilize their rule when holding elections? In a time when powerful states often act as black knights – that is, in support of authoritarian rule – rather than as promoters of democracy, we should also look into the autocracy-supporting effects of international interventions in national elections and not just the international community's support for democracy (see, for instance, Tolstrup 2015; Bubeck and Marinov 2017).

Fourth, authoritarian regime stabilization through elections also points to the issue of legitimacy. This book has focused on the argument that state capacity and economic control allow electoral authoritarian regimes to stabilize because they make certain strategies of electoral manipulation available to rulers. That such subtle manipulative strategies – or their absence – were indeed important for regime stabilization or breakdown by elections in Malaysia, the Philippines, and Zimbabwe was demonstrated in Chapters 5–6. However, it is entirely possible that state capacity, particularly administrative capacity, also affects stabilization through elections via another mechanism. It may be that autocrats with higher levels of administrative capacity are not only better able to manipulate voters but also better able to convince voters to vote for them because they simply perform better. Flores and Nooruddin (2016) argue that elections in autocracies with higher levels of legitimacy are more likely to turn democratic because rulers do not need to manipulate them in order to win. They highlight that previous experience with democratic rule, a larger fiscal space (understood as the government's ability to spend money on projects, etc.), and the absence of conflict enhance legitimacy, which in turn ensures that elections turn democratic over time. The lack of a democratic stock, limited ability to spend public money, and ongoing conflicts deprive states of legitimacy and make rulers more prone to manipulate elections, in turn inhibiting democratization.

It is indeed plausible that the ability to win elections without heavy manipulation makes autocrats more willing to democratize (see also Slater and Wong 2013). On the other hand, performance legitimacy may also keep electoral autocrats in power as they may win votes relying in part on their performance and in part on subtle electoral manipulation. Control over an efficient bureaucracy and coercive force is one way of securing output legitimacy based on, for instance, economic growth or the ability to secure peace. Thus, administrative capacity may secure stabilization by elections not only because it enables autocrats to manipulate elections, but also because it ensures autocrats more votes through better performance.

It is hard to ascribe President Mugabe's continued rule after the 2008 and 2013 elections and until late 2017 to output legitimacy. The elections occurred during periods of severe economic crisis and the coercive force played a large role in securing the ruling party's electoral victories. In other cases, such as Singapore, although subtle electoral manipulation has been argued to play an important part in the PAP's continued rule (Tan 2013; Li and Elklit 1999), the state's performance, for instance, in terms of economic growth, undoubtedly also affects electoral outcomes (Wong and Huang 2010). How state capacity enables electoral manipulation as well as performance legitimacy in autocracies – and how these different paths to electoral victory are chosen or combined by dictators – would form an interesting topic for future research on electoral authoritarianism.

Authoritarian elections, violence, and standards of living

This book has looked at the effect of authoritarian elections on the likelihood of regime breakdown. However, elections in autocracies may have a number of effects that fall short of regime change. Prominently featured in recent scholarship is the study of electoral violence. Numerous cases demonstrate a clear risk of violence during or following elections in both democracies and autocracies. The authoritarian elections in Zimbabwe in 2008 (discussed in Chapter 6) saw high levels of violence primarily carried out by the ruling front and targeted at opposition candidates and voters. Only one year earlier, the democratic elections in Kenya escalated into violence that left thousands of people dead.

On this background, scholars have investigated the drivers of election violence, the timing of election violence and its targets, as well as the risk of elections leading to outright civil war (e.g., Hafner-Burton, Hyde, and Jablonski 2014; Fjelde and Höglund 2016; Bhasin and Gandhi 2013; Wilkinson 2006; Cederman, Gleditsch, and Hug 2013). Scholars have established that in post-conflict societies, the risk of elections leading to violence is high (Brancati and Snyder 2013; Flores and Nooruddin 2012). However, the link between the holding of elections and overall levels of violence is debated. Recently, Harish and Little (2017) have argued that although violence may spike around election time in electoral regimes – what they term the political violence cycle – this does not mean that electoral regimes see more political violence than non-electoral regimes (see also Goldsmith 2015). Instead, it may simply imply that non-electoral regimes are as (or perhaps even more) violent than their electoral counterparts, but in electoral regimes, violence tends to lump around election time when political power is at stake and violence is most effectively employed to affect the process.

Although the new literature on election violence and elections as catalysts of violent conflict is promising, a number of questions on the link between elections and violence need to be explored. Do multi-party elections increase not just inter-ethnic violence but also the prevalence of government-directed violence in authoritarian regimes? Or do elections force rulers to give up on violent repression so as not to lose votes? In other words, is violence more or less common than in non-electoral or one-party electoral autocracies? And do elections have differing effects on violence in authoritarian and democratic systems, i.e., are competitive elections more or less likely to provoke violence than non-competitive elections – or do they perhaps instigate different types of violence? Many questions about the link between authoritarian elections and violence – not to mention how electoral violence may be prevented – remain unanswered.

Furthermore, the literature debates not only the potentially negative side effects of authoritarian elections but also their positive repercussions. For instance, it could also be argued that multi-party elections hold the potential to improve standards of living by increasing the responsiveness of the autocrat. Supporting this perspective, Miller (2015a) finds that the holding of elections as such does not affect policy choices. However, where autocrats perform poorly in elections, they respond by increasing social spending while cutting military spending. Thus, while this book has argued that the effect of elections on authoritarian regime stability is in part dependent on the capacities available to rulers, a wide range of questions about the broader effects of multi-party competition in authoritarian regimes remain unanswered.

What are the implications for the study and promotion of democracy?

When autocrats lack central capacities, holding elections increases the likelihood of regime breakdown. But what happens once the regime breaks down? The regime may be thrown into civil war or experience foreign occupation, it may give way to a new – and perhaps even more repressive – autocracy, or it may democratize. The result of an authoritarian regime breakdown is not trivial, but the question of what happens next has not been covered in the analyses of this book.

First of all, the findings of this book underscore Dahl's original warning that "it is a grave mistake to assume that if only leaders of a non-democratic country can be persuaded to hold elections, then full democracy will follow" (1992, 246). Authoritarian elections are not a safe road to democratization. Where authoritarian capacities are high, elections may stabilize authoritarian rule. On the other hand, the cross-national analyses also demonstrated that only a minority of autocracies possess the capacities to abuse elections to promote authoritarian stability. Thus, international pressure for elections could fruitfully be combined with reforms that limit electoral manipulation – and support democratic developments if the authoritarian regime collapses. For instance, Carothers stresses a number of reforms that domestic or international democracy promoters may push for to ensure that elections do not merely serve the will of the autocrat, including the introduction of an independent electoral commission and support for domestic election observers (Carothers 2007b, 26).

Second, if authoritarian regimes are more likely to democratize if they have held recent elections (Lindberg 2006; Brownlee 2009; Miller 2015b), and breakdowns are more likely to occur in electoral regimes with low levels of administrative capacity and economic control, we must inquire into the implications for the relationship between authoritarian capacities and the prospects for democratization. On the one hand, low levels of capacities may increase the likelihood that a transition will occur. On the other hand, a democratization process may be inhibited by low levels of capacities. This is the argument recently put forth by van Ham and Seim (2017). Is state capacity potentially a double-edged sword whose absence may spur authoritarian breakdown but also prevent processes of democratization?

The importance of state capacity for the transition to democracy, securing democratic survival, and ensuring electoral integrity has received increasing attention in recent years. Some researchers argue that certain levels of state capacity are necessary or at least beneficial to acquire prior to the introduction of multi-party competition in order for democracy to emerge (Zakaria 1997; Mansfield and Snyder 2007; Fukuyama 2007) or demonstrate that state capacity is an important factor in ensuring a high quality of elections (Norris 2015). Others criticize the call for democratic sequencing and argue that rather than wait around for dictators to reform their states, it is necessary to push for democratization, including the introduction of multi-party elections in authoritarian regimes, and then attend to state-building on the go (Carothers 2007b, 2007a). Sometimes, democratization processes may in fact be conducive to state-building (Carothers 2007b; Mazzuca and Munck 2014). Others again find that although we do not know how state capacity affects the prospect for democratization, it does promote stability of both authoritarian and democratic regimes (Andersen et al. 2014). The debate remains unsettled, but the findings presented here lend insight to the relationship between state capacity, elections, and democratization.

The type of capacity building will influence electoral dynamics and their effect on authoritarian rule. Studies emphasizing state capacity as instrumental for democratic development or electoral integrity often focus on administrative capacity and stress aspects such as an independent and meritocratic bureaucracy (Cornell and Lapuente 2014; Andersen et al. 2014; Norris 2015) or accept agreement on citizenship rights and a monopoly on the use of force as preconditions for a functioning democracy (e.g., Linz and Stepan 1996; Møller and Skaaning 2011). These conceptualizations of state capacity are different from the one employed in this book, where the administrative capacity of an authoritarian regime is perceived as higher if the bureaucracy is controlled by the autocrat rather than independent.

It may not be state capacity as such that both promotes authoritarian rule and supports democratization. Rather, different types of state capacity may be conducive to supporting authoritarian rule during elections and promoting democracy following authoritarian breakdown. Promoting state-building in electoral autocracies will not necessarily support authoritarian rule. As long as the focus of reforms is on restrictions to authoritarian rulers' control over the state apparatus and the economy, it can make them less likely to manipulate the electoral contest to their own advantage. Such limits to the autocrat's control could increase the chances that the authoritarian regime breaks down in the face of multi-party elections and at the same time ensure that the quality of the state apparatus is sufficient to support a potential process of democratization after the authoritarian regime has collapsed. As argued by Carothers, autocrats rarely take such initiatives without facing substantial pressure to do so (2007b). However, democracy promotion efforts in authoritarian contexts are increasingly focused on supporting pluralism and strengthening the market and the state independently of rulers (Carothers 2015, 62–3).

This book has argued that the effect of authoritarian elections on regime stability depends on the ruler's degree of state capacity and control over the economy. The findings do not offer concrete guidelines on how to promote democracy in authoritarian contexts. But if we are to support the millions of people living under authoritarian rule in their historical mission to break down dictatorship, we must understand the intricacies of authoritarian rule.

References

Albertus, Michael, and Victor Menaldo. 2012a. "If You're against Them You're with Us the Effect of Expropriation on Autocratic Survival." *Comparative Political Studies* 45 (8): 973–1003.
———. 2012b. "Coercive Capacity and the Prospects for Democratization." *Comparative Politics* 44 (2): 151–69.
Andersen, David, Jørgen Møller, Lasse Lykke Rørbæk, and Svend-Erik Skaaning. 2014. "State Capacity and Political Regime Stability." *Democratization* 21 (7): 1305–25.
Bhasin, Tavishi, and Jennifer Gandhi. 2013. "Timing and Targeting of State Repression in Authoritarian Elections." *Electoral Studies*, Special Symposium: The New Research Agenda on Electoral Integrity 32 (4): 620–31.
Boone, Catherine. 2014. *Property and Political Order in Africa*. New York: Cambridge University Press.
Brancati, Dawn, and Jack L. Snyder. 2013. "Time to Kill the Impact of Election Timing on Postconflict Stability." *Journal of Conflict Resolution* 57 (5): 822–53.
Brownlee, Jason. 2009. "Portents of Pluralism: How Hybrid Regimes Affect Democratic Transitions." *American Journal of Political Science* 55 (3): 515–32.
Bubeck, Johannes, and Nikolay Marinov. 2017. "Process or Candidate: The International Community and the Demand for Electoral Integrity." *American Political Science Review* 111 (3): 535–54.
Bunce, Valerie, and Sharon Wolchik. 2011. *Defeating Authoritarian Leaders in Postcommunist Countries*. New York: Cambridge University Press.
Carothers, Thomas. 2007a. "Misunderstanding Gradualism." *Journal of Democracy* 18 (3): 18–22.
———. 2007b. "The 'Sequencing' Fallacy." *Journal of Democracy* 18 (1): 12–27.
———. 2015. "Democracy Aid at 25: Time to Choose." *Journal of Democracy* 26 (1): 59–73.
Cederman, Lars-Erik, Kristian Skrede Gleditsch, and Simon Hug. 2013. "Elections and Ethnic Civil War." *Comparative Political Studies* 46 (3): 387–417.

Cornell, Agnes, and Victor Lapuente. 2014. "Meritocratic Administration and Democratic Stability." *Democratization* 21 (7): 1286–1304.
Croissant, Aurel, and David Kuehn, eds. 2017. *Reforming Civil-Military Relations in New Democracies: Democratic Control and Military Effectiveness in Comparative Perspectives*. New York, NY: Springer.
Dahl, Robert. 1992. "Democracy and Human Rights under Different Conditions of Development." In *Human Rights in Perspective: A Global Assessment*, edited by Asbjorn Eide and Bernt Hagtvet, 235–51. Oxford: Blackwell.
Davenport, Christian. 2007. "State Repression and Political Order." *Annual Review of Political Science* 10: 1–23.
Donno, Daniela. 2013. "Elections and Democratization in Authoritarian Regimes." *American Journal of Political Science* 57 (3): 703–16.
Escribà-Folch, Abel. 2013. "Repression, Political Threats, and Survival under Autocracy." *International Political Science Review* 34 (5): 543–60.
Fjelde, Hanne. 2010. "Generals, Dictators, and Kings Authoritarian Regimes and Civil Conflict, 1973–2004." *Conflict Management and Peace Science* 27 (3): 195–218.
Fjelde, Hanne, and Kristine Höglund. 2016. "Electoral Institutions and Electoral Violence in Sub-Saharan Africa." *British Journal of Political Science* 46 (2): 297–320.
Flores, Thomas Edward, and Irfan Nooruddin. 2012. "The Effect of Elections on Postconflict Peace and Reconstruction." *The Journal of Politics* 74 (2): 558–70.
———. 2016. *Elections in Hard Times: Building Stronger Democracies in the 21st Century*. Cambridge, New York, NY and Washington, DC: Cambridge University Press.
Fukuyama, Francis. 2007. "Liberalism versus State-Building." *Journal of Democracy* 18 (3): 10–13.
Geddes, Barbara. 1999. "What Do We Know about Democratization after Twenty Years?" *Annual Review of Political Science* 2 (1): 115–44.
———. 2003. *Paradigms and Sand Castles: Theory Building and Research Design in Comparative Politics*. Ann Arbor: University of Michigan Press.
Goldsmith, Arthur A. 2015. "Elections and Civil Violence in New Multiparty Regimes: Evidence from Africa." *Journal of Peace Research* 52 (5): 607–21.
Greene, Kenneth. 2007. *Why Dominant Parties Lose: Mexico's Democratization in Comparative Perspective*. Cambridge: Cambridge University Press.
Hafner-Burton, Emilie M., Susan D. Hyde, and Ryan S. Jablonski. 2014. "When Do Governments Resort to Election Violence?" *British Journal of Political Science* 44 (1): 149–79.
Harish, S. P., and Andrew T. Little. 2017. "The Political Violence Cycle." *American Political Science Review* 111 (2): 237–55.
Howard, Marc, and Philip Roessler. 2006. "Liberalizing Electoral Outcomes in Competitive Authoritarian Regimes." *American Journal of Political Science* 50 (2): 365–81.
Knutsen, Carl Henrik, and Hanne Fjelde. 2013. "Property Rights in Dictatorships: Kings Protect Property Better Than Generals or Party Bosses." *Contemporary Politics* 19 (1): 94–114.
Knutsen, Carl Henrik, Håvard Mokleiv Nygård, and Tore Wig. 2017. "Autocratic Elections: Stabilizing Tool or Force for Change?" *World Politics* 69 (1): 98–143.
Kuntz, Philipp, and Mark Thompson. 2009. "More Than Just the Final Straw: Stolen Elections as Revolutionary Triggers." *Comparative Politics* 41 (3): 253–72.
Levitsky, Steven, and Lucan Way. 2010. *Competitive Authoritarianism: Hybrid Regimes after the Cold War*. Cambridge: Cambridge University Press.

Li, Jinshan, and Jorgen Elklit. 1999. "The Singapore General Election 1997: Campaigning Strategy, Results, and Analysis." *Electoral Studies* 18 (2): 199–216.
Lindberg, Staffan. 2006. *Democracy and Elections in Africa*. Baltimore: The Johns Hopkins University Press.
Linz, Juan, and Alfred Stepan. 1996. *Problems of Democratic Transition and Consolidation: Southern Europe, South America, and Post-Communist Europe*. Baltimore: The Johns Hopkins University Press.
Lust-Okar, Ellen. 2006. "Elections under Authoritarianism: Preliminary Lessons from Jordan." *Democratization* 13 (2): 456–71.
Magaloni, Beatriz. 2006. *Voting for Autocracy*. New York: Cambridge University Press.
———. 2008. "Credible Power-Sharing and the Longevity of Authoritarian Rule." *Comparative Political Studies* 41 (4/5): 715–41.
Mansfield, Edward, and Jack Snyder. 2007. "The Sequencing 'Fallacy'." *Journal of Democracy* 18 (3): 5–10.
Mazzuca, Sebastián L., and Gerardo L. Munck. 2014. "State or Democracy First? Alternative Perspectives on the State-Democracy Nexus." *Democratization* 21 (7): 1221–43.
Miller, Michael K. 2015a. "Elections, Information, and Policy Responsiveness in Autocratic Regimes." *Comparative Political Studies* 48 (6): 691–727.
———. 2015b. "Democratic Pieces: Autocratic Elections and Democratic Development since 1815." *British Journal of Political Science* 45 (3): 501–30.
Møller, Jørgen, and Svend-Erik Skaaning. 2011. "Stateness First?" *Democratization* 18 (1): 1–24.
Norris, Pippa. 2015. *Why Elections Fail*. New York: Cambridge University Press.
Regan, Patrick M., and Errol A. Henderson. 2002. "Democracy, Threats and Political Repression in Developing Countries: Are Democracies Internally Less Violent?" *Third World Quarterly* 23 (1): 119–36.
Reuter, Ora John, and Jennifer Gandhi. 2011. "Economic Performance and Elite Defection from Hegemonic Parties." *British Journal of Political Science* 41 (1): 83–110.
Schedler, Andreas. 2013. *The Politics of Uncertainty: Sustaining and Subverting Electoral Authoritarianism*. Oxford: Oxford University Press.
Slater, Dan. 2010. *Ordering Power: Contentious Politics and Authoritarian Leviathans in Southeast Asia*. New York: Cambridge University Press.
Slater, Dan, and Sofia Fenner. 2011. "State Power and Staying Power: Infrastructural Mechanisms and Authoritarian Durability." *Journal of International Affairs* 65 (1): 15–29.
Slater, Dan, and Joseph Wong. 2013. "The Strength to Concede: Ruling Parties and Democratization in Developmental Asia." *Perspectives on Politics* 11 (3): 717–33.
Svolik, Milan W. 2012. *The Politics of Authoritarian Rule*. New York: Cambridge University Press.
Tan, Netina. 2013. "Manipulating Electoral Laws in Singapore." *Electoral Studies*, Special Symposium: The New Research Agenda on Electoral Integrity 32 (4): 632–43.
Tolstrup, Jakob. 2015. "Black Knights and Elections in Authoritarian Regimes: Why and How Russia Supports Authoritarian Incumbents in Post-Soviet States." *European Journal of Political Research* 54 (4): 673–90.
van Ham, Carolien, and Brigitte Seim. 2018. "Strong States, Weak Elections? How State Capacity in Authoritarian Regimes Conditions the Democratizing Power of Elections". *International Political Science Review* 39 (1): 49–66.
Weeks, Jessica L. 2012. "Strongmen and Straw Men: Authoritarian Regimes and the Initiation of International Conflict." *American Political Science Review* 106 (2): 326–47.

Wilkinson, Steven I. 2006. *Votes and Violence: Electoral Competition and Ethnic Riots in India*. Cambridge: Cambridge University Press.
Wong, Benjamin, and Xunming Huang. 2010. "Political Legitimacy in Singapore." *Politics & Policy* 38 (3): 523–43.
Wood, Reed. 2008. "A Hand upon the 'Throat of the Nation': Economic Sanctions and State Repression." *International Studies Quarterly* 52 (3): 489–513.
Wright, Joseph. 2008. "Do Authoritarian Institutions Constrain? How Legislatures Affect Economic Growth and Investment." *American Journal of Political Science* 52 (2): 322–43.
Zakaria, Fareed. 1997. "The Rise of Illiberal Democracy." *Foreign Affairs* 76 (6): 22–43.

Appendix

Table A Multi-party elections, coercive capacity, and regime breakdown – alternative controls

	1	2	3	4	5	7	8
Multi-party elections	0.335 (1.185)	−0.156 (1.050)	−0.398 (0.955)	−0.293 (1.090)	0.120 (1.232)	−0.108 (0.970)	−0.066 (0.977)
Military expenditure	−0.051 (0.095)	−0.011 (0.078)	−0.040 (0.079)	−0.027 (0.082)	−0.066 (0.089)	−0.047 (0.076)	−0.035 (0.080)
Elections* Military expenditure	0.009 (0.117)	0.067 (0.101)	0.088 (0.095)	0.074 (0.107)	0.033 (0.121)	0.066 (0.097)	0.057 (0.098)
Tax-to-GDP ratio	−1.759 (1.376)	−3.176** (1.387)	−3.570** (1.522)	−2.777** (1.297)	−2.768* (1.573)	−3.454** (1.409)	−3.138** (1.349)
GDP/cap	−0.209 (0.171)	−0.286* (0.148)	−0.294 (0.179)	−0.370** (0.182)	−0.203 (0.170)	−0.249* (0.145)	−0.262* (0.152)
Growth	−0.044** (0.017)	−0.039** (0.015)	−0.037** (0.017)	−0.034* (0.019)	−0.039** (0.017)	−0.040*** (0.015)	−0.039** (0.015)
Natural resource income	−0.029 (0.024)	−0.024 (0.026)	−0.013 (0.028)	−0.015 (0.027)	−0.008 (0.028)	−0.024 (0.025)	−0.024 (0.025)
War	−0.713 (0.886)	−0.630 (0.962)	−0.439 (0.908)	−0.931 (1.220)	−0.551 (1.031)	−0.592 (0.925)	−0.612 (0.945)
Military	1.361*** (0.304)						
Monarchy	−0.448 (0.500)						
Personalist	1.016*** (0.228)						
Media freedom		0.243 (0.322)					
Executive constraints			0.165 (0.112)				
ODA % GNI				−0.003 (0.003)			
Protests					0.230 (0.158)		
Post-Cold War						0.189 (0.292)	

	1	2	3	4	5	7	8
First election							0.327 (0.517)
Constant	1.328 (2.031)	2.632 (1.854)	2.644 (2.210)	3.453 (2.418)	1.714 (1.974)	1.644 (1.788)	2.715 (1.801)
N	2479	2479	2390	2136	2252	2479	2479
Breakdowns	108	108	96	88	91	108	108

Note: Dependent variable is regime breakdown. Logistic regression models with random effects and robust standard errors clustered on country in parentheses. Multi-party elections note whether at least one election was held in the past three years. Tax ratio and military expenditure are three-year running averages. Controls for time and regime age (cubed) are included (except Model 6) but not shown in the table. All covariates except time trends are lagged one year.

$*p < 0.10$
$**p < 0.05$
$***p < 0.01$

Table B Multi-party elections, military personnel, and regime breakdown

	1	2	3	4	5
	RE	RE	RE	FE	RE
Multi-party elections	0.576** (0.237)	0.590** (0.268)	0.620 (0.880)	1.171 (1.375)	0.493 (16.632)
Military personnel		−0.020 (0.075)	−0.018 (0.090)	−0.026 (0.150)	−0.120 (9.598)
Elections* Military personnel			−0.006 (0.148)	−0.110 (0.232)	0.048 (2.971)
Tax-to-GDP ratio		−2.990** (1.234)	−2.988** (1.237)	2.235 (2.600)	−4.941 (340.445)
Economic control (reduced index)					−0.113 (3.046)
GDP/cap	−0.308** (0.144)	−0.255* (0.137)	−0.254* (0.136)	0.159 (0.620)	−0.260 (20.413)
Growth	−0.036*** (0.013)	−0.038** (0.015)	−0.038** (0.015)	−0.034** (0.016)	−0.050 (0.740)
Natural resource income	−0.035 (0.024)	−0.030 (0.025)	−0.030 (0.024)	−0.111* (0.067)	
War	−0.637 (0.747)	−0.686 (0.980)	−0.687 (0.984)	−0.689 (1.229)	−0.130 (39.200)
Constant	3.024 (2.006)	2.583 (1.762)	2.573 (1.761)		7.431 (250.716)
Observations Breakdowns	2558	2558	2558	1807	1404

Note: Dependent variable is regime breakdown. Logistic regression models with robust standard errors clustered on country in parentheses. RE denotes random effects and FE fixed effects. Multi-party elections note whether at least one election was held in the past three years. Tax ratio, military expenditure, and economic control are three-year running averages. Controls for time and regime age (cubed) are included but not shown in the table. All covariates except time trends are lagged one year.

$*p < 0.10, **p < 0.05, ***p < 0.01$

Table C Multi-party elections (3 years), economic control, and regime breakdown – alternative controls

	1	2	3	4	5	6	7
Multi-party elections	0.302 (0.377)	0.376 (0.370)	0.522 (0.384)	0.507 (0.378)	0.347 (0.368)	0.377 (0.361)	0.361 (0.356)
Economic control	0.139 (0.431)	−0.028 (0.399)	0.389 (0.465)	0.070 (0.404)	−0.038 (0.383)	0.008 (0.388)	−0.009 (0.390)
Elections* Economic control	−0.653 (0.827)	−0.499 (0.764)	−0.795 (0.784)	−0.633 (0.803)	−0.480 (0.762)	−0.457 (0.737)	−0.493 (0.743)
Tax-to-GDP ratio	−3.903 (2.791)	−4.683** (1.869)	−5.781*** (1.858)	−3.639* (1.885)	−4.380** (1.843)	−4.830** (1.880)	−4.741*** (1.798)
Military expenditure	−0.329* (0.173)	−0.326** (0.128)	−0.403*** (0.142)	−0.384*** (0.144)	−0.325** (0.132)	−0.332*** (0.125)	−0.352*** (0.135)
GDP/cap	0.248 (0.262)	0.071 (0.228)	0.105 (0.261)	0.050 (0.249)	0.042 (0.231)	0.073 (0.220)	0.099 (0.233)
Growth	−0.058** (0.027)	−0.054** (0.024)	−0.041 (0.025)	−0.058** (0.024)	−0.049** (0.023)	−0.055** (0.022)	−0.053** (0.023)
Military	1.502* (0.852)						
Monarchy	−0.230 (0.851)						
Personalist	1.242 (1.029)						
Media freedom		0.258 (0.331)					
Executive constraints			0.268* (0.143)				
Foreign aid				−0.002 (0.004)			
Protests					0.322 (0.199)		
Post-Cold War						0.704** (0.337)	
First election							0.425 (0.684)
Constant	−0.400 (5.517)	1.627 (5.333)	−0.553 (6.473)	0.518 (5.831)	2.546 (5.172)	−0.881 (2.528)	1.811 (5.287)
N	1410	1410	1365	1314	1392	1410	1410
Breakdowns	59	59	51	56	58	59	59

Note: Dependent variable is regime breakdown. Logistic regression models with random effects and robust standard errors clustered on country in parentheses. Multi-party elections note whether at least one election was held in the past three years. Economic control, tax ratio, and military expenditure are three-year running averages. Controls for time and regime age (cubed) are included (except Model 6) but not shown in the table. All covariates except time trends are lagged one year.

*$p < 0.10$, **$p < 0.05$, ***$p < 0.01$

Table D Multi-party elections (5 years), economic control, and regime breakdown – alternative controls

	1	2	3	4	5	6	7
Multi-party elections	0.632 (0.517)	0.577 (0.421)	0.606 (0.466)	0.777* (0.422)	0.554 (0.422)	0.573 (0.405)	0.608 (0.392)
Economic control	0.413 (1.594)	0.195 (0.436)	0.535 (0.482)	0.318 (0.427)	0.178 (0.421)	0.226 (0.413)	0.219 (0.422)
Elections*Economic control	−1.323 (2.938)	−1.109* (0.610)	−1.189* (0.708)	−1.265** (0.613)	−1.024* (0.622)	−0.982 (0.605)	−1.073* (0.596)
Tax-to-GDP ratio	−1.587 (9.226)	−3.074 (2.056)	−4.616** (2.066)	−2.085 (2.049)	−2.616 (2.037)	−2.935 (2.135)	−3.176 (1.987)
Military expenditure	−0.379 (0.340)	−0.396*** (0.153)	−0.477*** (0.162)	−0.418** (0.176)	−0.377** (0.148)	−0.377*** (0.145)	−0.421*** (0.156)
GDP/cap	0.292 (0.395)	0.161 (0.268)	0.164 (0.295)	0.067 (0.290)	0.092 (0.266)	0.119 (0.256)	0.175 (0.268)
Growth	−0.055 (0.078)	−0.054** (0.025)	−0.039 (0.027)	−0.055** (0.026)	−0.047* (0.025)	−0.054** (0.024)	−0.052** (0.025)
Military	1.513 (5.421)						
Monarchy	0.377 (1.186)						
Personalist	1.472 (6.609)						
Media freedom		0.359 (0.355)					
Executive constraints			0.261 (0.165)				
Foreign aid				−0.003 (0.005)			
Protests					0.314 (0.217)		
Post-Cold War						0.685* (0.393)	
First election							0.392 (0.711)
Constant	−3.161 (7.479)	−2.034 (7.575)	−6.654 (8.530)	−3.489 (8.224)	−0.041 (7.335)	−1.311 (2.936)	−1.457 (7.538)
N	1267	1267	1227	1182	1253	1267	1267
Breakdowns	51	51	45	49	50	51	51

Note: Dependent variable is regime breakdown. Logistic regression models with random effects and robust standard errors clustered on country in parentheses. Multi-party elections note whether at least one election was held in the past five years. Economic control, tax ratio, and military expenditure are five-year running averages. Controls for time and regime age (cubed) are included (except Model 6) but not shown in the table. All covariates except time trends are lagged one year.

*$p < 0.10$, **$p < 0.05$, ***$p < 0.01$

Table E Multi-party elections (1 year), government spending, and regime breakdown – alternative controls

	1	2	3	4	5	6	7
Multi-party elections	3.623*** (1.289)	3.354*** (1.208)	3.639*** (1.217)	3.282** (1.453)	3.403** (1.340)	3.271*** (1.194)	3.396*** (1.128)
Government spending	0.206 (0.197)	0.100 (0.179)	0.125 (0.184)	0.175 (0.201)	0.070 (0.191)	0.124 (0.181)	0.117 (0.178)
Elections* Government spending	−0.954** (0.461)	−0.833* (0.438)	−0.928** (0.446)	−0.740 (0.525)	−0.811* (0.483)	−0.802* (0.426)	−0.802* (0.421)
Tax-to-GDP ratio	−2.280* (1.277)	−3.458*** (1.256)	−4.292*** (1.409)	−2.982** (1.228)	−2.754* (1.463)	−3.475*** (1.238)	−3.452*** (1.211)
Military expenditure	−0.006 (0.060)	0.041 (0.063)	0.039 (0.058)	−0.029 (0.063)	−0.055 (0.061)	0.013 (0.048)	0.013 (0.053)
GDP/cap	−0.570*** (0.216)	−0.552*** (0.176)	−0.610*** (0.193)	−0.530*** (0.184)	−0.407** (0.182)	−0.512*** (0.162)	−0.526*** (0.175)
Growth	−0.016* (0.008)	−0.014* (0.008)	−0.010 (0.008)	−0.030** (0.012)	−0.039** (0.017)	−0.014* (0.007)	−0.013* (0.007)
Military	1.499*** (0.324)						
Monarchy	−0.261 (0.494)						
Personalist	0.848*** (0.254)						
Media freedom		0.249 (0.314)					
Executive constraints			0.186* (0.111)				
Foreign aid				−0.003 (0.003)			
Protests					0.312* (0.174)		
Post-Cold War						0.152 (0.251)	
First election							−0.244 (0.450)
Constant	4.271 (2.828)	4.564** (2.204)	4.873* (2.491)	4.324 (3.085)	3.533 (2.195)	4.197** (2.051)	4.663** (2.251)
N	2550	2549	2448	2169	2298	2550	2550
Breakdowns	109	109	95	89	93	109	109

Note: Dependent variable is regime breakdown. Logistic regression models with random effects and robust standard errors clustered on country in parentheses. Multi-party elections note whether at least one election was held in the past year. Controls for time and regime age (cubed) are included (except Model 6) but not shown in the table. All covariates except time trends are lagged one year.

*$p < 0.10$, **$p < 0.05$, ***$p < 0.01$

Index

Note: Page numbers in *italic* indicate a figure on the corresponding page.

administrative capacity: effectiveness table 62; introduction 51, 53; Malaysia election 117–20, 128; Philippines election 117–20, 128; role in regime stability strategies 51, 53, 80–9, 81, 83, 84, *86*, *87*, 88; statistical methodology 73–80, *77*, *79*; tax extraction rates 74–7, 77, 81, 82–8, 83, 84, *86*, *87*, 88; Zimbabwe elections 135, 136, 146, 149–52; *see also* state capacity
Aquino, Benigno 125
Aquino, Corazon 125–29
authoritarian capacities: administrative capacity 51, 53; coercive capacity 51, 53; definitions 49–53, *50*, 53; economic control 51–3, 53; effects of low capacity 111, *112*; hypotheses on effectiveness of 59–62, 62; impacting voter choice 46–7, 53–8; increasing opposition costs 58–9; introduction to concept 2–8, 44–5; Malaysia 117–20, 128; Philippines 117–20, 128; possible scenarios derived from 63–6, 66; state capacity 50–1, 53; Zimbabwe 135–41, 146; *see also* authoritarian regime; multi-party elections; regime stability strategies
authoritarian regime: areas of future study 172–75; capacities 49–53, *50*, 53; effects of low capacity 111, *112*; existing studies on electoral impact 40–2; Georgia 3, 5, 35; hypotheses on effectiveness of capacities 59–62, 62; impacting voter choice 46–7, 53–8; increasing opposition costs 58–9; main actors threatening status quo 4–5, 36–40, 45–9, *46*; Malaysia 2–4, 35, 115–30, 128; multi-party elections considerations 9, *10*, *11*, *12*, 13–16, 17; non-multi-party elections considerations 16–17, *17*; paradoxical effect research 42–3; Philippines 1, 7, 115–30, 128; proliferation of elections 17–23, *18*, *19*, *21*; quantification of 8–12, *9*, *10*, *11*, *12*; regime subversion through elections 39–40; regime type considerations 23–7, *24*, *25*, 26; regional considerations *21*, 21–3; scope of book 2, 5–8, 27–9; Singapore 3, 4; stability factors 9, *10*, *11*, *12*, 12–13, 35–66, 38, *46*, *50*, 53, 62, 66; tax extraction rates 74–7, 77, 81, 82–8, 83, 84, *86*, *87*, 88; variety of consequences 1–4; Zimbabwe 2, 133–62, 146; *see also* authoritarian capacities; multi-party elections; regime stability strategies
autocracy *see* authoritarian regime
Autocratic Regimes Dataset *9*, 9–12, *10*, *11*, *12*

Barisan Nasional 3, 35
BN *see* Barisan Nasional
breakdown by election 64–5, 66; Philippines 120–21, 125–9

candidate choice 47–8; *see also* multi-party elections
Central Intelligence Organization 137, 140, 150; *see also* Zimbabwe elections
CIO *see* Central Intelligence Organization
coercive capacity: definition 51, 53; effectiveness table 62; Malaysia 115–30, 128; military spending 76–7, *77*, 81, 83, 84, 88, 90, 90–3, *92*, *93*, 94, 95; Philippines 115–30, 128; role in regime

188   Index

stability strategies 51, 53, 89–93, 90, 92, *93*; statistical methodology 73–80, *77*, *79*; Zimbabwe elections 137–8, 146, 149–52; *see also* state capacity
Coltart, David 154, 155, 157
co-optation *see* regime stability strategies
credible commitment *see* regime stability strategies
Cross, Eddie 155–6

DAP *see* Democratic Action Party
Democratic Action Party 121, 123
dictatorship *see* authoritarian regime

economic control: capacity hypotheses testing results 102–8, 103, 104, *106*, *107*, 111–12, *112*; definition 51–3, 53; effectiveness table 62; effects of low capacity 111, *112*; government spending 108–11, 109, *110*; Malaysia 115–30, 128; natural resource control considerations 101–2, 108, 109; Philippines 115–30, 128; regulatory power 108, 109; statistical methodology 100–1; subcomponents 108–11, 109, *110*; variables impacting 99–112, 103, 104, *106*, *107*, 109, *110*, *112*; Zimbabwe elections 138–41, 146, 149–52
electoral authoritarianism *see* multi-party elections
electoral survival 65, 66; 2008 Zimbabwe election 141–8, 146
exclusion *see* regime stability strategies

Georgia elections 3, 5, 35; Saakashvili, Mikheil 3, 35; Shevardnadze, Eduard 3, 35
gerrymandering 54–5; *see also* voter choice
Global Political Agreement 148–50, 153, 158
government spending 108–11, 109, *110*; *see also* economic control
GPA *see* Global Political Agreement

harassment of opposition: economic 58–9; physical 59

Ibrahim, Anwar 3, 123–4
IG *see* Inclusive Government
Inclusive Government 147, 148–53; *see also* Zimbabwe elections
increasing opposition costs 58–9
internal elites 4–5, 38, 38; regime subversion through elections 39–40

Joint Operations Command 137, 143–4, 149, 157; *see also* Zimbabwe elections

legitimation *see* regime stability strategies

Magaloni, Beatriz 52; *see also* economic control
Mahatir, Muhammad 7, 115, 117, 120–2
main actors threatening 4–5, 36–9
Malaysia elections 2–4, 35, 115–30, 128; Barisan Nasional 3, 35, 121–4; Democratic Action Party 121, 123; economic control overview 117–20; Ibrahim, Anwar 3, 123–4; New Economic Policy 118, 119; opposition considerations 121–4; patronage 119; *Reformasi* 3, 35, 123–4; stabilization by election 120, 121–4, 129–30; state capacity overview 117–20; summary of findings 129–30, 168–70; United Malays National Organization 3–4, 121–4
manipulation: of vote counting 57–8; of voters' preference expression 56–7; of voters' preference formation 55–6; *see also* voter choice
Marcos, Ferdinand 115, 118–20, 125–9
mechanisms of stability *see* regime stability strategies
Mexico elections 99
Migdal, Joel 51; *see also* state capacity
military regime *see* regime type considerations
military spending 76–7, *77*, 81, 83, 84, 88, 90, 90–3, 92, *93*, 94, 95; *see also* coercive capacity
monarchic regime *see* regime type considerations
monitoring and power distribution *see* regime stability strategies
Movement for Democratic Change: Coltart, David 154, 155, 157; Zimbabwe elections 133, 135, 142, 144–5, 150, 154, 157–59
Movement for Democratic Change-Tsvangirai: Cross, Eddie 155; Tsvangirai, Morgan 133, 135, 142, 144–5, 147–8, 159; Zimbabwe elections 2, 142, 144, 148, 150–2, 155–7, 159; *see also* Zimbabwe elections
Mugabe, Robert 2, 133–62, 146; 2008 election 141–8, 146; 2013 election 146, 148–60; administrative capacity overview 135–6, 146; Central

Intelligence Organization 137, 140, 150; coercive capacity overview 137–38, 146; economic control overview 138–41, 146; Global Political Agreement 148–50, 153, 158; harassment of the opposition 157–9; Inclusive Government 147, 148–53; introduction 133–4; Joint Operations Command 137, 143–4, 149, 157; Operation *Gukurahundi* 137, 155; patronage 139–41, 149–51; restricting access to the vote 156–7; Southern African Development Community 133, 147–9, 153, 159; summary of findings 160–2, 168, 170–2; systemic voter manipulation 153–5; Zimbabwe Electoral Commission 138, 144–5, 156–7

multi-party elections: definitions 13–15; effects of low capacity 111, *112*; existing studies on 40–2; hypotheses on effectiveness of capacities 59–62, *62*; impacting voter choice 46–7, 53–8; increasing opposition costs 58–9; main actors threatening status quo 4–5, 36–40, 45–9, *46*; measurement variables *9*, *10*, *11*, *12*, 15–16, *17*; paradoxical effect research 42–3; proliferation of elections 17–23, *18*, *19*, *21*; regime stability strategies *9*, *10*, *11*, *12*, 12–13, 35–66, 38, *46*, *50*, 53, 62, 66; regime type considerations 23–7, *24*, *25*, *26*; regional considerations *21*, 21–3; tax extraction rates 74–7, *77*, 81, 82–8, *83*, *84*, *86*, *87*, 88; *see also* authoritarian capacities; authoritarian regime; regime stability strategies

NAMFREL 126
natural resource control considerations: economic control overview 101–2, 108, 109; Malaysia 120; Philippines 120; state capacity overview 77, 81, 83, 84, 88, 90, 92
NELDA *9*, *10*, *11*, *12*, *18*, *19*, *21*, 24, *25*, 26
NEP *see* New Economic Policy
New Economic Policy 118, 119
non-multi-party elections considerations 16–17

Operation *Gukurahundi* 137, 155
opposition considerations 2–5, 27–8, 38, 39; harassment of 58–9; Malaysia elections 121–4, 128; mobilization of 45–9, *46*; Philippines elections 121–9, 128; regime subversion through elections 39–40, 42–4, 59–66, 62, 66; Zimbabwe elections 135, 140–2, 144–8, 146, 152–4, 156–60

PAP *see* People's Action Party
paradoxical effect research 42–3
party regime *see* regime type considerations
patronage 55–7; Malaysia 119; Philippines 115, 118–19; Zimbabwe 139–41, 149–51
People Power Revolution *see* Philippines elections
People's Action Party 3
personalist regime *see* regime type considerations
Philippines elections 1, 7; Aquino, Benigno 125; Aquino, Corazon 125–9; breakdown by election 120–1, 125–30, 128; economic control overview 117–20; Marcos, Ferdinand 115, 118–20, 125–9; NAMFREL 126; opposition considerations 125–9, 128; patronage 115, 118–19; restricting access to the vote 126, 129; state capacity overview 117–20; summary of findings 129–30, 168–70
populace considerations 4–5, 38, 39; regime subversion through elections 39–40
protester choice 48–9; *see also* multi-party elections

quantitative data analysis 73–80, *77*, *79*

Reformasi 3, 35, 123–24; *see also* Malaysia elections
regime breakdown *see* regime stability strategies
regime stability strategies *9*, *10*, *11*, *12*, 12–13, 35–66, 38, *46*, *50*, 53, 62, 66; administrative capacity role 51, 53, 80–9, 81, 83, 84, *86*, *87*, *88*; bias concepts 78–80; coercive capacity role 51, 53, 89–93, 90, 92, *93*; definitions 49–53, *50*, 53; economic control 51–3, 53; effects of low capacity 111, *112*; existing studies on 40–2; hypotheses on effectiveness of capacities 59–62, *62*; impacting voter choice 46–7, 53–8; increasing opposition costs

58–9; introduction to concept 2–8, 44–5; main actors threatening status quo 4–5, 36–40, 45–9, *46*; Malaysia 117–20; mechanisms involved 38, 38–40; paradoxical effect research 42–3; Philippines 117–20; state capacity role 50–1, 53, 73–4, 78–80; tax extraction rates 74–7, 77, 81, 82–8, 83, 84, *86*, *87*, 88; Zimbabwe 135–41, 146; *see also* authoritarian capacities; authoritarian regime; multi-party elections
regime subversion through elections 39–40
regime type considerations 23–7, 24, *25*, 26
regulatory power 108, 109
rent distribution *see* regime stability strategies
resource curse 52; *see also* economic control
restricting access to the vote 57; Philippines 126, 129; Zimbabwe 156–7; *see also* voter choice
Rose Revolution *see* Georgia elections

Saakashvili, Mikheil 3, 35; *see also* Georgia elections
SADC *see* Southern African Development Community
Sartori, Giovanni 14
scenarios derived from authoritarian capacities 63–6, 66; breakdown by election 64–5, 66; electoral survival 65, 66; stabilization by election 64, 66
Schedler, Andreas 4–5
Shevardnadze, Eduard 3, 35; *see also* Georgia elections
signaling *see* regime stability strategies
Singapore elections 3–4, 73, 94–5; People's Action Party 3, 73
Southern African Development Community 133, 147–9, 153, 159
stabilization by election 64, 66; Malaysia 120, 121–4; Zimbabwe 142–8
state capacity: definition 50–1, 53; effectiveness table 62; Malaysia 115–30, 128; Philippines 115–30, 128; statistical methodology 73–80, *77*, *79*; Zimbabwe 135–8, 146
summary of findings 167–78; direction of future research 172–5; election violence 175–6; Malaysia elections 168–70; Philippines elections 129–30, 168–70; promotion of democracy 176–7; Zimbabwe elections 168, 170–2
systemic voter manipulation 54–5; Zimbabwe 153–5

tax extraction rates 74–7, 77, 81, 82–8, 83, 84, *86*, *87*, 88
Tsvangirai, Morgan 133, 135, 142, 144–5, 147–8, 159

UMNO *see* United Malays National Organization
United Malays National Organization 3–4

voter choice: manipulation of vote counting 57–8; manipulation of voters' preference expression 56–7; manipulation of voters' preference formation 55–6; restricting access to the vote 57; systemic manipulation 54–5; *see also* multi-party elections

ZANU(PF) *see* Zimbabwe African National Union-Patriotic Front
ZAPU *see* Zimbabwe African People's Union
ZEC *see* Zimbabwe Electoral Commission
Zimbabwe African National Union-Patriotic Front 2, 133–62, 146; 2008 election 141–8, 146; 2013 election 146, 148–60; administrative capacity overview 135–6, 146; Central Intelligence Organization 137, 140, 150; coercive capacity overview 137–8, 146; economic control overview 57, 138–41, 146; Global Political Agreement 148–50, 153, 158; harassment of the opposition 157–9; Inclusive Government 147, 148–53; Joint Operations Command 137, 143–4, 149, 157; Movement for Democratic Change 133, 135, 142, 144–5, 150, 154, 157–9; Movement for Democratic Change-Tsvangirai 2, 142, 144, 148, 150–2, 155–7, 159; Mugabe, Robert 133–62, 170–1, 175; Operation *Gukurahundi* 137, 155; patronage 139–41, 149–51; restricting access to the vote 156–7; Southern African Development Community 133, 147–9, 153, 159; summary of findings 160–2, 168, 170–2; Tsvangirai, Morgan 133, 135, 142, 144–5, 147–8, 159; voter manipulation 153–5; Zimbabwe African People's Union 135, 137; Zimbabwe Electoral Commission 138, 142, 144–5, 156–7
Zimbabwe African People's Union 135, 137
Zimbabwe elections 2, 133–62, 146; 2008 election 141–8, 146; 2013

election 146, 148–60; administrative capacity overview 135–6, 146; Central Intelligence Organization 137, 140, 150; coercive capacity overview 137–8, 146; Coltart, David 154, 155, 157; Cross, Eddie 155; economic control overview 138–41, 146; Global Political Agreement 148–50, 153, 158; harassment of the opposition 157–9; Inclusive Government 147, 148–53; Joint Operations Command 137, 143–4, 149, 157; Movement for Democratic Change 133, 135, 142, 144–5, 150, 154, 157–9; Movement for Democratic Change-Tsvangirai 2, 142, 144, 148, 150–2, 155–7, 159; Mugabe, Robert 133–62, 133–162, 170–1, 175; Operation *Gukurahundi* 137, 155; opposition considerations 135, 140–2, 144–8, 146, 152–4, 156–60; patronage 139–41, 149–51; restricting access to the vote 156–7; Southern African Development Community 133, 147–9, 153, 159; summary of findings 160–2, 168, 170–2; systemic voter manipulation 153–5; Tsvangirai, Morgan 133, 135, 142, 144–5, 147–8, 159; Zimbabwe African People's Union 135, 137; Zimbabwe Electoral Commission 138, 142, 144–5, 156–7; *see also* Zimbabwe African National Union-Patriotic Front

Zimbabwe Electoral Commission 138, 142, 144–5, 156–7